# THE BETTERMENT MINDSET

## THE SECRET TO SUCCESS
### WHEN EVERYTHING FEELS OUT OF CONTROL

**ALISON EARL**

*Leadership Alignment and People Transformation*

**TALL POPPY**

Imprint: Tall Poppy Publishing
First published 2025

ISBN 978-1-7640766-0-9 (paperback)
ISBN 978-1-7640766-1-6 (e-book)

© ALISON EARL, 2025

The content of this book protected by copyright law. No part may be reproduced and reused for any commercial purpose without explicit written permission from the author.

Cover design by Global.Dezine on 99 Designs
www.99designs.com.au/profiles/GlobalDezine

Typeset and internal diagram design by Alicia Grady, Struck by Violet
www.struckbyviolet.com

Edited by Gail Tagarro, The Book Writing Coach
www.bookwritingcoach.com.au

 A catalogue record for this book is available from the National Library of Australia

*Dedication*

To my husband Jonas—life is infinitely better with you, Remi, and Finn by my side. And to my daughter Charlotte—your joy, curiosity, and adventurous spirit inspire me every day. Together, you remind me that life is full of endless possibility.

# Contents

**Introduction:** Mindset Shapes Everything — 9

## PART 1 THE MINDSET EVOLUTION—FROM MANAGEMENT TO BETTERMENT — 19

**Chapter 1** Mindset as Your Greatest Asset—Thriving in a World of Change and Uncertainty — 21

**Chapter 2** The Betterment Ladder—Steps from Surviving to Thriving — 39

**Chapter 3** Stress Mastery—An Essential Skill for Betterment in a Fast-Paced World — 59

## PART 2 RESPONSIBLE MINDSET— FROM OVERWHELM TO OWNERSHIP — 81

**Chapter 4** The Four States of Mind—Your Choice in the Storm — 83

**Chapter 5** The Anchor Within—Building Stability Through Empathy and Compassion — 101

**Chapter 6** The Power Shift—How Ownership Redefines Control — 119

## PART 3 WIN-WIN MINDSET—FROM COMPETITION TO COLLABORATION — 139

**Chapter 7** A Better Way—Moving Beyond Me Vs. You — 141

**Chapter 8** Beneath the Surface—Why Trust, Safety, and Respect are Non-Negotiable — 161

**Chapter 9** The Art of Alignment—Moving Beyond Stalemates to Shared Purpose — 181

## PART 4 OPPORTUNITY MINDSET—FROM PROBLEM TO POSSIBILITY — 207

**Chapter 10** Unlocking Potential—Transforming How You See Challenges — 209

**Chapter 11** Optimism—Opening New Doors to Opportunity
and Momentum … 233

**Chapter 12** Inspired Action—Expanding Possibility Through
Questions and Creative Problem-Solving … 251

## PART 5 BETTERMENT MASTERY—FROM LEADERSHIP TO LIFELONG IMPACT … 273

**Chapter 13** Betterment Leadership—Building Cultures of
Ownership and High Performance … 275

**Chapter 14** A Betterment Life—A Philosophy for Thriving
in Life and Relationships … 301

**Chapter 15** Betterment Beyond the Self—A Mission for a
Better World … 321

A Final Word … 339
Notes and References … 340
Acknowledgements … 362
About the Author … 363

# Introduction:
## Mindset Shapes Everything

### A Life-Changing Drive

The road stretched ahead, quiet and familiar. We were mid-conversation, laughing about something trivial, just another drive home after a long weekend away. Nothing out of the ordinary.

Then, in an instant, everything changed.

A car from the opposite direction veered across the median strip, heading straight for us. There was no time to react. No time to swerve. Just the brutal impact of a head-on collision. Our car flipped, over and over, for fifty metres. When we finally came to a stop, we were upside down and covered in petrol.

I was trapped, wedged in the wreckage, hanging awkwardly from my seatbelt. Blood was pouring out of my head. I don't remember much else. The smell of petrol. Voices blurring in and out. Sirens in the distance.

The paramedics, those incredible people, worked quickly to cut me out of the car. Later, I'd be told our car was barely recognisable, that we shouldn't have survived.

But somehow, we did.

**Two Paths, Two Outcomes**

In the days after the accident, I felt something unexpected: an overwhelming sense of gratitude. I thought that if I were meant to die, I would have died in that accident. Instead, I'd been given another chance, one not everyone gets. That thought was confronting but also energising. *I'm still here. That has to mean something.*

My boyfriend at the time saw it differently. He kept asking, *Why did this happen to us? Of all the cars on the road, why ours?* He was stuck in the randomness of it all, feeling as though we were so unlucky that this had happened to us.

Physically, I was very lucky. I was black and blue with bruises, but my injuries were nothing compared to what they could have been. I recovered quickly, pushing through the physio with determination. I wasn't pretending the accident wasn't traumatic; it was, but I saw it as something to move forward from, not something to hold me back.

But my boyfriend struggled. He carried the pain, both physical and emotional, for months. Every ache and twinge felt like a reminder of what had happened *to* him.

Same event. Two completely different experiences.

## Mindset Shapes Reality: In Life and in Work

That accident taught me something powerful: Mindset shapes everything.

This isn't about pretending things are fine when they're not. It's not about ignoring pain or denying reality. But when faced with challenge, change, or uncertainty, the way we choose to frame our experience can determine whether we move forward or remain stuck.

These days, I work with organisations going through major change and transformation processes, helping their people not just navigate uncertainty but also thrive in it.

For most people, workplace change feels like it's happening to them. Decisions are made at higher levels, yet these people are expected to show up, perform, and create important results. Time and time again, I'm reminded of my experience with the accident. Some people adapt readily, taking change in their stride. Others suffer and struggle, feeling powerless before the forces beyond their control.

But what if we didn't have to struggle? What if we could all learn to thrive, even when we face tough circumstances outside of our control?

## What to Expect from this Book

This book is designed to take you on a journey. It is a shift in how you see challenges, decisions, and opportunities. Change is inevitable, but struggle is not. When we learn to approach change with ownership, collaboration, and a focus on possibility, we don't just cope, we thrive.

The journey through the book is from personal awareness to collective impact. It starts with a better understanding of mindset as a tool and an asset, because the way we think shapes everything we do. From there, it explores taking ownership—focusing on what we can control rather than getting stuck in what we can't. Then, it shifts to how we work with others, building trust and collaboration instead of competition. Once that foundation is set, we expand into seeing opportunities where others see obstacles, learning to approach challenges with creativity and possibility. Finally, we bring it all together by applying these mindsets beyond ourselves, influencing teams, organisations, and the world around us in a way that creates lasting impact.

The book is structured in five parts.

**PART 1:** **The Mindset Evolution: From Management to Betterment**

Before we can change our results, we must first change how we think.

In a world of constant pressure and uncertainty, our mindset is the single most powerful tool we have to navigate challenges, unlock resilience, and thrive. Yet most of us are operating in reactive mode, managing stress, juggling demands, and firefighting problems without ever stepping back to ask, *Am I just surviving, or am I truly thriving*?

This section is about shifting that perspective. We learn why mindset isn't just about attitude. It's about how we interpret stress, how we show up under pressure, and how we take ownership of our experience. We discover the Betterment Ladder, a simple yet powerful framework to recognise where we are right now, whether we're feeling stuck in survival mode or pushing the limits of our growth, and how to move forward with intention. We also uncover the science of stress mastery, learning how to reframe pressure as fuel rather than a force that holds us back.

This is where our Betterment journey begins. By the end of Part 1, we'll have the tools to step out of reaction mode, shift our mindset, and take control of how we navigate change, challenge, and uncertainty. Everything that follows—how we take ownership, how we collaborate, and how we seize opportunities—starts here.

## PART 2: The Responsible Mindset—From Overwhelm to Ownership

How do we take charge of what we can control?

At some point, we all face moments where things feel out of our hands. Decisions are made above us, circumstances shift unexpectedly, and pressures mount. In these moments, it's easy to get caught up in frustration, blame, or helplessness. But what if the real game-changer isn't the situation itself, but how we respond to it?

This section is about reclaiming our sense of control, not by trying to control everything, but by developing a sense of agency and directing our energy to where it creates real momentum. The Responsible Mindset is about shifting focus away from what's beyond our influence and toward the choices, perspectives, and actions that shape our experience. We discover how to move from reacting to leading, using tools like the Four States of Mind, the CIA Model (Control, Influence,

Accept), and the shift from 'Little Me' to 'Big Me' to step into a more empowered way of thinking and acting.

Responsibility isn't just about taking action. It's also about how we treat ourselves in the process. Developing self-compassion and empathy, both for ourselves and others, allows us to navigate challenges without burnout or self-judgement. The ability to regulate stress, respond intentionally rather than impulsively, and shift from self-doubt to self-trust are at the heart of sustainable success. Through this section, we learn how to stay grounded under pressure, break free from unproductive cycles, and build resilience in both work and life.

By the end of Part 2, we'll have a stronger sense of ownership over our experience, the confidence to navigate challenges, and the mindset to create meaningful change, no matter what's happening around us. When we take ownership, we don't just adapt to change, we shape it.

## PART 3: Win-Win Mindset—From Competition to Collaboration

Success isn't a solo journey yet too often, we get stuck in a 'me vs. you' mindset, where competing positions lead to tension instead of progress. This section introduces the Win-Win Mindset, a shift from opposition to co-creation, where success comes from finding solutions that benefit everyone.

We explore how to move from rigid positions to shared purpose, ensuring conversations focus on what truly matters rather than getting stuck in deadlock. We gain strategies for replacing toxic competition with collaborative performance, where diverse perspectives fuel better outcomes rather than working against each other.

Trust, safety, and respect are the foundations of high-performing teams and relationships, but they don't happen by chance. We learn how to build alignment, foster psychological safety, and create an environment where people feel valued and engaged. Through practical tools like the ALIGN Model for negotiation, the Win-Win blueprint for understanding conflict styles, and the Positive No Sandwich for setting boundaries, we develop the skills to collaborate effectively, even in complex situations.

Of course, not every interaction will be smooth. We also cover how to handle difficult people, defuse tension, and maintain productive relationships, even under pressure.

The Win-Win Mindset isn't about compromise. It's about co-creating solutions that are better than what either party could achieve alone. By the end of this section, we'll have the tools to build stronger collaborations, create alignment, and turn tension into progress, whether at work or in life. When we stop asking, *How do I win?* and start asking, *What is our way?* we unlock new possibilities for everyone.

## PART 4: Opportunity Mindset—From Problem to Possibility

Challenges can be roadblocks or springboards, if we choose to see them that way.

Challenges are unavoidable, but struggle is optional. Some people face obstacles and see dead ends, while others see possibilities waiting to be unlocked. The difference? Mindset.

This section is about shifting from a reactive, problem-focused way of thinking to an opportunity-driven approach, one that helps us see constraints as catalysts for creativity, setbacks as stepping stones, and uncertainty as fuel for innovation. We learn how perspective shapes outcomes, and how small shifts in thinking can dramatically change what's possible.

We explore tools like the Opportunity Ladder, which helps us recognise whether we're stuck in survival mode, stabilising for progress, or ready to transform challenges into game-changing breakthroughs. We also learn how to break free from mental cages, the invisible beliefs and assumptions that keep us stuck in limitation rather than potential. We dive into the science of optimism, showing us how the way we explain events to ourselves can drive resilience, motivation, and long-term success.

Finally, this section introduces practical strategies for expanding possibility, from asking better questions and using creative problem-solving techniques like SCAMPER, to shifting from scarcity thinking to an abundance mindset. By the end of Part 4, we'll have the tools to turn obstacles into opportunities, think bigger, and take inspired action toward what's possible.

## PART 5: Betterment Mastery—From Leadership to Lifelong Impact

The greatest impact happens when we extend Betterment beyond ourselves into our teams, workplaces, and communities.

Betterment doesn't stop with personal growth. It becomes most powerful when it extends beyond the self. The way we lead, collaborate, and contribute doesn't just shape our own experience; it creates ripple effects in our teams, organisations, and communities.

This section is about taking everything we've explored—ownership, collaboration, and opportunity thinking—and embedding it into how we lead and live. We learn how to build cultures of ownership, where people don't just follow change but actively drive it. We explore strategies to balance high performance with well-being, ensuring that success is sustainable, not exhausting. And we see how small, intentional shifts in mindset and behaviour can transform not just individual teams, but entire systems and industries.

However, Betterment isn't just a leadership approach, it's a philosophy for life. In these final chapters, we are challenged to think about what Betterment means to us, beyond the workplace. What impact do we want to have? What values do we want to embody? What's the legacy we're creating through our daily choices?

This section guides us in shaping our Betterment Mission, a simple but powerful way to define how we contribute to making the world better, in whatever way feels meaningful to us. Betterment isn't about waiting for the perfect opportunity or the right conditions. It's about recognising that every interaction, every decision, and every small act of leadership has the power to create a lasting impact.

By the end of Part 5, we won't just see Betterment as a mindset but as a way of being. A way to lead, live, and shape the world around us with intention, generosity, and purpose.

## The Power of Real-World Examples: Protecting Privacy While Learning from Experience

Throughout this book, we find real-world examples from my work with leaders and teams. These stories showcase the challenges people face and the mindset shifts that helped overcome them.

To protect privacy, I've used aliases for both individuals and organisations. While the specifics may have been adapted, the core lessons and transformations are real.

These examples aren't just stories, they're blueprints. They show how the principles in this book have played out in high-stakes environments, during significant workplace changes, and in the daily challenges of leadership and teamwork.

I encourage you to see yourself in these stories. What would you have done? What lessons can you apply to your own experience?

## How to Engage with this Book

Reading alone won't change your mindset. Engagement, reflection, and application will.

The real power of this book comes from what you bring to it. The insights and tools are here, but how much you gain will depend on how actively you reflect, experiment, and apply these ideas in your own life.

We never stop growing.

No matter where you are in your career or personal journey, the opportunity for Betterment is always available. There is no final destination, just ongoing growth and learning.

Self-reflection is key.

Growth isn't just about learning new ideas, it's about integrating them.

## Journalling as a tool for change

One of the most effective ways to process and apply insights is through journalling. That's why at the end of each chapter there are reflection questions designed to help turn ideas into action. These aren't just prompts, they're an invitation to pause, reflect, and make these concepts your own.

As you read, engage fully. Take notes. Try out the tools. Reflect on the questions. Mindset isn't something you change once, it's something you shape daily.

## An invitation to take the first step

Mindset isn't something we're born with, it's something we shape.

That means we have the power to reshape it at any time. No matter where you are today, you have the ability to lead yourself through change, cultivate resilience, and create opportunities for growth, both for yourself and for those around you.

This book is your invitation to step into a new way of thinking, leading, and showing up in the world.

So, are you ready?

Let's begin.

# PART 1

# The Mindset Evolution—From Management to Betterment

# 1

# Mindset as Your Greatest Asset—
Thriving in a World of Change and Uncertainty

*'The pace of change has never been this fast, yet it will never be this slow again.' Justin Trudeau*[1]

Think about that for a moment.

We're living in a time where change is not just fast, it's relentless. Every day, new technologies disrupt how we work, global events reshape economies, and our personal and professional lives are constantly stretched by the demand to do more with less. Change is no longer something we experience in isolated bursts. It's a constant undercurrent shaping our lives.

This feels overwhelming for many of us. How do we keep up when the ground beneath our feet keeps shifting? The truth is that most of us are stuck in reactive mode. We manage, we firefight, we problem-solve, but we rarely pause to ask ourselves if we're doing more than just surviving.

And that's the real question, isn't it? In a world of endless complexity and pressure, is managing enough?

The answer is no. Managing alone keeps us in a cycle of coping, where we're focused on staying afloat but never moving forward. To thrive—to create, innovate, and grow—we need something far more powerful. We need to evolve how we approach the challenges of change itself.

This is where mindset comes in.

Mindset is the lens that shapes how we see the world around us. When life throws challenges our way, it's our mindset that decides whether we view these moments as chaos or as chances to learn and move forward. The really great thing is that our mindset isn't something set in stone; it's something we can actively work on and improve over time.

This chapter is about embracing that possibility. We explore why mindset matters more than ever, how it shapes our ability to thrive, and why the path to Betterment begins with rethinking how we respond to the demands of an ever-changing world.

## The Cost of Staying Reactive

Here's something you might not realise: uncertainty is more stressful to the brain than a known negative.

When you're waiting for important test results, what feels worse? Knowing the outcome, even if it's bad, or sitting in limbo, wondering what might happen? For most people, it's the waiting, the not knowing. Our brains are hardwired to crave certainty.

This isn't a personal flaw; it's biology. The human brain is designed to detect and respond to threats. When we come across situations filled with uncertainty, our bodies naturally kick into high alert mode, triggering the fight-or-flight response. The challenges we face today, however, are a never-ending flow of emails, changing priorities, and constant shifts in our environment. While it may feel threatening, in reality it's not. It can however make handling stress a real struggle in our day-to-day lives, as our bodies haven't evolved to distinguish between a life-threatening tiger and a mounting to-do list.

And so, we stay reactive. We focus on what's directly in front of us—the fire that needs extinguishing, the deadline that can't be missed—because that's what feels most urgent. But this approach often comes at a cost.

When we're stuck in reactivity, we lose the ability to see the bigger picture. We make decisions based on short-term relief rather than long-term impact. We prioritise tasks over purpose, action over alignment, and coping over thriving.

Have you ever had a day where you worked non-stop, ticking off one task after another, only to realise that at the end of it you didn't move the needle on anything that truly mattered? That's what living in a reactive state feels like. You're busy, but you're not better.

This is why reactivity, while natural, is limiting. Living in survival mode often means we're constantly trying to avoid risks and keep things as they are. However, just getting by isn't enough, especially in a world that requires us to be adaptable, creative, and ready for growth.

To really thrive in life, we need to change our mindset from reacting to the urgent to focusing on what matters. It's important to remember that while our natural stress reactions are a normal part of being human, and it's unlikely we can avoid them completely, we don't have to let them take over how we deal with challenges.

The good news is that reactivity isn't a permanent state. It's a habit, one that can be replaced with intentional responses.

## Mindset: The Lens that Shapes our Experience

Here's something pretty incredible. Our mindset doesn't just shape how we think, it actually affects how our body responds to the world around us.

Take stress. We're constantly told it's the enemy—something to avoid, manage, or get rid of altogether. But what if stress isn't the problem? What if the real issue is how we think about it?

A groundbreaking study of over 30,000 American adults uncovered a startling truth.[2] Participants were asked two questions: how much stress they had experienced in the past year, and whether they believed stress was harmful to their health. When researchers followed up eight years later, they found something remarkable.

The participants who reported high levels of stress and believed it was harmful had a 43% increased risk of premature death. But those who experienced high stress and didn't see it as harmful? They had some of the lowest mortality rates in the study, even lower than participants with little stress in their lives. The conclusion? Our beliefs about stress can be more dangerous than stress itself.

This isn't just a psychological effect; it's biological. In another experiment, Dr Alia Crum divided participants into two groups before exposing them to stressful tasks.[3] One group was primed to believe that stress was harmful. The other was primed to see stress as enhancing, and a source of focus, energy, and growth. The results were striking: the 'stress is harmful' group displayed a threat response, with heightened cortisol levels and poorer performance. However the 'stress is enhancing' group experienced a challenge response. Their bodies released not only cortisol but also dehydroepiandrosterone (DHEA), a hormone associated with resilience, learning, and long-term health.

What does this mean for us? It means that mindset isn't just a philosophical concept, it's a powerful biological force.

## The Stories we Tell Ourselves

This principle doesn't just apply to stress. It extends to other areas of life, like ageing and physical health. In one of Crum's other studies, hotel cleaners were told that the physical work they performed each day counted as exercise.[4] Over the next few weeks, their fitness levels improved, including reductions in body fat and blood pressure, all without any changes to their routines. The only thing that shifted was how they thought about their work.

Mindset also plays a critical role in healthy ageing. Research shows that individuals with a positive outlook on ageing live longer, have better cognitive function, and recover more quickly from illness.[5] Again, this isn't wishful thinking; it's the physiological impact of how we perceive our circumstances.

Think about that. The stories we tell ourselves about our experiences—whether stress will harm us, whether we're healthy, whether we're capable—don't just stay in our heads. They shape our bodies, our actions, and ultimately, our outcomes.

It's not about pretending life is easy or stress-free, it's about recognising the role our beliefs play in shaping our reality. It's about taking ownership of the lens through which we see the world and choosing a perspective that helps us thrive.

In Chapter 3, we explore how to move from managing stress to mastering it, using mindset as a tool to unlock resilience and growth. But for now, consider this: what beliefs are you holding onto about stress, change, or even your abilities? And how might shifting those beliefs unlock new possibilities?

The implications are profound. Your mindset can reshape your experience, not just mentally but biologically.

What does this mean in a world of constant pressure and uncertainty? It means that your mindset is not just an asset, it's a superpower. While you can't control every external event, you can control how you interpret and respond to them.

## The Betterment Mindset: Beyond Management

If mindset is our greatest asset, then the Betterment Mindset is how to activate it across all areas of our life.

At its core, the Betterment Mindset is about moving beyond mere management to creating better results in our life, relationships, work, and anything we set our mind to. It goes beyond how we think and feel about challenges and transforms the way we collaborate, solve problems, and create meaningful results.

Why does this matter? It's not enough to simply 'get by'. The pace of change is too fast, the pressure is too high, the challenges are too complex. To thrive in this reality, we need a new set of skills to drive creativity for advanced problem-solving and for collaboration, and we need the willingness to see challenges as springboards for growth.

The Betterment Mindset is built on three core pillars:

*Figure 1.*

1. **The Responsible Mindset**: Taking ownership of how we show up.
2. **The Win-Win Mindset**: Collaborating and creating value for everyone involved, rather than competing for limited resources.
3. **The Opportunity Mindset**: Seeing possibilities where others see problems and using them to innovate, grow, and evolve.

These pillars aren't abstract ideas, they're practical approaches that shape how we navigate every challenge, decision, and opportunity.

## Why Managing isn't Enough

Traditional management is about dealing with things. It's about solving today's problems and aiming to control the outcomes. While management is an important function, it keeps us locked in a cycle of firefighting, constantly reacting to what's urgent and leaving us more susceptible to losing sight of what's important.

In contrast, the Betterment Mindset is proactive. It's about stepping back to ask, *What does thriving look like here?* It's about making choices that align with our values, goals, and potential, even in the face of uncertainty.

For example, consider a leader managing a team through organisational change. A management mindset might focus on stabilising performance metrics, handling crises as they arise, and ensuring everyone does their job. Necessary? Sure. But Betterment asks a different set of questions: *How can we use this change to innovate? How can I empower my team to see this as an opportunity to grow, rather than as a problem to solve? How do we thrive together?*

The difference is profound. Management focuses on maintaining the status quo. Betterment focuses on creating something better.

## The Shift to Betterment: Small Changes, Big Impact

The good news is that Betterment isn't about perfection. It's about small, intentional shifts that add up to something much bigger over time.

When we adopt the Betterment Mindset, we're not trying to flip life upside down overnight. It's about small, intentional shifts; reframing a setback, asking a better question, or taking ownership of just one choice. On their own, these moments might seem minor, but over time, they stack up, creating real and lasting change.

This isn't just a nice idea; it's proven. Small improvements, made consistently, compound, leading to results far bigger than we might expect.

### Bryan Cranston's Breakthrough

*Bryan Cranston, best known for his role in Breaking Bad, credits a simple but powerful mindset shift with changing the course of his career.[6] Early on, he saw auditions as competitions, something to win. But over time, he realised that way of thinking was holding him back.*

*After nearly a decade of feeling the sting of rejection, he decided to shift his focus to the process itself: showing up, preparing intensely, and delivering the best performance he could. That small change completely redefined his experience. He no longer left auditions feeling drained or defeated, because he wasn't attached to the outcome. Ironically, it was this shift that allowed him to thrive, unlocking some of the biggest roles of his career.*

*<u>Cranston's Old Mindset:</u> An audition was like a job interview. The goal was to win the job.*

*<u>Cranston's New Mindset:</u> An audition was an opportunity to serve the script, to offer something truly unique that only he could bring to the character. Instead of trying to impress others, he realised he was there to give something, to share his interpretation of the role. Whether he was cast or not was beyond his control, but how he chose to show up was entirely within his power.*

*This wasn't an overnight change. It was a gradual shift in how he approached his craft. Instead of chasing a win, he focused on serving the story and bringing each character to life in a way that felt real. This shift gave him more confidence, creativity, and presence, allowing him to fully commit to the work, regardless of whether he landed the role.*

*As Cranston's mindset evolved, so did his career. He started with small parts, playing a paramedic, dubbing voices for animated films, and taking on guest spots in shows like Matlock and Hill Street Blues. But his new approach made him stand out, leading to bigger opportunities, such as his recurring role in Seinfeld as Dr Tim Whatley, and a pivotal role in Saving Private Ryan.*

*This Betterment approach eventually led to his breakthrough role as Hal in Malcolm in the Middle. But it was his performance in an episode of The X-Files that caught the attention of Vince Gilligan, who would later cast him as Walter White in Breaking Bad. Cranston's iconic portrayal of Walter White, a mild-mannered man who became a ruthless drug kingpin to provide for his family, won him multiple awards, including four Emmys and a Golden Globe.*

The learning for all of us is that his success wasn't due to a single, dramatic transformation. It was the small intentional shifts. By embracing Betterment, he moved beyond simply managing his career to becoming a visionary in his craft, driven by purpose rather than mere success.

By focusing on what's within our control, striving to help others, or contributing to a greater purpose while viewing obstacles as opportunities, we can shift from merely reacting to our circumstances to actively creating fulfilling and meaningful outcomes.

## Betterment in Business Outcomes

The Betterment Mindset isn't just a powerful tool for personal growth. It's equally transformative in an organisational context. While Bryan Cranston's story illustrates how small shifts can unlock extraordinary outcomes at an individual level, organisations that adopt a culture of continuous improvement see substantial gains in productivity, employee engagement, and innovation.

### The Toyota  Case Study

In the years following World War II, Japan grappled with a struggling economy and limited resources. Companies like Toyota had to find innovative ways to operate efficiently despite these constraints. During this challenging time, Toyota engineer Taiichi Ohno developed the principles of the Toyota Production System, anchored in the concept of kaizen, which means 'improvement' or 'change for better', and has been adopted in English to mean 'continuous improvement'.[9] This philosophy emphasises small, incremental improvements that, when consistently applied, can result in substantial progress over time.

Toyota's story provides a powerful example of how the Betterment Mindset can drive not only personal growth but also extraordinary organisational outcomes.

Toyota took a unique approach by involving every single employee, from factory floor workers to top executives, in the process of continuous Betterment. The company rejected the traditional notion that only senior management could drive innovation. Instead, it empowered employees at every level to suggest and implement improvements. Today, Toyota is known for generating nearly one million new ideas each year, most of which come from frontline workers. The impact of this relentless focus on improvement is profound: nearly 99% of these suggestions are implemented, demonstrating the company's commitment to turning ideas into action.[7]

## Driving a Culture of Ownership: The Responsible Mindset

One of the key elements that made Toyota's approach so effective was fostering a culture of ownership at every level. Workers were not just encouraged to do their jobs, they were empowered to take responsibility for improving how things were done. Employees were trained in problem-solving techniques and given the authority to stop the entire production line if they spotted an issue, a practice that was revolutionary in Western manufacturing at the time.

This empowerment to take action had transformative effects.

At the NUMMI (New United Motor Manufacturing, Inc.) plant, a joint venture between Toyota and General Motors, Toyota's approach to employee ownership led to remarkable results:

- The NUMMI plant, which had been previously deemed irreparably dysfunctional, transformed into one of the highest-performing plants in the industry.[8]

- Toyota recalled 79% fewer vehicles than Ford and 92% fewer than Chrysler.[7]

- Absenteeism rates, previously exceeding 20%,[7] dropped to just 3%, reflecting increased job satisfaction and engagement.[10]

By focusing on what they could control—small improvements in their daily tasks—Toyota's workers developed a strong sense of ownership over their work. This shift in mindset not only increased productivity but also created a culture where employees felt genuinely invested in the company's success. It's worth noting that this was all achieved with the same workforce, equipment, and facilities, simply by fostering a mindset focused on continuous Betterment and ownership.

## Collaboration for Mutual Success: The Win-Win Mindset

The success of Toyota's approach was not just about individual ownership; it was deeply rooted in collaboration. Toyota believed that a company's success depended on creating an environment where every employee felt valued and heard.

By introducing kaizen principles and simplifying the management hierarchy, Toyota created a culture where employees were not only workers but active contributors in the company's success.[7] The ability for every team member to stop the production line to fix issues demonstrated trust in their expertise and empowered them to make decisions that directly impacted quality. Team members were encouraged to suggest improvements, collaborate with supervisors, and take part in decision-making processes.

The collaborative spirit led to remarkable engagement:

- Over 85% of workers participated in submitting new ideas, resulting in nearly 10,000 actionable suggestions being implemented in a single year at the NUMMI plant.[10]

- The result was a radical transformation: absenteeism rates plummeted, job satisfaction soared, and operational efficiency and innovation improved dramatically.

This collaborative approach created a win-win environment where both the company and its employees thrived.

**Turning Challenges into Opportunities: The Opportunity Mindset**

One of the smartest aspects of Toyota's approach was how they handled employee suggestions. Instead of a typical suggestion box, where ideas often go to die, Toyota introduced 'idea coaches'. If a suggestion wasn't immediately workable, supervisors didn't just reject it, they coached employees to refine it into something actionable. The goal wasn't just innovation. It was creating a culture where every challenge was a chance to improve, not a roadblock.

The emphasis on small, consistent changes led to significant breakthroughs:

- Simple adjustments, like altering the height of shelves to improve efficiency, and changing the font size on safety signs, resulted in noticeable increases in productivity and safety.

- Over the course of two decades, Toyota gradually built a culture where every employee was expected to contribute at least two suggestions per year. This culture of continuous improvement became a standard across the company, propelling Toyota to the forefront of the automotive industry.

Toyota's story is a testament to the power of adopting a Betterment Mindset in a business context. By embracing the principles of ownership, collaboration, and continuous improvement, Toyota transformed itself into a global industry leader. The Responsible Mindset drove a culture of accountability; the Win-Win Mindset fostered collaboration; and the Opportunity Mindset turned everyday challenges into catalysts for innovation.

## Betterment: A Universal Driver of Success

Bryan Cranston's career-defining shift and Toyota's transformation into a global industry leader both show how the principles of Betterment can drive extraordinary outcomes across every level; personally, professionally, and even organisationally.

Whether we're leading a team, managing a project, or striving for personal growth, the same pillars apply: ownership, collaboration, and opportunity. The Betterment Mindset isn't about massive overhauls or unattainable perfection.

Just as Bryan Cranston transformed his career by shifting his focus to the process rather than the outcome, and Toyota empowered its employees to innovate through ownership, we, too, can create meaningful change in our life and work. The key lies in adopting the Betterment Mindset: seeing possibilities where others see problems to create a ripple effect of growth, innovation, and thriving, not just for us but for those around us.

## The Three Pillars of the Betterment Mindset

The three core areas of the Betterment Mindset—the Responsible Mindset, the Win-Win Mindset, and the Opportunity Mindset—create a framework for moving beyond simply managing life's challenges to actively making things better.

Let's break them down to understand why they matter and how they connect.

### The Responsible Mindset: Taking Ownership

At its core, the Responsible Mindset is about how we show up—owning our actions, choices, and attitudes. It's the foundation of Betterment. That doesn't mean trying to control everything or blaming ourselves when things don't go to plan. It's about focusing on what we can control and letting go of what we can't.

However, responsibility isn't just about better results; it also improves well-being. Research shows that when we focus on what's within our control, stress decreases, resilience grows, and our sense of agency strengthens.[11] Instead of reacting to whatever comes our way, we become active participants in shaping our experience.

### The Win-Win Mindset: Collaborating for Shared Success

The second pillar of the Betterment Mindset is about how we work with others. The Win-Win Mindset challenges the idea that success is a zero-sum game. Instead of competing for a bigger slice of the pie, it's about baking a bigger pie for everyone, creating outcomes where success is shared.

The Win-Win Mindset teaches us that when we stop seeing success as a competition and start embracing collaboration, trust, and shared purpose, we don't just lift others up, we expand our own potential in the process.

### The Opportunity Mindset: Seeing Possibilities in Challenges

The third pillar of the Betterment Mindset is about how we approach challenges. The Opportunity Mindset shifts our perspective. We see setbacks not as roadblocks, but as stepping stones for growth, learning, and innovation.

This mindset isn't about ignoring difficulties or pretending everything is positive. It's about staying curious, asking better questions, and focusing on what can be learned or improved. Research shows that when we adopt an opportunity-focused outlook, we boost creativity, decision-making, resilience, and adaptability, helping us navigate uncertainty with more clarity and confidence.[12]

## From Ownership to Opportunity: How the Mindsets Build on Each Other

The beauty of the Betterment Mindset lies in how these three pillars work together. When we take ownership of how we show up, we naturally improve our interactions with others. Collaborative, win-win relationships then create the trust and alignment needed to tackle challenges with creativity and resilience, which then open doors to new opportunities.

Whether we're navigating personal growth, leading a team, or solving a complex problem, these three mindsets provide the tools to move from firefighting to thriving. As we explore each pillar in greater depth, we discover practical ways to cultivate them in our own life and work.

# KEY INSIGHTS
## FOR BETTERMENT

- **Mindset is your greatest asset:** It shapes how you perceive and respond to challenges, influencing not just your mental state but also your biological and emotional resilience.

- **Reactivity keeps you stuck:** Operating in survival mode may feel necessary in the moment, but it prevents long-term growth and creativity.

- **Small changes drive transformation:** Incremental shifts, whether in mindset or action, accumulate to create profound personal and organisational outcomes over time.

- **The Betterment Mindset is built on three pillars:** These are the Responsible Mindset (taking ownership), the Win-Win Mindset (collaborating for shared success), and the Opportunity Mindset (seeing challenges as opportunities). Together, they provide a practical framework for thriving in an ever-changing world.

- **Your journey starts with awareness:** Recognising where you are now is the first step to moving toward Betterment.

# REFLECTIVE **QUESTIONS**

1. What beliefs about stress, change, or your abilities might be holding you back?
2. Where are you currently managing rather than thriving, and what small, intentional shifts could help you move forward?
3. Which of the three pillars—ownership, collaboration, or opportunity—feels most relevant to your current challenges?

**WHAT'S NEXT?** In the next chapter, we explore the Betterment Ladder, a practical framework to help you recognise where you are today and take intentional steps toward thriving.

# 2

# The Betterment Ladder—Steps from Surviving to Thriving

*'Knowing yourself is the beginning of all wisdom.'* Aristotle

## Self-Awareness is Freedom

### What Just Happened? The Story of Laura and Sam

*Laura was well known for her drive and ambition. She'd been clear with her boss, Sam, about her goals: she wanted a promotion and more responsibility, and she was ready to move up. But when he noticed her engagement had dropped lately—she was quieter in meetings, a bit withdrawn—he assumed she might be feeling unchallenged. He thought a new opportunity would give her exactly the boost she needed to feel reinvigorated.*

*So, Sam set up a meeting to propose a project he thought would be a perfect fit. It would expand her skills, stretch her responsibilities, and signal to leadership that she was ready for the next step. As he outlined the idea, he expected her typical reaction—enthusiasm, even gratitude. But that day was different. Laura sat quietly, her gaze fixed on her hands, and after a long pause, her eyes filled with tears and she snapped, 'I have enough on my plate, Sam, how do you expect me to get through all of this?'*

PART 1 THE MINDSET EVOLUTION

*What Sam didn't know was that outside of work, Laura's father's health had been declining, and she had become his main carer. With mounting personal responsibilities, even the simplest tasks felt overwhelming, let alone being given a new challenge. What Sam saw as a path for growth, Laura felt as another weight pulling her under.*

*Laura was in survival mode.*

We've all been Laura. And we've all been Sam.

The truth is, the way we behave—how we respond to challenges, relationships, and even ourselves—depends heavily on where we are mentally and emotionally. When we're in survival mode, our world becomes small. We react quickly, protectively, and often without the clarity we need to see the bigger picture.

It's completely different when we're thriving. We're excited and energised by the challenge and grab it with both hands.

The question is: how often do we need to pause to recognise where we are on that spectrum?

This is where the Betterment Ladder comes in. It's a tool for understanding our current state, not to judge ourselves, but to gain the awareness of where we are and what we need at any given point. Without self-awareness, we lose the ability to choose how we respond.

Before we can thrive, we have to understand where we're starting from.

## The Betterment Ladder: A Personal Mindset Strategy

Think of the Betterment Ladder as your personal strategy for navigating life's complexities. The framework serves as a guide to help you recognise your current position and identify what you need to move ahead with intention. This approach does not focus on attaining perfection or reaching the highest point in the shortest time. The Betterment Ladder helps you recognise where you are and take action toward meaningful growth.

For Laura, understanding the ladder would have meant realising that her defensiveness during the meeting with Sam wasn't about being overworked but about being in survival mode. For Sam, it would have been an opportunity to pause and ask Laura what support she needed to regain her balance.

The ladder also reminds us that our mindset isn't static. It's dynamic and influenced by how we engage with our experiences. While it's perfectly normal to find ourselves in survival or coping mode during challenging times, the goal is not to stay there by default. In the same way physical fitness demands regular practice, mastery of mindset does also, requiring planned and repeated effort. We develop this skill with practice over time, which helps us make intentional responses instead of letting events control us.

But this isn't just about managing stress or challenges. The Betterment Ladder is also a tool for growth. By identifying where we are today, we can take purposeful steps toward leveraging our strengths, embracing opportunities, and ultimately thriving in ways that feel meaningful and fulfilling.

## Self-Awareness is the First Step

The first step in using the Betterment Ladder is building awareness of what each level looks and feels like for us. What does surviving look like? How does it impact our energy, patience, or outlook? When we're just coping, what are the changes in these areas? When we're leveraging or thriving, what supports are in place, and what practices make that possible?

As we reflect on each level, we begin to craft a roadmap, a guide to help us respond intentionally to future challenges. The Ladder isn't about reaching a final destination. It's a dynamic tool for shifting upward with purpose, while also recognising that sometimes, growth begins with self-compassion. There are moments when the most powerful thing we can do is simply acknowledge where we are and give ourselves, or someone else, the grace to be there without judgement.

Our 'best' looks different at every level. When we're in survival mode, it might mean conserving energy and asking for help. When we're thriving, it might mean taking bold steps and embracing new challenges. The ladder helps us see where we are, understand what we need, and take small, meaningful steps toward growth, all while honouring the journey.

By recognising where we are at any given moment, we gain the power to shift upward with intention, or pause with compassion. Let's take a closer look at each level to see how the ladder can serve as both a mirror and a map for our Betterment journey.

## The Five Levels of the Betterment Ladder

### Surviving: Holding on by a Thread

Survival mode feels like treading water, using every bit of energy just to stay afloat. When life's demands outweigh our capacity, we are left mentally, emotionally, and physically drained. Small setbacks feel massive, decisions become overwhelming, and even the simplest tasks take effort.[1]

*James had always been the dependable one at work—respected, hardworking, and committed. But when his marriage ended, everything changed. Juggling a demanding career with the emotional and logistical challenges of co-parenting, he found himself stretched too thin. Deadlines that once felt easy now seemed impossible. He forgot meetings, missed emails, and started leaving early without explanation, just trying to get through the day.*

*His team noticed. Their frustration grew. Even his long-time supporters began to see him as unreliable. Meanwhile, his social life faded—texts went unanswered, and invitations felt like just another obligation. He wasn't trying to push people away; he was simply exhausted.*

Survival mode is a natural response to crisis, but staying there too long takes a toll.[2] It can damage relationships, erode trust, and make even the strongest people feel isolated. Recognising the signs—irritability, exhaustion, withdrawal—is the first step toward shifting out of it. While survival mode may be necessary in short bursts, no one is meant to stay there forever.

**Signals You're in Survival Mode**

- Frequent emotional breakdowns or tearfulness.
- Defensiveness or unpredictable reactions.
- Avoiding people, tasks, or responsibilities.
- Increased health issues over time (e.g., headaches, digestive problems, or frequent colds).
- Declining performance at work or home.
- Social withdrawal or strained relationships.

**Navigating Survival Mode**

Survival mode isn't about pushing harder. It's about recognising where you are and focusing on what will help you regain balance. Start small: prioritise rest, set boundaries, and ask for support. Even simple steps, like getting better sleep or tackling one task at a time, can help steady the ship.

Ask yourself: *Where is survival mode creeping into my life, and what small steps could help me move forward?* Recognising this state is the first step toward regaining control and progressing up the Betterment Ladder.

PART 1  THE MINDSET EVOLUTION

**Coping: Just Getting Through**

Coping mode is like living on autopilot, going through the motions without feeling truly engaged. We're physically present but mentally checked out, doing what's necessary to get by while waiting for a future moment when things will finally calm down. Over time, resentment builds toward our perceived 'source' of stress. It's a state of emotional exhaustion where escapism, whether through Netflix binges, scrolling endlessly on our phone, or pouring that extra glass of wine, feels like the only relief.

> *Layla, a corporate lawyer, knew this feeling well. Her days blurred together, packed with deadlines, last-minute client demands, and back-to-back meetings. She told herself she just needed to 'push through', but each morning she woke up already exhausted. Even small things like emails, conversations, and minor inconveniences felt heavier than they should. At night, she collapsed onto the couch, numbing her stress with TV and wine, promising herself that next week she'd get back to the gym, start meditating, or reconnect with friends. But 'next week' never came.*
>
> *At work, Layla became less patient, snapping at colleagues over small things. She skipped team lunches, avoiding social interactions that once felt energising. She wasn't unhappy, just detached, resentful, and tired. Coping mode had become her default.*

Coping is a natural response to prolonged stress, but when it becomes a way of life, it slowly drains our energy, relationships, and motivation. Recognising the signs—irritability, escapism, and disengagement—is key to moving forward. Real change doesn't come from waiting for life to slow down; it comes from taking small, intentional steps to re-engage before coping mode turns into burnout.

**Signals You're in Coping Mode**

- Feeling weighed down by responsibilities.

- Frequently feeling irritated with others or work in general.

- Relying on escapist habits like binge-watching TV or drinking more often 'to blow off steam'.

- Mentally checked out, feeling disengaged, and viewing relationships as burdens.

- Focusing on external factors as causes of stress, with scarcity-based thinking.

- Hanging out for holidays, often saying, *I just need to get through until…*

- Putting off self-care or meaningful activities for 'later'.

- Lacking enjoyment in what you do or feeling unsupported.

**Navigating Coping Mode**

Coping is a natural response to stress, but when it becomes a habit, it drains energy and builds resentment. Breaking free starts with small, intentional actions like setting boundaries, reconnecting with what recharges you, and taking breaks to prevent burnout.

Moving beyond coping isn't about waiting for life to calm down. It's about prioritising what you need now to create more space, energy, and fulfilment.

Ask yourself: *Where am I stuck in coping mode? What habits help me 'get through' but hold me back?* Recognising these patterns isn't about self-criticism, it's about self-compassion. The first step forward is simply acknowledging where you are and making one small, meaningful change.

**Managing: The Juggling Act**

Managing mode looks like balance from the outside—staying on top of work, family, and responsibilities—but inside, it feels like a constant struggle to keep everything from falling apart. We're getting things done, meeting expectations, and keeping the wheels turning, but there's no room for creativity, connection, or breathing space.[3] The pace is relentless, and even small disruptions feel like they could throw everything off track.

*Rachel, a CEO leading her organisation through a high-stakes review, was admired for her ability to stay composed under pressure. Her days were a blur, starting at 6 am and filled with back-to-back meetings, crisis management, and endless decision-making. She kept everything running, but at a cost. The demands of work left little room for strategic thinking, and even less for herself.*

*At home, the strain followed. She cherished being present for her children, but her mind was always elsewhere, thinking about the next report, the next meeting, the next problem to solve. One night, as she read her daughter a bedtime story, she caught herself reciting the words without absorbing them.*

*'I feel like I'm everywhere and nowhere at once,'* she later admitted. Managing mode is a trap of constant doing without real fulfilment. We keep up with the demands, but there's no breathing room, no space to fully engage in what matters most.[4] Recognising when we're stretched too thin is the first step to shifting from simply managing to truly living.

**Signals You're in Managing Mode**

- Delivering on responsibilities but feeling stretched and strained.
- Constantly feeling like there aren't enough hours in the day.
- Struggling to stay ahead of to-do lists or deadlines.
- Maintaining productivity but lacking creativity or big-picture focus.
- Feeling split between competing priorities at work and home.
- Skipping self-care routines, like exercise or rest, due to time constraints.

- Cancelling or rescheduling personal plans because of last-minute work demands.

**Navigating Managing Mode**

Managing mode keeps things moving under pressure, but it's not sustainable long term. Constantly juggling responsibilities without a break leads to exhaustion and a loss of perspective. The first step to regaining balance is by recognising when you're stuck in the cycle.

Moving beyond managing mode doesn't mean doing less. It means working smarter. Create breathing space with short breaks, delegate tasks, and set firmer boundaries to protect your energy. Small adjustments can restore balance without sacrificing productivity.

> Reflect: are you neglecting relationships or self-care just to keep up? Where do you feel most stretched, and what small shifts could ease the pressure? Managing mode keeps things running, but real fulfilment comes from aligning your priorities with what truly matters.

**Leveraging: Rising to the Challenge**

In Leveraging mode, stress isn't a burden, it's fuel. Instead of feeling overwhelmed, we use challenges to lift our game, sharpen our skills, and improve performance. Just like athletes who train under pressure to build resilience, those in Leveraging mode see obstacles as opportunities, not threats. This mindset shift turns stress into a driver for growth rather than something to endure.

*Jordan, who owned a construction firm, felt the weight of expectation when his company landed its biggest contract yet, a high-profile project that could make or break their reputation. The pressure was real, but instead of letting it overwhelm him, he saw it as a chance to lead with purpose. From the outset, he set a clear vision. He encouraged collaboration and gave his team the trust and ownership they needed to step up.*

*Rather than buckling under the demands, his team thrived.*

*Brainstorming sessions turned obstacles into creative solutions, and open conversations kept morale high. Instead of hovering over every detail, Jordan focused on backing his team, recognising their efforts and reinforcing a culture where challenges were seen as opportunities to grow.*

*By the time the project wrapped up, the impact wasn't just in the final build, it was in the team itself. They had grown more capable, confident, and invested in their work.*

Leveraging mode isn't just about delivering under pressure; it's about turning high-stakes moments into defining experiences that fuel long-term success.

**Signals You're in Leveraging Mode**

- Feeling energised by challenges and actively seeking them out.[5]
- Embracing stress as a driver of peak performance.
- Seeing challenges as opportunities for growth and learning.[6]
- Experiencing a strong sense of connection with others during difficult times.
- Achieving 'flow' state—feeling fully immersed and focused on what you're doing.[7]
- Learning, adapting, and staying open-minded with ease.
- Displaying high self-efficacy—maintaining an 'I can' mentality.[8]

**Navigating Leveraging Mode**

Leveraging mode is an exciting phase of growth, but sustaining it requires balance. Taking on challenges is valuable, but without limits and focus, it's easy to burn out or slip back into managing mode.

Peak performance demands energy. Strategic pauses for rest aren't signs of weakness but essential for maintaining momentum. Not every challenge is worth taking on. The most rewarding growth comes from choosing opportunities that stretch your capabilities while aligning with your values. Growth requires both discomfort and direction. Focus on what energises you and moves you toward your goals.

Leveraging mode also thrives on connection. Do challenges bring you closer to others, building trust and collaboration, or do they create division? The more you engage with others, the greater your capacity for growth.

Reflect: do you approach challenges with curiosity or overwhelm? How do you recharge when energy is low? Recognising what fuels your growth while maintaining balance allows you to progress toward the final level of the Betterment Ladder: Thriving.

## Thriving: Living with Purpose and Contribution

Thriving mode is when everything clicks, when our actions, values, and purpose all line up.[9,10] It's not about chasing big wins but about showing up with intention in the everyday moments. Challenges don't vanish, but they feel worthwhile because we're contributing to something bigger than ourselves. Thriving is about connection, fulfilment, and knowing that what we do genuinely matters.

*Mel, a customer service manager, had always been great at getting things done—solving problems, hitting targets, and keeping everything on track. But over time, she started to wonder: was she just being productive, or was she making a real impact?*

*Her perspective shifted when she stopped seeing her role as just fixing issues and started treating every client interaction as a chance to make someone feel heard and valued. Instead of rushing through conversations, she focused on connection. This shift extended to her team. She became more than a manager. She became a mentor, investing in their growth, celebrating their wins, and fostering a culture of support.*

*Success was no longer about ticking boxes; it was about making a difference. Mel found energy in seeing her team thrive, knowing her work had meaning beyond the daily tasks.*

Thriving isn't about external recognition. It's about alignment, contribution, and the deep satisfaction of knowing we're part of something bigger than ourselves.[11]

**Signals You're in Thriving Mode**

- You feel a strong sense of meaning, purpose, and alignment.
- Your actions reflect your values, creating deep fulfilment.
- You approach challenges with enthusiasm and curiosity.
- Each day feels energising, with a clear sense of contribution.
- You see how your efforts fit into the bigger picture.
- You focus on nurturing authentic connections with others.
- Challenges inspire growth rather than fear or avoidance.

**Embracing Thriving as a Path to Fulfilment**

Thriving isn't a destination, it's a way of being. It requires reflection, intention, and alignment with what matters most. Even in difficult times, thriving means living with purpose and finding fulfilment through meaningful contribution.

⎡ Reflect: where do you feel most aligned with your values? How do you contribute to others' well-being? What gives you a sense of purpose? ⎤

Thriving is about creating a life of connection, resilience, and impact, one that enriches both you and those around you. Each day offers a new opportunity to grow and make a difference.

## Beyond the Ladder: The Betterment Mindset

The Betterment Ladder is a framework for recognising our current state and providing clarity for what we need to do. When used as a tool for thriving, it helps us create better results in three key areas: our personal journey, our relationships, and our overall outlook on life. These three dimensions form the foundation of the Betterment Mindset, which we explore in greater depth throughout the book.

The ladder gives us a clearer understanding of our own experiences, helping us move from overwhelm to ownership. In survival and coping modes, it's easy to feel powerless when we're constantly reacting to life's demands without a sense of control. But as we move up the ladder, we shift to a more intentional way of operating, taking responsibility for our choices, habits, and mindset. This transition is at the core of the Responsible Mindset, which is explored in Part 2 of this book.

The ladder also sheds light on how we connect and work with others, guiding us from competition to collaboration. When we're stuck in the lower levels, stress, defensiveness, or a scarcity mindset can drive our interactions. But as we climb, we become more open, which fosters trust, teamwork, and shared success. This shift aligns with the Win-Win Mindset, which focuses on collaboration and mutual success, explored further in Part 3.

Finally, the ladder shapes how we see challenges, shifting our perspective from obstacles to opportunities for growth. In the lower levels, problems can feel overwhelming and draining. But as we climb, we develop a more empowered outlook, viewing setbacks as stepping stones for learning, improvement, and innovation. This reflects the Opportunity Mindset, which is all about turning problems into possibilities and is explored further in Part 4.

By using the Betterment Ladder as a guide, we build self-awareness and take intentional steps to cultivate ownership, collaboration, and opportunity in every aspect of our lives. It's a tool that empowers us to move beyond mere survival and create a more fulfilling, balanced, and purpose-driven life.

## PART 1 THE MINDSET EVOLUTION

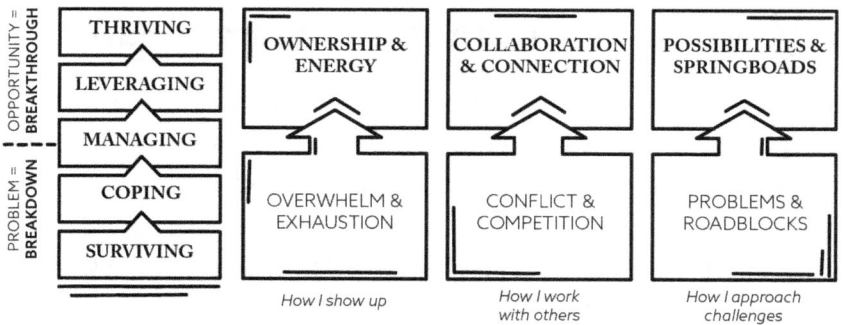

Figure 2.

## Building Your Betterment Mindset Strategy

Climbing the Betterment Ladder requires more than recognising where you are. It's about actively choosing how to respond to life's challenges. This isn't about perfection or racing to the top. It's about building a mindset that prioritises growth, balance, and intentionality. To help navigate this journey, the strategy is broken into three key steps: recognising where you are, understanding what you need, and committing to regular check-ins.

### Step One: Recognise Where You Are

Self-awareness is the foundation of growth and resilience. Just as we adjust our behaviour when we notice physical signs of strain, understanding where we are on the Betterment Ladder helps us respond more effectively to life's challenges.

Each level of the Ladder reflects a different part of the human experience. Recognising where we are isn't about judgement, it's about clarity. A new opportunity may feel exciting and energising when we're thriving, but overwhelming and burdensome when we're just surviving. By noticing where we are, we gain the freedom to act intentionally rather than reactively, to meet our needs in the present and create space for future growth.

THE BETTERMENT LADDER **CHAPTER 2**

Thriving may be the ultimate goal, but survival mode has its place too. It's a natural, protective response when life's demands exceed our capacity. Understanding these states enables us to approach our experiences with compassion and curiosity, transforming awareness into action.

> Everyone's experience is unique. Take a moment to reflect: what does each of these levels look like for you? How are you feeling, thinking, and behaving? What are your signals that indicate you are at a certain level? Personalising your understanding of each level allows you to recognise these states more quickly and respond with intention.

## Step Two: Identify What You Need

Once you recognise where you are, the next step is understanding what each level reveals about your needs and the actions that support you. Every position on the ladder is shaped by circumstances and choices, and each one calls for a specific kind of care and response.

In survival mode, your needs may be fundamental: rest, support, or simply a pause to regain your footing. In coping mode, you may need to reconnect with activities that restore energy or create stability. Managing mode often requires setting boundaries, delegating tasks, or carving out time for renewal, while leveraging mode encourages seeking meaningful challenges and opportunities for growth. Thriving, meanwhile, relies on sustaining alignment and staying intentional about your values and priorities.

Understanding your needs isn't just about reflection. It's about taking actionable steps to meet them. If you feel stretched in managing mode, it might mean saying 'no' to one commitment to protect your energy. If you notice you're withdrawing in coping mode, reconnecting with a friend or enjoying a hobby could help break the cycle. These actions don't have to be dramatic. Sometimes, the smallest adjustments—prioritising an early night, a walk outside, or a meaningful conversation—can create powerful momentum.

Take a moment to consider: what do you need at each level and what actions help you meet these needs? Understanding your needs gives you the clarity to act with intention, creating space for growth and alignment.

## Step Three: Develop a Practice for Checking in

Growth isn't a one-time event, it's an ongoing cycle of awareness and adjustment. The final step in building a change mindset is making regular check-ins a habit. This simple practice helps you stay aware of where you are on the ladder and what you need to keep moving forward.

It doesn't have to be complicated. A quick daily pause—*Where am I right now? What do I need?*—can offer valuable insight. You might build this into your routine, like during your morning coffee, at the end of your workday, or before bed. Journalling can also help, giving you a space to spot patterns, track progress, and clarify your thoughts over time.

It's also important to recognise that your position on the ladder can shift throughout the day. A morning spent thriving might give way to coping after a tough conversation or a stressful setback. Checking in regularly helps you notice these shifts and respond before stress becomes a default state.

This practice creates a foundation for resilience and intentionality. By routinely reflecting on your experience, you remain connected to your values and can navigate life's demands with clarity and purpose.

## Tips for Building Your Betterment Mindset Strategy

Recognising where you are on the Surviving-to-Thriving Ladder is just the start. Thriving comes from creating the right conditions for growth. Here are five key ways to build a resilient, sustainable mindset:

### 1. Balance Across Life Domains

Thriving isn't about excelling in one area while neglecting others. It's about alignment. If work is flourishing but relationships or well-being are suffering, imbalance will catch up with you.

**Reflect:** Are you investing too much energy in one area at the expense of others? What small adjustments could bring more balance?

## 2. Focus on What You can Control

External stressors—work, personal challenges, unexpected setbacks—can push you up and down the ladder. Resilience comes from anchoring yourself in what you *can* control: your mindset, actions, and responses.

**Ask yourself**: *Am I letting outside factors dictate my experience? How can I stay grounded despite uncertainty?*

## 3. Know when to Seek Support

Growth doesn't mean doing everything alone. Those who embrace help, whether from a mentor, friend, or professional, move forward with greater ease and resilience.

**Consider:** Where in your life could support make a meaningful difference? What's one small step you could take to reach out?

## 4. Practise Self-Compassion

You won't always be thriving, and that's okay. Every stage—struggle, progress, rest—plays a role in growth. Treat yourself with the same kindness you'd offer a friend.

**Reflect:** How do you speak to yourself when facing challenges? Are you allowing yourself the grace to grow?

## 5. Stay Curious and Adaptable

Growth isn't linear. It requires flexibility. Instead of resisting change, look for unexpected opportunities to turn hardship into possibility.

**Ask yourself**: *Where in my life could curiosity help me adapt and grow?*

**Final Thought: Thriving is a Journey, not a Destination**

A change mindset strategy isn't just about getting to the next level. It's about embracing the process with curiosity, patience, and a sense of fulfilment along the way. True growth takes time, effort, and a commitment to showing up for yourself consistently. By balancing different areas of life, creating inner stability, seeking support, practising self-compassion, and staying open to new possibilities, you build a journey that's not just productive, but genuinely meaningful.

Wherever you find yourself on the ladder today, remember that progress isn't a race. It's the small, intentional steps, those everyday moments of learning, adjusting, and appreciating, that create a life of fulfilment and resilience. Thriving isn't just a destination; it's the way we engage with the present, celebrate our wins, and embrace each challenge as an opportunity to grow.

# KEY INSIGHTS
## FOR BETTERMENT

- **Self-awareness is the foundation for growth:** Recognising where you are on the Betterment Ladder helps you respond with intention, making small but meaningful shifts that align with your goals and values.

- **Balance across life domains is essential:** Thriving in one area of life while neglecting another is unsustainable. True fulfilment comes from creating alignment across personal, professional, and relational aspects of life.

- **The Betterment Ladder is a tool for growth across every dimension:** It helps you take ownership of your experience (Responsible Mindset in Part 2), strengthen your relationships (Win-Win Mindset in Part 3), and expand your outlook (Opportunity Mindset in Part 4).

- **Meeting your needs accelerates progress:** Each level of the ladder reveals unique challenges and opportunities. Identifying your needs at each stage empowers you to take intentional action toward Betterment.

- **Progress is an ongoing journey, not a final destination:** Checking in with yourself regularly helps you stay aligned with your values, adapt to challenges, and sustain meaningful growth.

# REFLECTIVE QUESTIONS

1. Where do you currently find yourself on the Surviving-to-Thriving Ladder, and how does it impact different areas of your life?
2. How well balanced are your personal, professional, and relational domains? Where might you need more alignment?
3. Which aspect of the Betterment Mindset—ownership, collaboration, or opportunity—feels most relevant to your current challenges?
4. What specific needs do you have at your current level, and what actions can you take to support yourself?
5. How can you incorporate regular check-ins to ensure you're progressing intentionally rather than reacting to life's demands?

**WHAT'S NEXT?** In the next chapter, we dive into the critical role stress plays in shaping our daily experience. Stress is an unavoidable part of modern life, but how we manage it determines whether we remain stuck in survival mode or move toward thriving. We explore practical tools and strategies to navigate stress more effectively. Mastering stress is not just about coping; it's about using it as a catalyst for growth and Betterment.

# 3

# **Stress Mastery**—An Essential Skill for Betterment in a Fast-Paced World

*'You cannot control the waves, but you can learn to surf.'*
*Jon Kabat-Zinn*

## The Reality of Stress: Why it Matters more than Ever

### When Stress and Progress Collide

Life is increasingly demanding. We're expected to do more, achieve more, and keep up with relentless change, leaving many of us feeling stretched thin and running on empty.

The challenge? Growth and Betterment require energy, focus, and creativity, qualities that are eroded by unchecked stress. The more we strive to improve, the more stress pulls us into survival mode, making us reactive, defensive, and exhausted.

A chief marketing officer at a leading tech company I worked with captured this perfectly: 'This is the first time in my career I've had to completely change my strategy in less than a year. The pressure is relentless. We want to focus on growth, but my people are in pure survival mode. Stress and burnout are our biggest challenges right now.'

Sound familiar?

PART 1 THE MINDSET EVOLUTION

When progress and pressure collide, it's easy to feel stuck, uncertain, and even to question whether Betterment is possible at all.

## A Personal Turning Point: My Own Experience with Stress

*I always believed I thrived under pressure. My time as an elite basketball player taught me to embrace both physical and mental challenges, and I carried that mindset into my career, building businesses in Sydney, London, and New York. Long hours, high expectations, and relentless deadlines felt normal. Stress never seemed like a problem—until it was.*

*During four fast-paced years in New York, I started experiencing inexplicable health issues. After countless specialist appointments, I was diagnosed with proctitis, an inflammatory condition with very embarrassing symptoms that my doctor said I'd have to manage for life. He advised cutting out alcohol, adopting a strict diet, and, most importantly, reducing stress.*

*But stress wasn't something I could just 'reduce'. I loved my work and wasn't willing to slow down. I tried everything—diet changes, medication, even restructuring my schedule—but my symptoms persisted. I began planning my days around them, making excuses to leave meetings, and feeling the need to hide what I was going through.*

*At one point, I wondered if this was just my new normal. But deep down, I wasn't ready to accept that. I needed a different approach.*

*Then something unexpected happened. My symptoms disappeared almost overnight. Despite my doctor saying it wasn't possible, I found myself back to living the life I wanted—drinking socially, enjoying meals out, and tackling new challenges—all without the physical toll of stress. The difference? It wasn't my lifestyle; it was my mindset.*

*I had spent years treating stress as the enemy, something to battle or eliminate. But stress wasn't the problem; it was part of the life I wanted to live. Once I stopped fearing it and started seeing it as a challenge to rise to, everything changed. I learned to rebound faster from high-stress moments and let go of the emotional weight I'd been carrying for years.*

This experience taught me two powerful lessons:

1. **Stress is part of a meaningful life.** Big goals come with stress. It's unavoidable. Trying to eliminate it is disempowering. The key is learning to work with stress, not against it.
2. **Unchecked stress always takes a toll.** Whether stress manifests as burnout, exhaustion, or strained relationships, running on adrenaline isn't sustainable. We must build a healthier relationship with stress, one that fuels performance without sacrificing well-being.

## The Case for Stress Mastery: Why it's an Essential Skill for Betterment

Mastering stress isn't about avoiding it; it's about creating the ability to navigate it with greater awareness and control. That's why this chapter is so important. By developing the right tools and mindset, we can stop stress from being something that drags us down and instead use it to propel us forward.

If we don't learn to master stress, it will continue to drive us into a reactive cycle, one that limits our potential in every aspect of life. When stress takes control, it:

- **Reduces responsibility**: Instead of taking ownership, we fall into patterns of avoidance, blame, or overwhelm.

- **Strains relationships**: Stress can divide and isolate us, making it harder to collaborate effectively and achieve win-win outcomes.

- **Narrows our perspective**: Under stress, we default to short-term thinking, making it difficult to see opportunities or think creatively.

By mastering stress, we reclaim our ability to take responsibility for our actions, build meaningful connections, and pursue growth with clarity and purpose.

## Stress isn't the Problem, Our Relationship with it is

As we explored in Chapter 1, our mindset plays a profound role in shaping our experience of stress. We often see stress as the enemy, something to be avoided or eliminated at all costs. In fact, over the past two decades, our beliefs about what constitutes a healthy level of stress have gone down.[1] However, research suggests that our beliefs about stress may be more harmful than the stress itself.[2]

The groundbreaking study explored in Chapter 1 found that individuals who viewed stress as harmful had a significantly higher risk of negative health outcomes. However, those who saw stress as a challenge, not a threat, experienced better health, greater resilience, and improved performance.

This shift in perspective is crucial because, let's face it, stress isn't going anywhere. Reducing stress entirely isn't a realistic solution, but mastering it is. As Kelly McGonigal highlights in her book *The Upside of Stress*,[3] changing how we think about stress can transform our experience of it. When we learn to work with stress rather than against it, it becomes a force for focus, energy, and growth.

What if we saw stress as an essential part of the journey?

## A New Approach: The Betterment Mindset for Stress Management

If stress isn't something we can simply reduce or eliminate, then the question becomes, how do we work with it in a way that fuels rather than depletes us?

The key lies in adopting a new approach to stress mastery, one that focuses on building resilience in real time rather than waiting for the perfect conditions to appear. This approach isn't about 'stress reduction'. It's about equipping ourselves with the tools and mindset to manage stress in a way that aligns with our goals and ambitions, rather than against them.

The Betterment Mindset approach to stress management is built around three essential steps, which I call the 3Rs:

1. **Respond:** Shifting from reacting to stress to responding with intention. This step focuses on recognising stress for what it is—a sign that something matters—and learning how to reframe it in a way that enhances focus and performance rather than triggering survival mode.
2. **Rebound:** Recovering and re-energising throughout the day to prevent exhaustion from creeping in. Instead of waiting until burnout hits, we can leverage practical, science-backed techniques to reset and recharge in small, consistent ways.
3. **Release:** Letting go of the emotional and physical weight of stress to ensure it doesn't accumulate over time. Unprocessed stress lingers in our bodies and minds, creating long-term impacts. Releasing stress intentionally helps us move forward with clarity and focus.

Each of these steps is designed to help us take ownership of our stress experience, transforming it from something that drains us to something that drives us.

## 1. Respond: Shifting from Reacting to Taking Control

When stress hits, most of us react instinctively. We go into fight, flight, or freeze mode, our minds racing, our emotions heightened, and our actions often driven by impulse rather than intention. This automatic reaction is deeply wired into our biology; it's how our ancestors survived threats in the wild. But in today's world, where the 'threats' we face are more psychological than physical—tight deadlines, difficult conversations, or the pressure to perform—our default stress response can do more harm than good.

The good news? We have the power to shift from reactivity to response-ability—the ability to pause, assess, and respond in a way that aligns with our goals and values.

## The Science of Stress: Why Our Brains Get it Wrong

The fight-or-flight response is our built-in survival system, kicking in when the amygdala senses danger. Adrenaline surges, heart rate spikes, and cortisol fires up our energy reserves, preparing us to react fast. In real emergencies, it's exactly what we need.

With today's more psychological stressors—overflowing inboxes, tough conversations, looming deadlines—our brains fail to distinguish real threats from perceived ones, keeping stress hormones elevated for far too long.

For many of us, the threat stress state becomes the default, leading to:

- **Poor memory.** Stress prioritises immediate action over recall, making forgetfulness common.

- **Shallow breathing.** Fast, chest-level breaths replace the deep breathing needed for calm.

- **Sleep issues.** A racing mind prevents quality rest.

- **Low heart rate variability (HRV).** Chronic stress reduces HRV, keeping the nervous system on high alert.

Left unchecked, prolonged stress contributes to burnout, anxiety, digestive issues, and chronic pain. The key? Recognising threat mode and shifting to a more constructive response.

## From Threat to Challenge: Reframing Stress for Growth

While the threat response helps us survive, the challenge response allows us to thrive. When we shift into a challenge mindset, our bodies still produce adrenaline and cortisol, but they also release a powerful hormone called DHEA (dehydroepiandrosterone). DHEA supports brain function, growth, and repair, helping to counteract some of the negative effects of cortisol and enabling us to learn and grow from high-pressure experiences.[4]

The balance between cortisol and DHEA is often referred to as the growth index, which plays a crucial role in determining how we perform under pressure. A higher growth index, meaning more DHEA relative to cortisol, is linked to:

- Improved focus and problem-solving abilities.
- Greater emotional resilience in challenging situations.
- Enhanced ability to recover from setbacks.

The good news? We don't need supplements or drastic lifestyle changes to improve our growth index. The key lies in shifting our perception of stress and adopting practical strategies to leverage it as fuel for growth rather than seeing it as a force to fear.

## Mindset Matters: The Power of Seeing Stress as Helpful

Groundbreaking research by Dr Alia Crum and her colleagues has shown that how we think about stress shapes our body's response to it. In a well-known study, participants were divided into two groups and exposed to different messages about stress.[5]

One group was told that stress is harmful and should be avoided.

The other was told that stress can enhance performance and build resilience.

When faced with a high-pressure task afterward, the 'stress is harmful' group exhibited a typical threat response, with heightened cortisol levels and poorer performance. In contrast, those who were primed to see stress as helpful experienced a challenge response, complete with a beneficial release of DHEA that supported focus and problem-solving.

Crum's findings don't just apply to health. They've been replicated across a range of contexts, from performance to relationships and beyond. Whether participants were asked to consider stress in the context of their careers, personal relationships, or academic pursuits, the results were remarkably consistent: those who believed stress could be helpful performed better, built stronger connections, and felt more capable of handling challenges. In contrast, those who viewed stress as harmful were more likely to experience anxiety, disengagement, and lower overall satisfaction.

> The takeaway is clear: our beliefs about stress are powerful. When we see stress as a challenge to overcome rather than as a threat to escape, our bodies respond in kind, providing the energy and focus we need to rise to the occasion.

**Shifting from Reactive to Responsive**

This understanding of stress is essential for mastering it. Instead of letting stress hijack our thinking and decision-making, we can train ourselves to pause and reframe the situation and the stress to engage our challenge response.

This is where the **R.O.A.R. technique**, a simple framework designed to help shift our stress response in real time and harness it as a tool for growth, comes in.

### The R.O.A.R. Technique—A Tool for Performance

The **R.O.A.R. technique** offers a simple, four-step framework to ensure you have a healthy physiological response to stress, rather than reacting impulsively, and to set you up to perform at your best:

1. **Reframe the Stress:** Instead of seeing stress as a threat, view it as your body's way of preparing you to perform. When you feel your heart racing before a big presentation, remind yourself, *This is my body gearing up to help me focus.*

2. **Own the Opportunity:** Stress usually means something important is at stake. Instead of letting it overwhelm you, ask, *What does this stress signal about what matters most to me?* Take a moment to connect with a positive motivation.

3. **Activate the Energy:** Harness the energy that stress provides and channel it into meaningful progress. Whether it's tackling a task, having a crucial conversation, or focusing on solutions, use stress to drive constructive action.

4. **Recharge and Reward:** After pushing through a stressful moment, it's vital to take a pause, acknowledge your effort, and recharge. Small recovery moments throughout the day help prevent burnout and reinforce resilience.

A study conducted with employees at a Fortune 500 company tested the impact of this type of intervention during a high-stress period.[6] Participants were asked to practise the core principles at least once a day over a two-week period, whenever they felt stressed.

The results were impressive.

Employees reported a noticeable shift in their mindset. They felt better equipped to handle stress with greater confidence and clarity. They experienced reductions in anxiety and depression and improvements in physical health, and they reported feeling more focused, creative, and engaged in their work. Most importantly, these benefits weren't fleeting. The positive effects were sustained well beyond the initial intervention.

**Building the Habit of Responding with Intention**

Just like any skill, learning to respond to stress intentionally takes practice. Here are a few small shifts you can start making today:

- **Pause before reacting.** When stress arises, take a deep breath and give yourself a moment to assess before reacting.

- **Reframe your internal dialogue.** Instead of thinking, *I can't handle this,* try asking, *How can I use this stress to perform at my best?*

- **Use physical cues to reset.** Do you notice tension in your shoulders, shallow breathing, or racing thoughts? These are signals to pause and respond mindfully.

By adopting a response-driven mindset, we not only navigate stress more effectively but also unlock greater confidence, clarity, and control in all areas of our life.

## 2. Rebound: Recovering Quickly to Sustain High Performance

As we get better at managing stress, one key skill stands out—the ability to rebound quickly. It's not about getting rid of stress altogether, but learning to shift between high and low states with ease. Stress helps us focus and perform, but without intentional recovery, it leads to burnout, exhaustion, and fatigue. Learning to rebound quickly allows us to sustain high performance without draining our energy.

### Heart Rate Variability—Our Built-in Resilience Gauge

HRV measures how well the body shifts between fight-or-flight (threat) and rest-and-digest (recovery).[7] High HRV signals adaptability and resilience, while low HRV suggests chronic stress and slower recovery.

Prolonged stress lowers HRV, increasing fatigue and cognitive fog. The good news? Simple practices—breathwork, movement, and mindfulness—can boost HRV, helping us recover faster and stay in control.

## Becoming a 'State Shifter'

Many of us are familiar with the long-term habits that support resilience—getting quality sleep, maintaining a healthy diet, and exercising regularly. While these are essential, they often fall by the wayside during high-stress periods. This is why it's crucial to develop quick, practical techniques that allow us to shift our state in the moment, helping us stay composed, energised, and focused throughout the day.

Whether we need to calm down after a high-stress moment or energise ourselves before an important task, these 'state-shifters' are science-backed strategies that can be used anytime, anywhere.

## Seven Science-Backed Tools to Shift Your State

### Smile—Even if You Fake it

Smiling triggers endorphins, reducing stress and improving mood, even when forced. Studies show it lowers heart rate and promotes calmness.[8]

**Quick tip:** Make smiling a habit, on walks, in meetings, or during stressful moments.

### Breathe with Intention

Deep breathing calms the nervous system, counteracting stress. Try the **4-6 method**: inhale for four counts, exhale for six.[9]

**Quick tip:** Extend your exhale when tension builds, especially before meetings or challenges.

### Strike a Power Pose

Expansive postures boost confidence and reduce cortisol. Standing tall signals strength to your brain.[10]

**Quick tip:** Before high-pressure situations, hold a power pose (e.g., 'Wonder Woman' stance—standing tall with shoulders back, hands on hips and feet hip distance apart) for two minutes.

### Take a Walk in Green Spaces
Nature reduces stress hormones and improves focus. Even looking at nature images can have a calming effect.[11]
**Quick tip:** Step outside for fresh air or keep a nature image nearby to reset your mind.

### Listen to Uplifting Music
Music affects mood, focus, and energy. Upbeat tunes boost motivation, while calming melodies enhance relaxation.
**Quick tip:** Create playlists for focus, relaxation, and energy boosts.

### Move Your Body
Physical movement reduces cortisol, improves circulation, and releases endorphins. Even small movements help.
**Quick tip:** Do a quick stretch or take a brisk walk when stress feels overwhelming.

### Engage in a Creative Activity
Creativity relaxes the mind and fosters clarity. Writing, drawing, or playing music shifts focus away from stress.
**Quick tip:** Spend a few minutes on a creative task—doodle, journal, or play an instrument.

By incorporating these quick, science-backed techniques into your day, you become more intentional about how you manage your stress state, allowing you to stay energised, focused, and adaptable.

## Transform Your Mind and Body in Ten Minutes a Day

Most people feel they don't have time for meaningful change, but resilience is built through small, consistent actions.

The **2x5=10 method** is simple. Take a two-minute state-shifter five times a day—just ten minutes total. These micro-rebounds help you reset, refocus, and train your nervous system to shift between high and low states. Like athletes strengthening muscles through short, consistent workouts, these small pauses build long-term resilience and stress adaptability.

**Making it a Habit: The Power of 'When-Then' Plans**

New habits need intention and consistency. 'When-then' plans link a specific situation (when) to a specific action (then), creating automatic triggers for stress management. Research shows they boost follow-through by up to 80%, making it easier to stay consistent even on busy days.[12]

Examples:

- When I make my coffee, then I'll stand in a power pose for two minutes.
- When I finish a meeting, then I'll take a deep breath and stretch.
- When I feel overwhelmed, then I'll do a gratitude pause.

Repeating these actions reinforces stress-regulation habits, making them second nature. Visual cues like phone reminders or sticky notes can help until they become automatic.

### 3. Release: Letting Go of Stress Before it Accumulates

Stress is a natural part of life and experiencing it, even with negative emotions, isn't necessarily a problem. In fact, short-term stress, when processed effectively, can be motivating and can help us rise to challenges. The real issue arises when stress and the emotions that come with it linger, when we carry them from one day to the next.

Studies have shown that lingering negative emotions associated with stress can have long-term effects on our health.[13] They are also associated with chronic conditions up to ten years later. When we don't actively release the emotional weight of stress, it can accumulate, showing up in our bodies, thoughts, and behaviours, often without us realising it.

Letting go isn't about ignoring stress or pretending it doesn't exist. It's about acknowledging it, processing it, and moving forward in a way that allows us to stay mentally and emotionally free.

**Three Proven Techniques Release Stress and Negative Emotions**

Releasing negative emotions requires both awareness and action. The goal is to process the emotions connected to stress rather than allowing them to accumulate and weigh us down. Below are three highly effective techniques that can help us let go and regain a sense of balance.

**1. Expressive Writing: Getting it out of Our Head and onto Paper**

Research shows that expressive writing changes brain activity in ways that help regulate emotions effectively, making it a powerful technique to support both direct action and emotional processing.[14]

Engaging in expressive writing activates the right prefrontal cortex, the area of the brain associated with effortful control over emotional states. This activation helps to 'turn off' parts of the brain linked to strong negative emotions, such as the amygdala, which is responsible for our fight-or-flight response. By putting emotions into words, expressive writing helps blunt the intensity of these feelings, allowing us to approach the situation with greater clarity and calm.

**How to practise expressive writing**

- **Set Aside Time:** Dedicate fifteen to twenty minutes to writing freely about the situation. Don't worry about grammar or structure. Just let the thoughts flow.
- **Describe Your Feelings:** Write openly about why the situation is bothering you. This is your chance to vent and release emotions.

- **Shift to Responsibility:** Spend the last five minutes retelling the story from a place of total responsibility. Imagine you are in complete control of the outcome, and reflect on what actions you could take to improve it.

Expressive writing isn't just a way to vent. It helps you process emotions and gain clarity on your next steps. By getting thoughts out of your head and onto paper, you can tackle challenges with a clearer, more focused mindset.

## 2. Forgiveness and Letting Go: Releasing Emotional Baggage

Writing a forgiveness letter can be powerful when we're holding onto past hurts that are getting in our way, causing ongoing stress and keeping us stuck in a cycle of negativity.[15] Learning to let go of what no longer serves us is a crucial part of releasing stress. Forgiveness, both for ourselves and others, has been shown to lower stress levels and contribute to greater emotional resilience.

Forgiving doesn't mean excusing or forgetting; it means choosing to move forward without carrying the emotional burden.

### Structure for a forgiveness letter

1. **Create a Calm Space.** Set aside fifteen to twenty minutes in a quiet, private space. Take a few deep breaths, allowing yourself to feel grounded and centred. Focus on the intention of releasing the hurt and reclaiming your emotional energy.

2. **Acknowledge the Hurt.** Begin the letter by writing down the name of the person you're forgiving. Then, express everything that hurt you. Be as honest and detailed as possible about their actions, how they made you feel, and how those feelings impacted your life. Allow yourself to experience these emotions fully, acknowledging the pain without judgement.

**PART 1** THE MINDSET EVOLUTION

*Example:* 'Dear [Name], I want to express how much your actions hurt me. When you [describe specific action], it made me feel [emotion]. I've carried this pain with me for a long time, and it has affected me in ways I didn't always realise. I felt [add more feelings], and it has been hard to let go.'

3. **Recognise the Impact.** Now, reflect on how holding onto this hurt has influenced your energy, mindset, or daily life. Write down how the person's actions have affected you over time. This helps to externalise the burden and recognise the power their actions have had over you.

   *Example:* 'Holding onto this pain has drained my energy, affected my peace of mind, and sometimes made me doubt myself. It has influenced my mood, relationships, and ability to fully experience joy in certain situations. I realise now that continuing to hold onto this hurt gives your actions more power over me than I'm willing to allow.'

4. **Shift the Focus to Yourself.** Write a transition sentence where you begin to shift the focus from their actions to yourself. Acknowledge that while you cannot change the past or control their behaviour, you can control how you let it affect you going forward.

   *Example:* 'I understand now that I can't change what happened or control how you behave, but I can choose how I respond from now on. I refuse to let your actions hold me back any longer.'

5. **Express Forgiveness.** Take a moment to release the anger or bitterness you've been holding. Forgiveness doesn't mean that what they did was okay; it means you are choosing to

free yourself from the weight of it. Write a few sentences of forgiveness, not for them, but for yourself.

> *Example:* 'I forgive you, not because you deserve it, but because I deserve peace. By forgiving you, I am taking back control over my emotions and my energy. I am choosing to release the bitterness and free myself from the weight of this pain.'

6. **Reclaim Your Power.** End the letter by focusing on your strength, healing, and empowerment. Affirm that you are taking back your emotional energy and will no longer let their actions define your present or future.

    > *Example:* 'From now on, I reclaim my power. I will no longer let your actions dictate my happiness or well-being. I am strong, and I choose peace, healing, and joy. My energy is now focused on my growth, and I release this pain fully.'

7. **Optional: Letting Go Ritual.** After writing the letter, you may want to symbolically release it. You can tear it up, burn it safely, or fold it and place it in a special place to remind yourself that you've let go of the burden. This physical action can serve as a powerful symbol of your emotional release.

## 3. Physical Release: Moving Stress out of the Body

Stress isn't just a mental experience; it's stored in the body as well. When we experience stress, our muscles tense up and our nervous system stays on high alert long after the stressful event has passed. Physical movement is one of the most effective ways to release lingering stress and return the body to a state of balance.

Whether it's stretching, a short walk, playing a sport, or shaking out tension, moving the body helps regulate stress hormones and supports emotional release.

## CONNECT: Why Relationships are the Ultimate Stress Buffer

We've explored the 3Rs—Respond, Rebound, and Release—but there's another key to stress mastery: connection. Stress often makes us feel like we must handle everything alone, but reaching out to others is one of the most effective ways to build resilience and thrive.

### The Science of Support: The Tend-and-Befriend Stress Response

For years, stress research focused on fight-or-flight, but another response, tend-and-befriend, originally proposed by Dr Shelley E. Taylor and her colleagues in 2000, reveals that humans instinctively seek connection in stressful times.[16] Studies show that offering and receiving support isn't just comforting, it's biologically wired for resilience, growth, and Betterment.

Our brains release oxytocin (the 'bonding hormone') when we engage in meaningful conversations, shared experiences, or acts of kindness.[17] Oxytocin counteracts stress hormones such as cortisol, promoting calm and trust. Instead of isolating ourselves in stressful moments, reaching out fosters security, shared resilience, and well-being.

Seeking support isn't dependence but a sign of emotional intelligence. Strong social networks improve problem-solving, stress recovery, and mental clarity.

Supporting others, through mentorship, caregiving, or small gestures, activates the brain's reward system, releasing oxytocin and reducing stress hormones. Research shows that those who regularly help others experience:

- Greater emotional resilience
- Lower anxiety and depression
- A stronger sense of purpose

- Longer lifespans.

One study found that job candidates who reflected on how their success could benefit others performed better and had lower stress levels than those focused solely on personal gain.[18]

This highlights a simple but powerful truth: it's in our own self-interest to focus on the interests of others.

**Activating the Power of Connection**

While oxytocin is often associated with physical connection, like a hug, handshake, or eye contact, it can also be triggered by adopting a 'bigger-than-self' mindset. When we focus on contribution and the well-being of others, we create meaningful connections that help us navigate stress more effectively.

Here are a few practical ways to activate the tend-and-befriend response:

**1. Shift Your Focus to Others**

When stress kicks in, take a moment to reflect on how your actions support others, whether it's your team, family, or community. Recognising your impact can shift stress from feeling like a burden to something purposeful, while also triggering a boost of oxytocin.

**Try this**: Ask yourself, *How does my work positively impact those around me?*

**2. Practise Compassionate Thinking**

Supporting others, whether by listening, offering encouragement, or lending a hand, doesn't just help them, it helps you too. It activates your body's stress-relief system, fostering connection and shifting your mindset from isolation to shared experience.

**Try this:** Reach out to a friend or colleague and offer support, even if it's just a few kind words.

### 3. Strengthen Social Bonds

Building meaningful relationships, whether through a supportive chat or tackling challenges together, helps take the edge off stress. Connecting with others who are in the same boat creates a sense of solidarity, making tough times easier to navigate.

**Try this:** Make a conscious effort to engage with someone who may also be experiencing stress, and share experiences openly.

### 4. Adopt a Purpose-Driven Mindset

When under pressure, remind yourself of the broader purpose behind your efforts. Studies show that individuals who connect their work to a higher mission experience lower stress levels and greater motivation.[19]

**Try this:** Reframe your current challenge by asking, *How does this contribute to a larger mission?*

## Contribution as a Pathway to Betterment

Stress can often feel self-focused. We worry about our responsibilities, pressures, and expectations. But true Betterment happens when we shift our focus outward. Contribution, no matter how small, creates a positive ripple effect that enhances our sense of purpose and fulfilment.

When we focus on contributing to others, we:

- Build stronger, more supportive relationships.
- Feel a deeper sense of meaning and accomplishment.
- Develop greater emotional resilience and adaptability.

Betterment is not a solo pursuit; it's a shared journey. When we focus on enriching the world around us, we create better results, not just for ourselves, but for everyone.

# KEY INSIGHTS
## FOR BETTERMENT

- **Response-Ability is a game-changer:** Stress itself isn't the problem. It's how you respond to it that matters. Shifting from being reactive to responsive helps you stay in control and channel stress productively. The **R.O.A.R. technique** provides a simple, actionable framework to reframe stress, take ownership, and activate energy in a positive way.

- **Small shifts create big impact:** Recovery doesn't require major lifestyle changes; it's the small, intentional actions that build resilience. The **2x5=10 method**, which involves two-minute micro-rebounds throughout the day, helps prevent burnout and improves focus and energy levels.

- **Letting go is essential for long-term well-being:** Experiencing stress and negative emotions isn't the issue. Holding onto it is. Lingering negative emotions can have long-term health impacts, but by using techniques such as expressive writing, physical movement, and forgiveness, you can release what no longer serves you and create space for clarity and renewal.

- **Connection is a hidden superpower:** Stress can make you feel isolated, but embracing the tend-and-befriend response helps you feel supported and resilient. Seeking support, offering help, and focusing on contribution not only reduces stress but also enhances your sense of purpose and fulfilment.

# REFLECTIVE QUESTIONS

1. How do I typically respond to stress, and how can I start building more response-ability in my daily life?
2. Which small recovery actions could I incorporate into my routine to sustain my energy and avoid burnout?
3. What sources of stress am I holding onto, and which release techniques could help me move forward?
4. How can I strengthen my connections and better leverage social support to manage stress?
5. Where in my life am I feeling overwhelmed, and how can taking ownership help me regain control?

**WHAT'S NEXT?** Mastering stress is a critical step in Betterment, but sustainable growth requires more than just managing challenges as they arise. In Part 2, we take the next step in our self-mastery journey by exploring the Responsible Mindset, a mindset that shifts us from overwhelm to ownership. Through practical strategies and mindset shifts, we learn how to take full responsibility for our actions, decisions, and impact, creating a foundation for long-term success and fulfilment.

# PART 2

# Responsible Mindset— From Overwhelm to Ownership

# 4

# The Four States of Mind—Your Choice in the Storm

*'You have power over your mind—not outside events. Realise this, and you will find strength.' Marcus Aurelius*

## Betterment Begins Within: Finding Solid Ground in Chaos

Imagine standing on shifting ground and trying to steady yourself, like on loose sand during a storm. You grasp for stability, but the more you scramble, the less control you have.

In times of rapid change, when the world around us seems to be moving faster than ever, it's easy to feel that the ground is being pulled out from under us. This is the paradox of overwhelm; the more we try to control the chaos, the more it seems to control us.[1] The secret isn't to fight the storm but to find solid ground within ourselves, a foundation that we build, brick by brick, from the inside out.

Here's the thing: Betterment begins within. The first step to thriving in an uncertain world isn't about learning to control everything around us, but about taking ownership of the one thing we can control—ourselves. It's about being so grounded that, like a deep-rooted gum tree, we can sway with the winds of change without breaking. True stability isn't about being rigid; it's about being anchored. When we cultivate that inner steadiness, we can weather any storm, bending when needed but always standing strong, ready for whatever comes next.

Too often, we rush to fix what's happening outside of us—our teams, projects, or circumstances—when in reality, the work needs to begin internally. Just like we wouldn't build a house without first laying a strong foundation, we can't effectively collaborate, innovate, or lead if we're not standing on solid ground within ourselves. Taking ownership of our mindset and our emotional state is that foundation. It's what allows us to show up fully, with clarity and intention, no matter how chaotic the world around us might be.

But let's be honest: taking ownership when everything feels out of control can be confronting. It's much easier to blame the external—be it the boss, the market, or that impossible deadline—than to pause, reflect, and ask ourselves, *What part of this can I truly own?* That initial resistance is normal. It can feel unfair or even infuriating to take responsibility when so much is outside our control. Yet, paradoxically, it's the very act of claiming ownership over our response that brings us back to solid ground.

As we journey through this chapter, we'll see that embracing this Responsible Mindset isn't about being rigid or trying to control everything. It's about feeling grounded enough to adapt, respond, and grow no matter what comes our way. It's about standing firmly rooted, not so we can stay the same, but so we can flex and flow without losing our footing.

The good news? There are practical tools and strategies designed to help us cultivate that sense of internal stability. Whether it's learning to reframe our perspective, practising mindful reflection, or using techniques to focus on what we can control, these tools will guide us to an anchored, responsible state. No matter how turbulent the world may feel, we can begin to reclaim a sense of control, not by changing what's outside, but by mastering what's within.

THE FOUR STATES OF MIND **CHAPTER 4**

## A Resilient CEO: Leading Through Uncertainty

*Imagine leading an organisation where, at any moment, everything you've built could be dismantled. That was the reality for a CEO I worked with. She was tasked with doubling her workforce while simultaneously facing the threat of her agency being abolished in the upcoming election. The opposition party had publicly committed to shutting it down, turning her entire organisation into a political chess piece.*

*Her team was feeling it. Morale had taken a hit under constant media scrutiny and the looming threat of job cuts. Partnering departments started pulling away, some making throwaway comments like, You won't be here much longer anyway. Even those who believed in the mission found it hard to stay motivated when the future felt so uncertain.*

*For her, the pressure was suffocating. Every decision, every comment, was twisted into headlines, some even attacking her personally. In her previous roles in the private sector, success had been measured by results and integrity. But here? It felt like she was playing a game where truth didn't matter, only perception did. She promised herself she wouldn't get dragged into politics, yet every day was an exhausting test of that resolve.*

*At a breaking point, she made a pivotal decision. Instead of fixating on the chaos she couldn't control, she would refocus on what she could.*

*She gathered her team and set a new tone: We can't control the politics. We can't control the headlines. But we can control how we show up every day.*

*She encouraged her team to channel their energy into their work, their professionalism, and their support for one another. Whenever tensions flared, she repeated a simple mantra: Don't go down to their level. Be bigger.*

*By embodying this mindset shift herself, she found clarity. Instead of wasting energy fighting battles she couldn't win, she doubled down on leading with integrity, resilience, and purpose. The results were remarkable. Her team, once weighed down by fear, started showing up with renewed focus and commitment. They became a force of stability amid the chaos, delivering results that made them impossible to ignore, regardless of political games.*

Her story is a powerful testament to the Responsible Mindset. We may not be able to control external circumstances, but we always have the power to choose our response. When we anchor ourselves in our values, focus on what we can influence, and refuse to get dragged into distractions, we build inner strength that carries us through any storm.

## Understanding how We Show up: The Four States of Mind

There are two key factors that tend to influence whether we're operating from a Responsible Mindset or slipping into unhelpful states: focus (where we direct our energy),[2] and agency (our belief in our ability to impact outcomes).[3] These factors are not just theoretical. They powerfully shape how we show up in different situations. When these factors are misaligned, we can find ourselves operating from less effective states, which can impact not only our own growth but also the dynamics of our teams and organisations.

Let's break this down further:

- **Focus** is about what we choose to pay attention to. Are we consumed by what's beyond our control, or are we channelling our efforts into what we can influence?

- **Agency** reflects our belief in our ability to make things happen. When we feel a sense of agency, we're more likely to take ownership, step up, and drive change. Without it, we may feel disempowered or stuck.[4]

## THE FOUR STATES OF MIND CHAPTER 4

Depending on how these two factors show up for us, we can find ourselves in one of four states:

### 1. Victim Mode: When Everything Feels out of Control

*Low agency, externally focused.*

Before we dive in, let's clarify something important: Victim Mode is not about dismissing real hardship. People face genuine injustices, traumas, and setbacks. This isn't about blaming those who've suffered. It's about recognising a state of mind where we feel powerless, convinced that nothing we do will change our situation.[5]

Victim Mode generates anxiety. When life feels unfair, it's natural to think, *Why is this happening to me?* But staying in this mindset keeps us stuck, fixated on what we can't control rather than what we can influence. It's the difference between fault and responsibility.

When we're in Victim Mode, we focus on what's happening *to* us, blaming the economy, our boss, or difficult colleagues. But the more we dwell on external factors, the more powerless we feel. Breaking free starts with a shift in focus: instead of asking, *Why me?* we ask, *What can I do?*

For example, if your team is struggling due to budget cuts or leadership changes, instead of dwelling on the unfairness, consider, *How can I support my team's morale?* or *What creative solutions can I implement within new constraints?*

This shift isn't easy. It requires moving from justified frustration to proactive ownership. It doesn't mean ignoring real challenges. It means focusing on where you have influence.

⎡ Even if all you can control is your mindset, that's still a powerful place to start. The next time you feel overwhelmed by things outside your control, pause and ask, *What's one thing I can control in this situation? How can I show up differently?* ⎦

Shifting from blame to ownership is the first step toward reclaiming your power and moving forward with purpose.

## 2. Helpless Mode: When Self-Doubt Holds Us Back

*Low agency, internally focused.*

The Helpless State is marked by deep insecurity and self-doubt. It's the feeling of being paralysed, convinced that no effort will be enough. Instead of seeking solutions, we turn inward, repeating thoughts like, *I'm not enough* or *I can't do this*.

This isn't to dismiss real challenges. Life can be overwhelming. But Helpless Mode is more than just a feeling that we're falling behind; it's a mindset where insecurity drains our energy, trapping us in inaction.

Take James from Chapter 2. A high-performing professional, he was once a pillar of reliability. But during his painful divorce, juggling shared custody and a demanding career, he felt like he was failing everyone. Rather than asking for help, he withdrew, convinced he was letting people down. His once-dependable presence faded. Colleagues noticed he was physically there but emotionally absent.

Well-meaning co-workers tried to motivate him. *Come on, we want the old James back.* But instead of lifting him, it made things worse. He admitted, *I don't know if I am that person anymore.* The more he questioned himself, the more he pulled away, turning down projects he once thrived on because he no longer believed he could deliver.

Helpless Mode feeds isolation. When we feel unworthy, we shy away from risks, resist opportunities, and retreat from challenges, cementing the belief that we're not capable. Over time, *I'm not good enough* becomes the very thing holding us back, slowly wearing down our confidence and self-belief.

So, how do we break the cycle? Small steps. We may not be able to control everything, but we can rebuild confidence by focusing on what we can influence. Setting realistic goals and recognising progress, no matter how small, shifts our mindset from helplessness to possibility.

⎡ Next time you catch yourself thinking, *I can't handle this* or *I'm not capable*, pause and ask, *What's one step I can take right now to move forward?* ⎤

Even the smallest step can begin to break the cycle, turning doubt into growth. It's not about holding onto who you once were, it's about discovering who you can become.

## 3. Controlling Mode: When Holding on too Tightly Backfires

*High agency, externally focused.*

The Controlling Mode stems from a deep desire for things to go perfectly. We fear that if we loosen our grip, everything will unravel. While this often comes from good intentions—wanting to ensure success or protect others—it leads to frustration. The tighter we hold on, the more we suffocate the process, often creating the very problems we were trying to prevent.[6]

This need for control shows up everywhere. At work, it can look like micromanaging—double-checking others' work, redoing tasks ourselves, or feeling like no one else can do things 'properly'. While it may seem productive, it disempowers the team, making them disengaged and dependent. Conversely, if you've been on the receiving end of micromanagement, you know how it feels to have someone constantly looking over your shoulder. It's frustrating and demotivating.

But control isn't just a workplace issue. It seeps into everyday life. Take my daughter, Charlotte. She loves helping in the kitchen. One morning, she eagerly wanted to crack the eggs for breakfast. But I was in a rush, expecting guests, and didn't have time for a mess. Instead of letting her help, I distracted her with an episode of *Bluey*. Ironically, the episode was called 'Omelette', where Chilli (the mum) tries to make an omelette for Bandit's birthday. The storyline hit a little too close to home. Chilli was trying to keep everything neat and perfect, but after seeing how deflated Bingo felt, thinking she wasn't good enough, she had to rethink her priorities and encourage Bingo to help, even if it meant broken eggs and a less-than-perfect omelette. Watching it, I realised I'd prioritised control over growth, missing a chance to let Charlotte contribute and build her confidence.

This urge to control sneaks into small, everyday moments—reloading the dishwasher because someone else 'did it wrong', planning every detail of a night out because you 'know the best spots'. These habits might seem harmless, but they can make others feel excluded or undervalued. When we don't allow others to contribute, we not only carry all the stress ourselves, we also miss out on different perspectives and unexpected joy.

The way out of Controlling Mode starts with recognising that letting go doesn't mean failure. Things might not happen exactly as we envisioned, but that doesn't mean they won't turn out well.[7]

> Next time you feel the urge to micromanage, pause and ask, *What's really at stake if this isn't perfect? Am I prioritising control over growth, connection, or trust?*

By loosening our grip, even slightly, we reduce stress, empower others, and create space for collaboration. When we stop trying to control every little detail, we often find that the outcome surprises us in the best way.

## 4. Responsible Mode: Stepping into Ownership

*High agency, internally focused.*

The Responsible Mindset is where we find our true power. It's about stepping into a place of ownership, where we recognise that while we may not control everything around us, we always have control over our actions and responses. This isn't about being perfect or always getting it right. It's about choosing to show up with intention, even when circumstances are challenging. The underlying emotion here is confidence, the quiet assurance that, no matter what happens externally, we have the ability to steer our own experience.

Unlike the other mindsets where we might be driven by fear, frustration, or insecurity, operating from a Responsible Mindset means we're grounded in self-awareness and resilience. It's the belief that, no matter the starting point, whether it's feeling overwhelmed, helpless, or overly controlling, we always have the power to shift toward a more empowered state. This mindset is about taking control of how we show up, aligning our actions with our values, and focusing on what we can influence.⁸

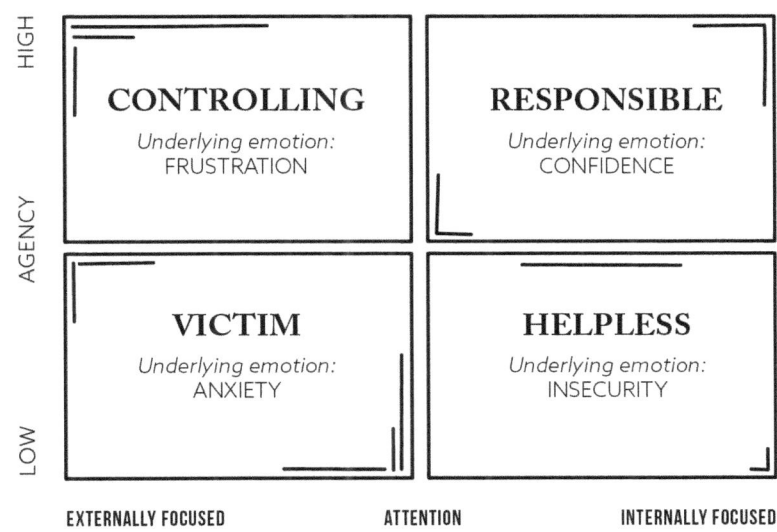

Figure 3.

## The Iconic Example of Nelson Mandela: From Anger to Acceptance

*Few stories embody the Responsible Mindset like Nelson Mandela's.⁹ As a young activist, he was fiery and determined, willing to take on the injustices of apartheid South Africa head-on. In those early years, his fight was relentless, even if it meant using extreme measures.*

*But everything changed when he was imprisoned for nearly twenty-seven years. During those decades behind bars, Mandela had every reason to be consumed by bitterness and anger. He had been unjustly imprisoned, was separated from his family, and was forced to live in harsh conditions. For someone who had been so determined to fight, it would have been easy for him to come out of prison filled with rage, ready to stoke the fires of division even further. But Mandela chose a different path.*

*By the time he was released in 1990, Mandela had transformed. Prison hadn't broken him. It had given him clarity, patience, and a deeper sense of purpose. He emerged not as the fiery young activist he once was, but as a measured, grounded leader who understood that while he couldn't change the past, he could choose how to shape the future. Instead of seeking revenge, he chose reconciliation, dedicating himself to healing a nation scarred by decades of racial oppression.*

*Mandela realised that holding anger and resentment would only continue the cycle of hatred. He directed his attention toward elements he could control, including his actions, words, and influence on others. The time he spent in prison remained irreversible, along with the wrongs he and his community endured. He had the power to respond with compassion and use his past experiences to lead his people toward unity and peace. Through his decision to forgive his jailers, he showed he wasn't excusing their actions, but he reclaimed his power and chose to lead.*

The story of Mandela demonstrates that having a Responsible Mindset does not mean being passive or abandoning our aspirations for change. It requires us to direct our energy toward our core values to create meaningful outcomes that transcend personal gain. Mandela demonstrated authentic leadership by selecting acceptance over anger and responsibility over blame. This allowed him to turn his suffering into positive influence, while proving that effective leadership means taking control of reactions despite facing wrongs.

We all have the capacity to show up with the Responsible Mindset in every moment of every day, in both big and small ways. While Mandela's choice transformed a nation, and arguably the world, our daily choices can transform a relationship, or simply bring more joy into our lives.

### The Daily Choice: Small Shifts, Big Impact

*A friend of mine went through a painful divorce. After discovering her husband's affair, her twenty-year marriage ended abruptly. To make things worse, he soon became engaged to the 'other woman' and made co-parenting difficult. She had every reason to be angry and bitter.*

*One day, he emailed her demanding payment for the kids' haircuts, even though she had already covered the last three. Her initial reaction was rage. She wanted to lash out, to tell him exactly what she thought. But instead, she took a deep breath and responded calmly, thanking him for taking the kids and even acknowledging that his new partner was a positive influence in their lives.*

*Talk about being the bigger person.*

*Her ex softened his tone. The tension eased. Over time, they were able to co-parent with less hostility and more focus on their children. Her decision to respond with intention rather than to react with emotion changed their dynamic, not instantly, but significantly.*

Does this mean every attempt to mend a strained relationship will work? No. But it gives us the best chance. Even if the situation doesn't improve, choosing to act with integrity allows us to move forward without bitterness.

Ultimately, the greatest impact of this choice is how we feel about ourselves. Instead of becoming resentful or combative, we can take comfort in knowing we showed up in a way that aligns with our values.

This is the Responsible Mindset in action. No, it didn't end apartheid, nor did it change the past for my friend. But it did change the way she experienced the present. Sometimes, small, intentional choices create the most meaningful change.

## Bridesmaids and Mind Shifts: A Comedic Look at Responsibility

Talking about mindsets, ownership, and personal responsibility can sometimes feel a little heavy. But who says we can't learn and laugh at the same time? That's where the brilliance of *Bridesmaids* comes in. Beneath its comedic genius, the film offers profound insights into the different mindsets we navigate through life.

Using humour to explore how these dynamics show up is a great way to shine a light on important lessons, while breaking down the barriers that might keep us from seeing ourselves in the characters. Each character represents a journey from disempowerment to ownership, illustrating how we can all shift into a Responsible Mindset. Let's dive into the stories of Annie, Helen, Lillian, and Megan, exploring how they each overcome their struggles in their own hilarious, relatable ways.

**Annie's Journey: From Victim to Responsible**

*There's a brilliant scene in Bridesmaids that bluntly, yet hilariously, portrays the shift to a Responsible Mindset. At rock bottom, Annie (Kristen Wiig) has lost her bakery and her relationship, and is stuck in a job she hates. Life feels like one misfortune after another, and instead of taking action, she wallows in self-pity and resentment, convinced she's powerless.*

*Enter Megan (Melissa McCarthy), storming into Annie's pity party with tough love. She doesn't offer sympathy; she calls Annie out. You're your problem, Annie. And you're also your solution. Megan sees what Annie won't admit: her biggest obstacle isn't her circumstances, it's her refusal to take responsibility.*

*What follows is both hilarious and profound. Megan slaps Annie repeatedly, yelling, Snap out of it! a ridiculous yet spot-on metaphor for what Annie needs. The message? Life will knock you down, but how you respond is up to you.*

*Annie's shift to the Responsible Mindset isn't instant. Her problems don't magically disappear. But she stops blaming her ex, her bad luck, and the past, and starts asking, What's my next step? Instead of spiralling into Why me? questions, she makes small, intentional choices—rebuilding friendships, opening up to new relationships, and finding pride in what she can control.*

*Megan's tough-love intervention reminds us that sometimes, what we need isn't comfort. It's a reality check. In the end, we are both our problem and our solution.*

## Helen's Journey: From Control to Authenticity

*Helen (Rose Byrne) enters Bridesmaids as the picture-perfect bridesmaid, effortlessly polished and determined to pull off the ultimate wedding for Lillian. From the engagement party to the bridal shower, she meticulously plans every detail, but beneath the flawless exterior is a deep fear of not being enough.*

*Her need for control isn't just about making things run smoothly; it's about proving her worth. She believes that if everything is perfect, she will be valued. But her relentless grip on every detail pushes Lillian and the bridesmaids away, turning what should be a joyful celebration into a stressful power struggle.*

*The turning point comes when Annie finally calls her out, forcing Helen to drop the façade. In a rare moment of vulnerability, she admits that behind her glamorous, curated life is deep loneliness. For the first time, she realises that her need to control wasn't about Lillian's happiness. It was about her own insecurity.*

*This realisation changes everything. Instead of micromanaging, Helen lets go. She swallows her pride and reaches out to Annie, choosing connection over control. It's a small but powerful shift, one that teaches her that showing up and supporting others matters far more than creating a picture-perfect event.*

*By the end of the film, Helen embraces authenticity over image. She discovers that true friendship isn't about grand gestures or flawless execution. It's about showing up, being real, and allowing others in. Letting go of control doesn't mean lowering standards. It means recognising that genuine strength comes from vulnerability and trust.*

### Lillian's Struggles: From Helpless to Ownership

*Lillian (Maya Rudolph) may seem like the picture-perfect bride, but beneath her calm exterior, she's silently struggling. Unlike Annie, who fights against her circumstances, Lillian's challenge is internal. She feels out of place in Helen's world of country clubs, extravagant parties, and high-society expectations. Instead of asserting herself, she goes along with it all, afraid that speaking up will expose that she doesn't truly belong.*

*The 'dreaded dress' scene, where she is standing in a stunning bridal gown yet completely losing control thanks to an unfortunate bout of food poisoning, is a hilarious metaphor for her helplessness. She looks the part but feels powerless and exposed.*

*Rather than making decisions for herself, Lillian hands over control to Helen, convinced that others know better, even when it leaves her with a dress she hates. Deep down, she's not blaming anyone. She simply doesn't believe she has the power to change things.*

*Her turning point comes when she reconnects with Annie before the wedding. In a simple yet symbolic moment, they cut up the dress to make it more her style, a small act of reclaiming agency.*

*Lillian's true shift into a Responsible Mindset happens on her wedding day. While it's too late to change the elaborate details, she chooses peace over regret. Instead of dwelling on what she should have done differently, she steps into the moment, embracing what she can control—her attitude, her presence, and how she moves forward.*

*It's a quiet but powerful realisation: even when things don't go as planned, owning your experience can change how you feel.*

### Megan: The (not so) Quiet Power of Unshakeable Self-Ownership

*Megan (Melissa McCarthy) is the most unexpected embodiment of the Responsible Mindset in Bridesmaids. At first, she seems like the outrageous, overly blunt comic relief, completely unfazed by high-society expectations. Unlike Helen, she's not polished; unlike Annie, she's not filled with self-doubt. Beneath her larger-than-life personality is someone who's deeply grounded in who she is.*

*Megan's strength comes from owning her story. She openly shares that she was bullied in high school for being different, but instead of letting it defeat her, she used it as fuel. 'They couldn't break me,' she laughs. She never chased validation. She owned who she was, embracing her quirks and using her resilience to push forward.*

*Her pity party scene with Annie is both absurdly funny and profound. Slapping Annie out of her self-pity, Megan delivers the ultimate truth: Life is messy, unfair, and unpredictable, but you always have the power to choose how you respond.*

*Unlike the other characters, Megan doesn't wait for permission or validation. She takes full ownership of how she shows up, focusing on what she can control—her attitude, her actions, and how she supports those she cares about.*

*Megan may not fit the traditional mould of 'responsible', but she's a powerful reminder that responsibility isn't about being polished or perfect. It's about embracing who you are, stepping up when it matters, and using every setback as a stepping stone for growth.*

## Lessons from *Bridesmaids*: A Journey into Responsibility

The stories of Annie, Helen, Lillian, and Megan in *Bridesmaids* offer hilarious yet profound lessons on stepping into a Responsible Mindset. Each character begins in disempowerment, whether feeling like a victim, drowning in helplessness, or clinging to control out of fear. And then there's Megan, who, from the very start, embodies unshakable self-ownership, serving as a model of resilience for the others.

By the end of the film, each woman makes a shift into responsibility, proving that this mindset isn't a fixed trait but a choice, one we can all step into, regardless of where we start.

**PART 2** RESPONSIBLE MINDSET

- **Annie** stops blaming the world and starts taking ownership of her life.
- **Helen** lets go of control, embracing authenticity over perfection.
- **Lillian** reclaims her voice, choosing to own her experience rather than shrink in self-doubt.
- **Megan** doesn't change, but she earns the respect of those around her by staying true to herself when everyone else is spiralling.

⎡ The real lesson? Responsibility isn't about never falling into victimhood, helplessness, or control. It's about recognising when we do and choosing to step out of it. These characters remind us that no matter where we find ourselves, we always have the power to reclaim our agency. ⎤

But perhaps the most powerful insight is the role of empathy and compassion. None of these women made their shift alone.

- Megan's tough-love intervention helped Annie realise her potential.
- Helen's shift came when she finally allowed herself to be vulnerable.
- Lillian found her voice through Annie's support, making her wedding truly her own.

The film reminds us that empathy isn't just about kindness to others. It's about compassion for ourselves, especially when we feel like we're falling short.

In the next chapter, we explore how empathy and compassion help shift mindset, helping us navigate life's challenges with greater resilience and deeper connection. The journey into responsibility isn't one we have to take alone. It's one where the support of others helps light the way forward.

# KEY INSIGHTS
## FOR BETTERMENT

- **Stability starts from within:** When everything around us feels uncertain, the key to thriving isn't trying to control it all, it's finding steadiness within ourselves. By owning our mindset and emotional state, we create a strong foundation that keeps us grounded and adaptable, no matter what comes our way.

- **Ownership creates clarity and control:** When we take ownership of our thoughts, emotions, and actions rather than blaming external factors, we regain a sense of control and agency. This shift in focus empowers us to respond intentionally rather than to react impulsively.

- **We always have a choice:** Even when circumstances feel overwhelming, we can choose how we show up. By recognising our ability to focus on what we *can* control, we create a sense of empowerment that fuels progress and well-being.

- **Betterment is about anchoring, not resisting:** Stability doesn't mean resisting change; it means anchoring ourselves deeply enough to stay flexible. A strong internal foundation enables us to remain steady while embracing growth and new opportunities.

# REFLECTIVE
# QUESTIONS

1. How do I typically respond when faced with uncertainty, and what steps can I take to create more internal stability?
2. In what areas of my life am I focusing too much on what I can't control? How can I shift my focus to what I can influence?
3. What habits or routines help me feel grounded, and how can I reinforce them in my daily life?

**WHAT'S NEXT?** Building internal stability is a crucial step in self-mastery, but to truly embody Betterment, we must take ownership of how we show up in all aspects of life. Next, we explore how empathy, both for ourselves and others, can serve as a powerful anchor, helping us navigate the challenges of life with greater clarity, resilience, and connection. Through practical strategies, we learn how to strengthen our emotional foundation and cultivate deeper, more meaningful relationships.

# 5

# **The Anchor Within**—Building Stability Through Empathy and Compassion

*'The great gift of human beings is that we have the power of empathy.' Meryl Streep*

## Why Empathy and Compassion are Hidden Superpowers

People often associate superpowers with abilities such as strength and intelligence or creative talents. But when it comes to navigating life's challenges and maintaining stability, two unexpected superpowers stand out: empathy and self-compassion. In the context of the Responsible Mindset, these qualities serve as powerful anchors, helping us stay grounded, resilient, and adaptable in the face of prolonged stress and uncertainty.

True Betterment requires us to be empathetic, not just toward others but also toward ourselves. When we embrace empathy and self-compassion, we create a steady internal foundation that helps us stay purposeful and in control during times of pressure. Without these inner anchors, we can easily drift into self-criticism, overwhelm, or disengagement, losing sight of our goals and values.

The role of empathy in Responsible Mindset is essential because it moves us from isolation into connection, while reminding us that we are not alone. During extended periods of stress, we need this connection because we naturally become overwhelmed and can feel disconnected from ourselves and others. Studies demonstrate that even a minor negative social interaction can impact our health by weakening the immune system and heightening the risk of stress-related illnesses.[1] The development of empathy and self-compassion leads to better emotional regulation, which improves our stress management capabilities and boosts our overall well-being.[2]

Empathy is far more than a feel-good approach. It's a practical tool to maintain stability. Empathy enables us to stop and reflect and then respond with consideration instead of acting on impulse. Developing empathy leads to emotional stability, which enables us to manage our problems effectively without feeling overwhelmed.

## Empathy and the Responsible Mindset: Why it's More Than 'Being Nice'

Embracing empathy is not just about being 'nice' or avoiding conflict. It's about taking ownership of how we show up in the world. A Responsible Mindset requires us to approach ourselves and others with openness, understanding, and a willingness to engage with reality as it is, not as we wish it to be. Without empathy, we risk falling into patterns of blame, avoidance, or burnout.

Cultivating empathy and self-compassion is a lifelong practice, but it's one that pays off in countless ways:

- **Emotional Stability:** Empathy helps us process challenges without being overwhelmed by them, providing a sense of calm and perspective even in difficult situations.

- **Greater Self-Awareness:** When we reflect on thoughts, feelings, and behaviours with compassion we learn to take ownership while avoiding negative self-criticism.

- **Stronger Relationships:** When we approach others with

empathy, we foster trust, collaboration, and meaningful connections that act as a buffer against stress.

## The Science of Empathy: Why it's Good for You

Our physical and mental health benefit deeply from empathy beyond just better relationships. Studies show that practising empathy and self-compassion can:[3]

- Reduce stress-related hormones such as cortisol, which helps maintain our balance during stressful situations.

- Strengthen the immune system, making us more resilient to illness and burnout.

- Enhance our emotional regulation skills so we can behave more thoughtfully instead of reacting impulsively.

When we make empathy a priority, we're not only creating healthier relationships but also fostering a healthier self. This is the essence of the Responsible Mindset: taking ownership of how we show up, both for ourselves and those around us, while cultivating a mindset of compassion and resilience.

## Empathy as the Anchor to Betterment

As we continue exploring the principles of the Responsible Mindset, remember that empathy is the anchor that keeps us steady. It allows us to face our challenges with grace, acknowledge our shortcomings without judgement, and still choose to show up as the best version of ourselves.

By bringing empathy and self-compassion into our daily lives, we create a more resilient, connected, and compassionate way of being, one that supports us on our Betterment journey, no matter what challenges we face.

PART 2 RESPONSIBLE MINDSET

# Empathy for Self: Building an Internal Foundation

## Understanding Your Triggers

One of the most overlooked aspects of empathy is the need to extend it toward ourselves. When we're constantly pushing to be resilient, it's easy to fall into the trap of self-criticism. We berate ourselves for not being strong enough, not coping well enough, or not having it all together. But self-compassion is essential if we want to sustain our energy and well-being. Acknowledging our own hardships is the first step to truly understanding where we are and what we need.

Through self-empathy we learn to stop denying our feelings and instead, take the time to identify triggers with a curious mindset. When work demands are overwhelming, empathy helps us discover the underlying reasons for our feelings. Are we feeling undervalued? Are we afraid of failing? By understanding these underlying emotions, we can respond more thoughtfully, rather than reacting out of frustration or self-doubt. This shift from self-judgement to self-compassion is what allows us to return to a Responsible Mindset more quickly.

## You're not Alone: Embracing Common Humanity

Recognising our shared human condition forms a vital part of self-empathy. It's easy to feel alone and struggling due to some kind of personal failure. This isolated way of thinking intensifies our shame and feelings of inadequacy, which trap us in our current state. But common humanity reminds us of an important truth: everyone struggles. Everyone faces setbacks, disappointments, and hardships. Struggling doesn't mean we're failing. It means we're human.

Embracing common humanity helps us see our challenges as part of a shared human experience rather than as a unique burden. For instance, instead of asking, *Why is this happening to me?* common humanity encourages us to think, *This is hard, but I'm not alone in feeling this way.* Research shows that people who adopt this perspective are more resilient and less prone to burnout.[4] They're also more likely to seek support and find meaning in their struggles, which helps them move through adversity with greater strength and self-compassion.

By shifting from isolation to connection, common humanity helps us let go of the unrealistic expectation that we should always have it all together. Instead, we can approach ourselves with the same kindness we'd offer a friend. This creates a powerful foundation for resilience, as it transforms the way we process hardship. Recognising that our struggles are shared doesn't diminish their importance. It softens the sting of shame and opens the door to healing.

When we practise empathy, we create a space for personal growth and learning. Rather than responding to difficulties with severe self-criticism, we need to stop to reflect and react according to the Responsible Mindset. Self-compassion and common humanity teach us that struggling is natural, while providing us with strategies to face those difficulties with strength and poise. In the end, these practices not only help us to recover more quickly but also to show up more fully for ourselves and others.

---

## *Self-Compassion in Action: A Simple Reflection Exercise*

When you're struggling with a difficult experience and feeling isolated, it can be helpful to pause, reflect, and reconnect with your emotions in a way that fosters both empathy and self-compassion. Use this reflection to help you move through tough moments with greater understanding and kindness—toward yourself and others.

1. **Recognise Your Pain**
   Take a moment to think about the difficult experience you're facing. What has been tough for you recently? Is there

something you feel you've missed out on, or a challenge that has caused you pain or suffering?

Allow yourself to feel whatever thoughts and emotions arise. Acknowledge the underlying feelings—whether they're anxiety, anger, sadness, disappointment, rejection, or fear. Write them down if it helps to give them form.

2. **Make Space for Your Emotions**
   Let yourself fully experience the emotion without denying or pushing it away. It's okay to feel pain. It's a natural response to difficulty. As you hold space for your emotions, imagine that you're sitting with them as you would with a friend.

3. **Imagine Sharing with Someone Who Cares**
   Picture yourself sharing these feelings with someone who loves you—a good friend, a family member, or someone you trust deeply. Imagine that this person simply listens to you without judgement, offering only understanding and care. They hear you and say, *I understand. You are not alone. I'm glad you told me.*
   Allow yourself to feel the comfort and connection in being heard and validated.

4. **Embrace Common Humanity**
   Now consider that your experience, while unique to you, is also part of the shared human condition. The pain you feel—whether it's stress, regret, sadness, injustice, or fear—is something countless others have experienced too. Take a moment to bring an example to mind: someone who, while their situation may not be identical to yours, is likely feeling the same kind of pain.
   Imagine stepping into their shoes. How might this challenge be affecting them? What would they be thinking or

feeling? Allow yourself to feel a sense of connection to this shared human experience. Recognising this commonality can ease the weight of isolation and replace it with empathy, for yourself and for others.

(5.) **Affirm Your Strength**
As you close this reflection, take a deep breath and remind yourself: May I know my own strength. May I treat myself with kindness. May I feel connected to others who walk this same path.
Carry this sense of empathy and compassion with you, knowing that you're not alone in your struggles and that each step forward is an act of courage.

# Empathy for Others: The Power of Connection

## Why Compassion Creates Stronger Teams and Relationships

Empathy doesn't just benefit our relationship with ourselves. It profoundly transforms how we relate to others. Rapid-paced environments that prioritise results can lead to a preoccupation with tasks and deadlines, which makes it easy to forget about the people who perform these work functions. The strength of empathy emerges from its power to build real connections, which transform workplaces into supportive communities where everyone feels appreciated and acknowledged.[5]

### The Impact of a Single Act of Compassion: John's Story

*My client John shared a story that beautifully illustrates a life-altering moment of compassion at work. One of his previous employees sent him a LinkedIn article she had written about his compassion. She shared how, years before, her father had suffered a second stroke while he was in the UK, 12,000 miles away from her in Australia. In the middle of a critical project at work, she made the immediate decision to fly across the world, knowing that if she didn't go, she would regret it for the rest of her life.*

*But there was a significant obstacle. Her boss was away, and she needed urgent approval from the managing director to take leave. Feeling anxious, she knocked on the MD's door, only to be told John was busy and to come back later. As she began to walk away, she became overwhelmed by her emotions and broke down in tears. The interaction, which could have remained purely procedural, took an unforeseen turn. John stood up at once, ushered her into his office, and gave her his complete attention.*

*John's response went beyond a mere expression of sympathy. After listening to her situation, he insisted she travel to be with her father. Not only did he give her the time off, but he also asked his executive assistant to book her flight and cover the cost so she could focus on packing and getting to her family as quickly as possible.*

*Compassion obviously came naturally to John, as when she showed him her article years later to illustrate how his compassion had changed her life, he had no memory of the event. For her, this experience became a defining life event that has stayed with her forever. Her perception of workplace leadership and human connection fundamentally changed because of this simple act of compassion. It wasn't about grand gestures. It was about seeing someone in need and responding with kindness and understanding.*

This story is a powerful reminder that, while we may not always be able to go as far as John did, we all have the capacity to show compassion when the opportunity arises. It's often these small, spontaneous acts of kindness that create the most profound impact, leaving people feeling seen, valued, and supported. In the context of the Responsible Mindset, empathy and compassion are not just nice-to-have qualities.

They are essential for building resilient teams and fostering a culture of mutual support.

### Empathy as a Business Advantage: The Microsoft Case Study

Empathy is often dismissed as a 'soft skill', something nice to have but not essential in driving hard business results. However, the story of Microsoft's cultural transformation under CEO Satya Nadella challenges that misconception. Under Nadella's leadership, empathy wasn't just a feel-good concept; it was a strategic lever that drove one of the most significant corporate turnarounds in recent history.[6] Microsoft's journey demonstrates that the Responsible Mindset, one rooted in empathy, collaboration, and trust, can produce not only a healthier workplace culture but also outstanding business outcomes.

Microsoft faced serious problems when Satya Nadella became CEO in 2014. The company that used to lead the tech industry saw no growth and its market relevance had declined amid rising competition. The internal environment had turned aggressive and employees sought survival above all else.[6] According to accounts from that time, employees were more focused on competing with one another than on collaborating to drive the company forward. In his memoir, Hit Refresh, Nadella described Microsoft's culture as one where 'innovation was being replaced by bureaucracy' and 'teamwork was being replaced by internal politics'.[7] It was a toxic environment that stifled creativity and progress.

Recognising that the root of Microsoft's challenges was cultural, Nadella set out to rebuild the company's foundation. He didn't start with a flashy new strategy or sweeping layoffs. Instead, he began by focusing on what many would consider a 'soft skill': empathy. He used a straightforward yet effective approach by showing humility and actively listening to his workforce to create a collaborative environment. Through his emphasis on trust and transparent communication, Nadella established the foundation for Microsoft's comeback.

Nadella's leadership style focused on empowering employees to bring their best selves to work. But where Nadella truly excelled was by showing up with a Responsible Mindset. He recognised that his ability to influence outcomes was sometimes limited, but he maintained control over his leadership style by demonstrating empathy, authenticity, and accountability.

Nadella's focus on empathy not only created a kinder workplace but also served as a strategic business decision that produced measurable outcomes. He empowered employees with new purpose through collaboration and the elimination of siloed structures. Microsoft's vast workforce gave Nadella a remarkable 95% approval rating in an internal survey, which demonstrated the trust and admiration he inspired.[8] The revitalised employee engagement at Microsoft directly resulted in business innovation and company growth. Under his leadership, Microsoft's market value grew from $300 billion in 2014 to beyond $2 trillion, which positioned Microsoft among the world's most valuable companies.[6]

The transformation didn't stop with financial metrics. People actually wanted to work at Microsoft again, and teamwork flourished. He supported team innovation through trust, which allowed them to take risks and learn from their failures. The transition from a strict 'command and control' culture to one that emphasised trust and empowerment led to widespread changes across the company, including everything from product development to customer relationships.

This case study illustrates the transformative power of the Responsible Mindset, built on empathy and self-awareness, to change not only individual behaviour but whole organisations. Through his journey, Nadella proved how empathy functions as a strategic advantage. By prioritising how he showed up, Nadella created a culture where people were inspired to also show up as their best selves.

Empathy, when combined with a Responsible Mindset, has the power to turn around not just failing businesses, but also struggling teams and individuals. It's a lesson that extends beyond the boardroom: by focusing on what's within our control—how we show up and how we treat others—we can transform the environments in which we operate, whether at work, at home, or in our communities.

## Practical Ways to Strengthen Empathy

### When Perspectives Clash: Staying Grounded During Conflict

Everyone at some point has experienced intense, visceral emotional responses to other people's views or behaviours. Our instinctive reaction to view things as 'wrong' often emerges during workplace debates with co-workers, or through personal arguments with family members, or when something is unfamiliar. People tend to react most strongly when personal stakes are high. Developing the ability to pause and practise empathy during these situations proves vital not only for conflict resolution but also for safeguarding our mental health.

Research underscores the significant impact that prolonged interpersonal conflict can have on our health. A study by researchers at Portland State University's Institute on Aging found that 'stable negative social exchanges', such as repeated or prolonged conflict, were significantly associated with poorer self-rated health, increased physical limitations, and a higher number of health conditions.[9] Simply put, unresolved conflict doesn't just strain relationships; it takes a measurable toll on our bodies and minds. This makes practising empathy not just an emotional exercise but a vital tool for reducing stress and fostering healthier interactions.

### The Water Glass Technique: Stepping into Another's Perspective

One way to cultivate empathy when we feel a strong impulse to reject another viewpoint is through a technique inspired by acting training: the Water Glass Exercise. It helps us step into someone else's shoes and consider their perspective, even when it feels completely at odds with our own.[10]

Here's how it works. Imagine waking up after a long, restful sleep, feeling parched. You see a glass of water on your bedside table. But there's a catch. The water has been sitting there for five days. Would you drink it? Most people have a strong, instinctive reaction to this scenario. It's often a hard 'yes' or 'no', with very little middle ground. Those who say 'yes' might reason that it's just water and unlikely to do any harm, while those who say 'no' may find the idea unthinkable, imagining the dust and bacteria that could have accumulated.

In acting schools, this technique is helpful when actors need to take on the perspective of a character for whom they hold a strong opposite perspective. If they're a firm 'yes', they must argue why someone might refuse to drink the water. If they're a hard 'no', they must explain why someone else might choose to drink it. The purpose isn't to change their minds but to help them develop empathy for a viewpoint that initially felt incomprehensible.

You can apply this same technique to real-life situations where you feel resistance or rejection toward another person's perspective. When you find yourself thinking, *How could they possibly think that?* or *This makes no sense to me,* pause and ask yourself:

- Why might their viewpoint make sense to them?
- What experiences or values might be influencing their perspective?
- What would it feel like to see the situation through their eyes?

The goal isn't to adopt their opinion as your own. It's to approach the situation with greater understanding, which can diffuse tension and open the door to more productive conversations. By stepping outside of your visceral response and considering an alternative perspective, you're better equipped to engage with others from a place of curiosity and respect, rather than defensiveness or dismissal.

When we resist another's viewpoint, it often triggers a 'threat mode' in the brain, amplifying stress and making us more adversarial. Practising empathy through techniques like the Water Glass Exercise can help interrupt this cycle, allowing us to approach disagreements with a more grounded and open mindset. This not only improves the quality of our relationships but also reduces the harmful effects of prolonged stress.

Empathy doesn't require us to agree with everyone we encounter, but it does ask us to consider their humanity. The ability to hold space for perspectives that different from our own helps strengthen our connections with others and also protect our health and well-being. In the process, we create the conditions for deeper understanding, collaboration, and mutual respect, key ingredients for both personal and collective growth.

**Breaking Free from Assumptions: The Power of Mentalisation**

It's human nature to make assumptions about others, especially in moments of frustration or conflict. Perhaps someone doesn't respond to an email, misses a deadline, or gives short answers in a meeting. Without even realising it, we may jump to conclusions: *They're lazy. They don't care. They're out to make my life harder.* These automatic assumptions can quickly spiral into a vicious cycle, where negative thoughts about someone's intentions become self-fulfilling, deepening frustration and widening the gap in understanding each other.

The trouble is, these assumptions are often just that, assumptions or stories, not facts. When our story becomes our version of the truth, we risk turning minor misunderstandings into entrenched conflicts that are difficult to break. We need to step back and question our assumptions with a more open, curious mind. This is where mentalisation becomes a powerful tool.

Mentalisation is the practice of thinking about thinking, pausing to reflect on what might be driving someone's behaviour, instead of leaping to conclusions.[11] It invites us to separate the facts of a situation from the story we're telling ourselves about those facts.

For example:

- **Fact**: A colleague didn't respond to your email.
  **Story**: *They're ignoring me because they don't care about this project.*

- **Fact**: A friend cancelled plans at the last minute.
  **Story**: *They're unreliable and don't value my time.*

- **Fact**: Your spouse didn't clean up after cooking.
  **Story**: *They don't respect all the effort I put into keeping the house tidy.*

By identifying the story you've created, you give yourself the chance to rewrite it, or at least question its validity. The next step is to ask yourself:

1. **Do I really know this to be true**? Are there other possible explanations for their behaviour? Perhaps your colleague was tied up in meetings, your friend is overwhelmed by other responsibilities, or your spouse simply forgot after a hectic day.
2. **What might I be missing**? Could there be context or factors influencing them that you're not aware of?
3. **How can I find out more about their perspective**? Instead of making assumptions, consider engaging with them directly. Ask a simple, curious question. *How are things going for you lately?* or *Is there anything getting in the way of your progress?* These kinds of open-ended questions create space for dialogue rather than conflict.

**From Vicious Cycles to Virtuous Ones: Changing the Narrative**

When we assume the worst in others, it doesn't just strain the relationship; it also impacts our own emotional state. Negative assumptions trigger frustration, defensiveness, and even cynicism, all of which make it harder to find common ground. By practising mentalisation, we can shift from a vicious cycle of judgement to a virtuous cycle of curiosity, empathy, and understanding.

Consider this. Instead of assuming a team member isn't pulling their weight because they're disengaged, what if you asked them how they're doing? You might discover they've been struggling with a personal issue, or juggling competing priorities. Similarly, rather than jumping to the conclusion that your spouse leaving the kitchen a mess is a sign of disrespect, consider asking what's been on their mind. You might learn they had a stressful day or simply forgot in the rush to get dinner on the table. These small moments of inquiry don't just reveal new insights, they also de-escalate tension and help you respond with compassion.

The process of mentalisation should not be used to excuse poor behaviour or to avoid holding people accountable. We must address poor behaviour no matter who it comes from, including colleagues, friends, and spouses. The approach we take during these discussions determines everything. Basing our approach on assumptions, which take the worst possible view, blocks the path to meaningful resolutions. But when we approach with curiosity and openness, we're far more likely to uncover the real issue and work toward a productive path forward.

This process is particularly important as we build toward adopting both the Win-Win Mindset and the Opportunity Mindset, themes we explore in later sections of this book. Both require us to operate with openness, clarity, and empathy, and they start with the ability to challenge our assumptions. Whether in a professional setting or a personal relationship, turning a vicious cycle into a virtuous one helps us create deeper understanding, better solutions, and stronger connections with those around us.

# KEY INSIGHTS
## FOR BETTERMENT

- **Empathy and self-compassion are powerful anchors for stability:** These qualities provide an inner foundation that helps us navigate uncertainty and stress with resilience. When we embrace them, we stay grounded, adaptable, and better equipped to handle life's challenges.

- **Self-empathy fosters emotional stability and self-awareness:** Understanding our triggers and embracing common humanity allows us to approach setbacks with curiosity rather than judgement, preventing self-criticism from undermining our progress.

- **Connection through empathy strengthens relationships and resilience:** When we extend empathy to others, we foster trust, collaboration, and deeper connections that help buffer us against stress and uncertainty.

- **Empathy fuels the Responsible Mindset:** Taking ownership of how we show up, both for ourselves and for others, requires a foundation of empathy. It shifts us from reactivity to thoughtful, intentional responses that align with our values.

- **Betterment requires balancing strength with compassion:** True resilience isn't about pushing through challenges alone; it's about recognising when to offer ourselves and others kindness and support.

# REFLECTIVE QUESTIONS

1. **When do I find it easy to show compassion to others, and when do I find it more difficult?** What patterns do I notice, and how can I begin to approach challenging situations with more empathy?
2. **Think of a time when I was at odds with someone.** Can I step into their shoes and consider their perspective? How might greater empathy have changed the outcome of that situation?
3. **How do I typically respond to my mistakes or setbacks?** What would it look like to replace self-criticism with self-compassion in those moments?

**WHAT'S NEXT?** Empathy and compassion provide the foundation for emotional stability, but the next step in our Betterment journey is taking ownership of our actions, choices, and mindset. Next, we explore practical tools to take ownership. By redefining what control means and embracing ownership, we can create meaningful progress in all areas of life.

# The Power Shift—How Ownership Redefines Control

*'Between stimulus and response, there is a space. In that space is our power to choose our response. In our response lies our growth and our freedom.' Viktor E. Frankl*

## The Game-Changer: Owning What's in Your Control

In the previous chapter, we explored how empathy and self-compassion create an inner anchor, helping us stay grounded during life's challenges. But stability alone isn't enough. True Betterment comes when we take ownership of our responses, actions, and mindset. This shift in perspective is what allows us to move from feeling stuck to taking purposeful action.

Taking ownership is more than just accepting responsibility; it's a power shift. Instead of wasting energy on things we can't control, it shifts our focus to what we can—our choices, actions, and mindset. It's about recognising that while we may not always have control over external events, we always have control over how we respond.

Too often, we waste time and mental energy dwelling on things beyond our reach, whether it's workplace dynamics, personal relationships, or external circumstances. This fixation can leave us feeling overwhelmed, frustrated, and powerless. But ownership offers a new perspective, one that reframes challenges as opportunities to take meaningful action.

## Wrong Zone of Focus

*One example of this comes from a team I worked with who were stuck in what I'd call the 'wrong zone' of focus. They were a small HR group in an organisation of about fifty people and shared HR systems with a much larger organisation with over 30,000 employees. They were frustrated about the restrictions imposed upon them and were pouring time and energy into trying to convince the larger organisation to adapt its systems, but their efforts weren't gaining traction. Instead of feeling productive, they were deflated and stuck.*

*However, once they accepted the reality of this situation, their creative juices started flowing. They brainstormed practical solutions they could implement right away to adapt to and work around the restrictions. The energy in the room transformed. They went from feeling drained to laughing, collaborating, and generating ideas. This is the power of focusing on the right zone: it generates energy, creativity, and a renewed sense of agency.*

The key to this power shift is knowing where to direct our energy. The CIA model—Control, Influence, Accept— was originally developed by Neil and Sue Thompson.[1] It helps us clarify what we can change, where we can make an impact, and what we need to let go of. When we apply this mindset, we reclaim our sense of control, reduce unnecessary stress, and create meaningful progress.

By embracing ownership, we take charge of our Betterment journey, not through force, but through focus and intention.

## The CIA Model: A Framework for Focus

How do we know if we're focusing on the wrong things? One way is to pay attention to how we feel. If we're hitting dead ends or notice a drain on our energy, it's often a sign we're putting our attention on the wrong things. However, when we're focused on what we can control or influence, we start to feel a sense of momentum and clarity.

To make this distinction clearer, it's helpful to break things down into three zones:

1. **Control:** These are the things we have direct power over—our actions, words, and decisions. For example, how we structure our day, how we communicate, how we respond to a challenging situation.
2. **Influence:** These are areas where we don't have full control but can have an impact. For instance, influencing team dynamics or offering suggestions to shape a decision.
3. **Accept:** These are things completely outside our control, like other people's behaviours, larger systemic issues, or past events. Here, the goal is to accept the reality of the situation and adapt our approach rather than resist what we can't change.

Sometimes, recognising what's in our control comes with a surprising amount of clarity, and sometimes, with tough truths.

### The Story of a Toxic Employee

*A leader in early childhood education I worked with experienced this firsthand. She had a toxic employee whose behaviour was dragging down the whole team. For a long time, she felt stuck, frustrated, exhausted, and convinced she had no choice but to tolerate it.*

*When we stepped back and looked at the situation differently, she realised something important: while she couldn't control the employee's behaviour, she did have control over who worked at her centre. This was her organisation, her team, and her responsibility. Owning that wasn't easy. It meant stepping into the discomfort of making a tough call.*

*But once she embraced that responsibility, everything shifted. She stopped feeling stuck and started taking action. More than just solving one issue, this moment was a turning point where she reclaimed her sense of agency and put her energy where it could actually make a difference.*

*With this newfound clarity, she approached the situation with confidence rather than fear. Instead of tiptoeing around the issue or hoping things would improve on their own, she took practical steps to address the toxic behaviour head-on. She set clear expectations, held firm boundaries, and had the tough conversations she'd once avoided. In the end, she made the decision that was best for the team—whether that meant coaching the employee towards change or letting them go. What mattered most was that she was no longer stuck. She'd reclaimed her authority, her energy, and her vision for the kind of culture she wanted to create. And that made all the difference.*

The key is to start at the top and work our way down. If we have direct control, we can take action. If not, we can look at what we can influence. If neither is possible, we focus on how to adapt to or reframe the situation. Some challenges may span all three zones, requiring us to break them down.

## 1. Control: Where Action Begins

The first zone of the CIA Model is control—what's directly within our power to change or act on. This includes our choices, mindset, behaviour, and responses. If we have control over an aspect of a challenge, this is where our energy should go first.

For instance, imagine you're feeling overwhelmed at work because of tight deadlines. While you can't always control the deadlines, you *can* control how you plan your time, how you communicate with your manager about priorities, and how you set boundaries to stay focused. Starting with what's in your control not only reduces overwhelm but also builds momentum, helping you feel more empowered and less stuck.

## 2. Influence: Shaping Outcomes

If we don't have direct control over a situation, the next question is, *What can I influence?* Influence is about shaping decisions, outcomes, or perspectives, even when we're not the one making the final call.

For example, say your team is struggling with low morale. You might not be able to overhaul the entire workplace culture overnight, but you can influence it. You can start positive conversations, advocate for small but meaningful changes, and role-model the kind of support and mindset you want to see. Small actions add up, and influence often creates a ripple effect. Influence requires creativity and collaboration, thinking about who needs to be involved and how to make a compelling case for change.

Recognising your sphere of influence is about finding leverage points. It's about saying, *I may not control everything, but I can contribute in a meaningful way.*

## 3. Accept/Adapt: Letting Go and Reframing

When we've worked through control and influence but find there are elements of the challenge that remain outside our reach, it's time to move into acceptance. This isn't about giving up. It's about letting go of resistance to things we can't change and finding ways to adapt.

Imagine a parent dealing with a child who's struggling in school. While they can control how they support their child at home and influence their engagement with teachers, they ultimately cannot control how their child feels about learning. Acceptance might look like recognising this limit and focusing instead on creating a nurturing environment that fosters resilience and confidence in their child.

Acceptance is powerful because it shifts our perspective from *Why is this happening to* me? to *What can I learn from this?* It frees up emotional energy for growth and allows us to respond with grace rather than frustration.[2]

## Breaking Challenges Down: When Control, Influence, and Acceptance Overlap

It's important to recognise that many challenges aren't confined to a single zone; they're layered. There may be aspects we can control, others we can influence, and still others we need to accept.

Take the example of a manager dealing with a high-performing team member who has suddenly become disengaged.

1. **Control:** The manager can control how they approach the conversation, ensuring it's constructive and supportive.
2. **Influence:** They can influence the team member's engagement by offering mentorship, flexibility, or resources.
3. **Accept/Adapt:** They must accept that the ultimate decision to re-engage lies with the team member. The manager may need to adapt by preparing for alternative outcomes.

Breaking challenges down in this way helps us see where our energy can be most effective, preventing us from falling into frustration or helplessness.

---

### *An Exercise to Shift Your Focus*

If you're feeling stuck or overwhelmed, take a moment to apply the CIA Model to a current challenge. This exercise will help you clarify where to direct your energy and create a path toward more effective action.

1. **Write Down the Challenge.** Start by identifying a specific situation that's consuming your energy. Write it down in one or two sentences.
   For example:
   *I'm frustrated because my team isn't meeting deadlines.*
   *I feel drained by a conflict with a close friend.*
   *I'm anxious about upcoming changes in my organisation.*

2. **Control.** Ask, *What aspects of this challenge are entirely within my control?*

   These might include your actions, decisions, words, or mindset. Write down anything that you have the direct power to change.

   Follow-up questions:

   *What outcome do I want to create?*

   *What's the first small step I can take to move in that direction?*

   *How can I show up in a way that reflects my values?*

   Example. If your team isn't meeting deadlines, you might identify that you can control how you communicate expectations, the tools or processes you use to track progress, and the support you provide to your team members.

3. **Influence.** Next, consider, *What can I influence?*

   These are areas where you don't have direct control but can shape outcomes or behaviours. Think about the people, processes, or decisions you can impact through communication, collaboration, or support. Write down your opportunities for influence.

   Follow-up questions:

   *Who else is involved, and how can I engage them constructively?*

   *What information or perspective could I share to make a positive impact?*

   *What relationship dynamics or shared goals can I leverage?*

   Example. If you're feeling drained by a conflict with a friend, you might identify that while you can't control their emotions, you can influence the relationship by opening up a dialogue, expressing your perspective with kindness, or finding common ground.

4. **Accept/Adapt.** Finally, reflect, *What is completely outside my control or influence?*

These are the aspects of the situation you cannot change, no matter how much you wish you could. Write down what you need to let go of and think about how you can adapt to the reality of the situation in a way that supports your well-being and overall needs.

Follow-up questions:
*What am I resisting, and how is it affecting me?*
*How can I reframe this situation to find peace or growth?*
*What's one thing I can do to adapt positively to this reality?*
Example. If you're anxious about upcoming changes in your organisation, you might identify that while you can't control leadership decisions, you can adapt by focusing on building your skills, maintaining strong relationships, or seeking clarity about your role.

## The Real Power of the CIA Model

The real power of the CIA Model is how it shifts our energy, from what drains us to what drives us. When we focus on what's in our control, we take action. When we identify what we can influence, we create opportunities for collaboration and change. And when we accept what we can't change, we let go of frustration, making room for growth and resilience.

This shift isn't just about solving problems. It's about reclaiming our power and focusing our energy where it matters most.

# Choosing how We Show up: The Ultimate Ownership Move

## The Power of Intentional Responses

At every moment, in every situation, one thing we always control is how we show up. This choice isn't always easy, especially in difficult or emotionally-charged situations, but it's the ultimate expression of self-responsibility. It's about owning how we respond, rather than being swept up in the tide of our reactions.

Let's be honest. There are times when we don't show up as our best selves. We're reactive, defensive, or overly focused on protecting ourselves. These moments are a normal human experience, but they rarely leave us feeling good about ourselves. Snapping at a colleague in a tense meeting, avoiding a tough conversation with a loved one, or getting caught up in justifying our actions, these reactions usually come from fear, insecurity, or frustration. In the moment, they might feel justified, even satisfying. But they rarely lead to the best outcomes, or reflect the person we want to be.

Then there are times when everything just clicks. We feel calm, grounded, and completely in sync with ourselves. We show up with empathy and clarity, staying focused on solutions while remaining true to our values. There's no need to justify our actions or second-guess our choices. We're comfortable in our own skin and confident in how we respond. These are the moments when we're at our best, and they don't just feel good. They lead to better outcomes, stronger relationships, and a lasting positive impact.

## Little Me vs. Big Me: Getting to know our 'selves'

The reality is, we all oscillate between these two states, Little Me vs. Big Me, often without even realising it. The question is not whether we'll face triggering situations. The triggers will always be there. A challenging colleague, a difficult family member, an unexpected setback, these factors will continue to show up in our lives. Real self-mastery involves maintaining control over our responses despite external influences. The key lies in recognising those moments when we need to stop and make conscious choices about how we show up.

It's this ability to choose, this intentionality, that defines ownership.

When we take responsibility for how we show up, even in difficult situations, we reclaim our power and set the stage for better outcomes.

**Recognising the Signs of Little Me vs. Big Me**

The first step to choosing how we show up is understanding the difference between Little Me and Big Me. Recognising what each looks like in our own lives allows us to catch ourselves in Little Me mode before it takes over, and actively channel our Big Me in moments that matter most.

**Little Me** is reactive. It's the version of ourselves that's quick to defend, act impulsively, or shut down. Little Me feels driven by fear, insecurity, or frustration, often leading to behaviours that don't reflect who we truly want to be. Think of Annie from *Bridesmaids* at her lowest—blaming others, lashing out, and spiralling into negativity. Or Helen, letting her need for control isolate her from those around her. Little Me is about self-protection in the moment, but it rarely leads to long-term success or makes us feel proud. We're small.

**Big Me**, on the other hand, is intentional. It's the version of ourselves that pauses, takes a breath, and chooses a response that aligns with who we want to be. It focuses on solutions over blame, stays open to different perspectives, and acts in line with our values, even when it's tough. It's Annie taking ownership of her life, or Helen letting down her guard and reaching out for help. Big Me creates clarity, strengthens relationships, and brings out the best in ourselves and those around us.

It's important to remember that what Little Me and Big Me look like is deeply personal, unique to each of us. For one person, being quiet in a meeting might signal Little Me at work, reflecting a lack of confidence or fear of sharing an opinion. For another, that same quietness could be Big Me in action, demonstrating thoughtful consideration before speaking.

The key is knowing what these states look like for us. What does it feel like when we're reactive or defensive? How do we show up

THE POWER SHIFT **CHAPTER 6**

when we're calm, confident, and solutions-focused? Recognising the difference helps us catch ourselves in Little Me mode and consciously redirect toward Big Me.

**Become an Expert Spotter**

Recognising the difference between Little Me and Big Me becomes even clearer when we see how these moments play out in real life. Here are a few examples of how people show up in both states, and the powerful shifts they experienced when they consciously chose to move from reactive to intentional.

**Little Me**: Sends a sharp response to an email from a colleague they felt was undermining them. The impact: reactivity only escalated tension, making collaboration more challenging.

> **Big Me**: Reflects on the situation and decides to address the concern calmly and directly in person. The impact: discussing intentions openly led to mutual understanding and better teamwork.

**Little Me**: Micromanages their team when under pressure, feeling the need to control every aspect of the process. The impact: the fear of failure led to frustration for their team and themselves.

> **Big Me**: Empowers and trusts their team to take ownership. The impact: improved morale, creativity, and better outcomes.

**Little Me**: Snaps at their spouse over small things, like leaving dirty dishes in the sink. The impact: unnecessary conflict, resentment, and strain on the relationship.

> **Big Me**: Consciously pauses and reflects on their trigger and takes the time to express their feelings more constructively. The impact: deeper connection instead of unnecessary conflict.

**Little Me**: Blames external factors, like market conditions and company policies, for poor performance during a project. The impact: a cycle of helplessness and inaction.

> **Big Me**: Redirects their energy toward aspects they can

influence, such as improving internal processes and communication. The impact: boosted confidence and tangible improvements in project outcomes.

**The Power of Choice**

These examples illustrate the key difference between Little Me and Big Me. Little Me is reactive, focused on self-protection, and often rooted in fear or frustration. Big Me, on the other hand, is intentional, proactive, and grounded in values.

The shift from Little Me to Big Me isn't automatic; it's a choice. As these stories show, it's a choice that leads to better outcomes, stronger relationships, and a deeper sense of alignment with who we truly are. By recognising our triggers and actively channelling our Big Me, we can show up as the person we aspire to be, even in the most challenging situations.

**Catching Triggers and Redirecting to Big Me**

We all have triggers, moments or situations that spark Little Me responses. These might include:

- Feeling unappreciated at work
- A loved one saying something that hits a nerve
- A project derailed by unexpected challenges.

The goal isn't to eliminate these triggers, as they're inevitable. Instead, it's about learning to catch ourselves in the moment. When we feel the pull of Little Me, we need to pause and reflect:

- What's triggering me right now?
- What's the best version of myself in this situation?
- How can I align my response with the outcome I want to create?

THE POWER SHIFT **CHAPTER 6**

This process isn't about perfection, it's about progress. Each time we consciously shift into Big Me, we build the habit of showing up intentionally, even in challenging situations.

---

### *Exercise: Get to Know Your Selves*

This exercise will enable you to understand how your behaviour changes between Little Me situations and Big Me events. Recognising the distinct traits and behaviours that characterise each state enables you to detect Little Me mode and deliberately transition into Big Me.

**Step 1: Reflect on Your Little Me**
Take a moment to think about times when you've been reactive, defensive, or impulsive, when your Little Me was in charge. Ask yourself:
*How was I being in those moments?*
*What behaviours or attitudes showed up?*
*What emotions or triggers were driving my reactions?*
Get a piece of paper and write down the words that come to mind to describe your little Me (see Column 1 on Figure 4).

**Step 2: Reflect on Your Big Me**
Now, think about moments when you've shown up as your best self—when you were intentional, grounded, and aligned with your values. Ask yourself:
*How was I being in those moments?*
*What behaviours reflected my values?*
*How did I engage with people and challenges?*
Write down these qualities that embody your Big Me in action (see Column 2 on Figure 4), focusing on how your values and beliefs influence your behaviours.
For example:

PART 2  RESPONSIBLE MINDSET

*Figure 4.*

**Step 3: Recognise the Power of Choice**
Once you've filled out both columns, step back and reflect on the contrast. What stands out about your Little Me versus your Big Me? How does it feel to see these qualities side by side?

The purpose of this exercise isn't to judge yourself. It's to recognise and own both aspects of how you show up. When you see your Little Me and Big Me clearly, you can catch yourself in reactive moments and intentionally choose to respond as your Big Me.

**Step 4: Apply it in Real Life**
Keep your list somewhere accessible and revisit it regularly. The next time you feel triggered, take a moment to pause and ask:
*Which version of me is showing up right now?*
*What would my Big Me do in this situation?*

By practising this awareness, you'll strengthen your ability to align your actions with your values, creating better outcomes for yourself and those around you.

### A Practical Exercise: Moving from Little Me to Big Me
To put this into practice, try this journalling exercise:

1. **Reflect on a Recent Little Me Moment:** Write about a situation where you reacted defensively or impulsively. What triggered your reaction? How did you respond?

2. **Define Your Big Me Response:** Revisit the same situation through the lens of Big Me. How would you have responded differently? What values or priorities would have guided your actions?

3. **Prepare for Future Challenges:** Identify an upcoming situation where you might feel triggered. Write down how you plan to approach it as Big Me. What mindset, actions, or behaviours will you focus on?

## Emotional Mastery: Taking Ownership of Your Inner World

### Why Emotional Ownership Matters

Mastering our emotions becomes crucial as we advance toward developing a Responsible Mindset. Emotions determine our thinking patterns and behaviours and influence our interactions with the surrounding world. Without proper emotional regulation, our judgement becomes impaired, our resilience decreases, and stress cycles develop that harm our health.[3] However, when we take ownership of our emotional experience by learning to regulate negative emotions and stimulate positive ones, we gain greater control, opening ourselves up to creativity, resilience, and well-being.[4]

Emotional mastery doesn't mean suppressing negative emotions or forcing ourselves to stay positive. Suppressing emotions often leads to them resurfacing later, sometimes with greater intensity. Negative emotions serve an important purpose. They alert us to challenges and boundaries but if left unregulated, they can overwhelm us, leading to prolonged stress that impacts both our mental and physical health. Studies show that unresolved negative emotions can linger for years, increasing the risk of conditions such as cardiovascular disease, immune dysfunction, and depression.[5]

The goal of emotional mastery is twofold:
1. **To regulate negative emotions in a healthy way,** ensuring they don't take over our experience or drain our energy.
2. **To intentionally cultivate positive emotions,** which broaden our perspective, improve our well-being, and enhance our ability to respond constructively to challenges.[6]

By balancing these two aspects, we create an emotional foundation that supports our ability to take ownership of our actions and decisions.

## Regulating Negative Emotions: Staying in the Driver's Seat

Negative emotions, such as anger, frustration, and fear, are not inherently bad. They provide valuable information about our needs and boundaries. However, due to the brain's negativity bias, we tend to focus more on negative experiences than positive ones.[7] This bias, while useful in helping our ancestors avoid danger, can lead to rumination, stress, and fixation on setbacks in our modern lives.

This means that unless we take proactive steps to regulate our thoughts and emotions, they can unconsciously steer us toward stress and anxiety.

### Why Regulating Negative Emotions Matters

- **Health consequences:** Lingering negative emotions are linked to chronic health conditions such as cardiovascular disease and immune dysfunction.

- **Cognitive impact:** Persistent negative emotions impair focus, decision-making, and creativity.
- **Emotional well-being:** Unregulated emotions can lead to burnout, disengagement, and relationship strain.

The key to regulating negative emotions lies in recognising them, understanding their purpose, and applying effective strategies to manage their intensity.

**Practical Strategies**

1. **Name it to Tame it:** Recognising and naming emotions helps reduce their power over us. Simply acknowledging, *I'm feeling overwhelmed right now,* creates space for intentional responses.
2. **Expressive Writing:** Writing down thoughts and feelings helps to process negative emotions and reframe situations with a clearer mindset.
3. **Reappraisal:** When facing a situation outside our control, shifting our perspective can help us find opportunities for growth rather than getting stuck in frustration.

## Stimulating Positive Emotions: The Key to Thriving

While managing negative emotions is essential, actively fostering positive emotions is equally important. Positive emotions expand our cognitive abilities, helping us think more creatively, connect more deeply with others, and enhance our resilience. According to Barbara Fredrickson's 'broaden-and-build' theory,[6] experiencing emotions such as joy, gratitude, and optimism broadens our perspective and helps us build personal resources over time.

## The GLOW Method: A Daily Tool to Stimulate Positive Emotions

The GLOW method—Gratitude, Laughter, Optimism, and Wonder—offers a practical way to intentionally cultivate these super emotions:

- **Gratitude:** Regular gratitude practice has been shown to improve sleep, reduce stress, and increase life satisfaction.[8] Simple habits like journalling three things we're grateful for can shift focus from what's lacking to what's working.

- **Laughter:** Laughter releases endorphins and reduces stress hormones, promoting a sense of connection and relaxation.[9] Seeking out moments of humour in daily life can serve as a natural stress reliever.

- **Optimism:** Training ourselves to view challenges as temporary and opportunities as possible fuels resilience and motivation. We explore optimism more in Part 4 of this book.

- **Wonder:** Taking moments to appreciate beauty or the unexpected, or to be in awe, enriches our experience and reminds us of the bigger picture, promoting a sense of calm and inspiration.[10]

When we make these practices a habit, we create a positive ripple effect, boosting our well-being and strengthening our ability to take ownership of our lives.

As we move forward on our Betterment journey, embracing emotional mastery allows us to redefine control, not as something exerted over our circumstances, but as something we cultivate within ourselves.

# KEY INSIGHTS
## FOR BETTERMENT

- **Ownership is a power shift, not just a responsibility:** True ownership is about focusing our energy on what we can control and influence, rather than dwelling on what we can't. This shift brings clarity, momentum, and a renewed sense of agency.

- **The CIA Model provides a framework for action:** By categorising challenges into what we can Control, Influence, or Accept, we direct our efforts productively, reducing stress and fostering meaningful progress.

- **The choice to show up intentionally is always ours:** Recognising the difference between reactive 'Little Me' and intentional 'Big Me' helps us take charge of how we respond in any situation, aligning our actions with our values.

- **Emotional mastery enhances ownership:** Taking responsibility for our emotions, regulating negative emotions and stimulating positive ones empowers us to respond intentionally rather than to react impulsively.

- **Betterment begins with self-awareness and intentional action:** Ownership isn't about having all the answers; it's about consistently showing up, learning, and adapting in ways that align with our goals and values.

# REFLECTIVE **QUESTIONS**

1. **What areas of my life am I currently focusing on that may be outside my control?** How can I shift my attention to what I can influence or accept?
2. **When do I find it easiest to show up as my 'Big Me,' and when do I tend to fall into 'Little Me' reactions?** What patterns do I notice, and how can I shift toward responding with greater intention and ownership?
3. **What's my ratio to positive vs. negative emotions?** How might emotional mastery help me achieve a more productive balance?

**WHAT'S NEXT?** Taking ownership is a powerful step toward Betterment, and an essential step to allow us to collaborate more effectively with others. In Part 3: Win-Win Mindset—From Competition to Collaboration, we explore how shifting from a 'Me vs. You' mentality to a collaborative, mutual success approach unlocks greater opportunities, stronger relationships, and better results for everyone.

# PART 3

# Win-Win Mindset—From Competition to Collaboration

# 7

# **A Better Way**—Moving Beyond Me Vs. You

*'If you want to go fast, go alone. If you want to go far, go together.' African Proverb*

## Shifting from Me vs. You to Win-Win

In so many situations, whether at work or at home, we instinctively fall into a 'Me vs. You' mindset, where what we want seems to clash with what others want. But when we shift our focus from competing positions to shared interests, we uncover a better way forward. This is the Win-Win Mindset in action.

Take something as simple as planning a family holiday. One person wants to relax on a tropical beach, another is after an adventure in the city, and someone else just wants to save money and stay home. If they dig a little deeper, they might find that what really matters is quality time, relaxation, and a sense of adventure, not necessarily the exact location. Instead of arguing for individual preferences, they could co-create a solution that meets the needs of all, even if it's not exactly what anyone first imagined.

So far, we've explored how taking ownership of our thoughts, emotions, and actions helps us show up with more intention and impact. Now, we take that further, moving from self-mastery to collaboration.

## PART 3 WIN-WIN MINDSET

The Win-Win Mindset applies these same ownership principles to relationships, helping us find solutions that work for everyone.

A Win-Win approach isn't about everyone getting exactly what they want. It's about uncovering shared priorities and values. Whether in families, workplaces, or communities, this mindset transforms conflicts into opportunities for collaboration, trust, and progress.

That doesn't mean forcing an impossible compromise. If one person insists on earning a million dollars while working ten hours a week, while their employer requires full-time commitment to lead a major innovation, no mindset shift will magically make both possible. But the Win-Win Mindset invites us to look deeper, beyond fixed positions to the real drivers underneath: financial security, balance, purpose, growth. By focusing on these, we explore creative solutions that, while not perfect for anyone, meet the most important needs of all.

In leadership, teamwork, and negotiations, moving beyond 'Me vs. You' thinking is critical to meaningful progress. By focusing on shared values and long-term goals, we build trust, collaboration, and better solutions.

At its core, the Win-Win Mindset reframes how we approach challenges. It moves beyond 'my way vs. your way' and instead asks, *What is our way?* It's not about compromise. It's about co-creating solutions that go beyond what any individual could achieve alone. This mindset doesn't just strengthen relationships. It also fuels innovation, trust, and sustainable progress, even in the toughest situations.

With this lens, let's explore why the Win-Win Mindset isn't just an ideal but an essential framework for thriving in today's fast-moving, interconnected world.

### The Cost of Toxic Competition

*What happens when two teams, both working toward the same ambitious goal, get stuck in a cycle of blame and misalignment? This was the challenge faced by a client mine, a major insurance company launching an innovative policy aimed at disrupting the market. The conflict? Underwriting and Sales, two teams that couldn't succeed without each other but were operating like adversaries.*

*On paper, their mission was aligned: develop and sell a competitive new policy that balanced affordability with risk management. But in practice, their competing priorities turned this shared purpose into a tug of war. Sales wanted aggressive pricing and flexible policies to attract new customers, while Underwriting insisted on tight risk controls to protect the business from excessive payouts. Instead of working together to find a solution, they were locked in a battle, one that was slowing down approvals, frustrating clients, and threatening the success of the entire initiative.*

## When Alignment Breaks Down

*For Sales, the problem was clear: Underwriting was too slow and too rigid. 'We bring in high-value clients, but Underwriting knocks them back or drags their feet on approvals,' one sales executive vented. 'How are we supposed to hit targets if we can't even get policies through?'*

*Meanwhile, Underwriting had its own frustrations: Sales was making promises they couldn't keep. 'They push deals that expose us to massive risks,' an underwriting lead argued. 'We're the ones who have to manage claims down the track, and we can't just approve policies to keep Sales happy.'*

*The lack of alignment fuelled frustration, slowed down deals, and created a toxic blame culture. Meetings became battlegrounds, with both teams more focused on defending their side than on finding a way forward. 'Every discussion starts with finger-pointing. You're blocking deals! You're putting us at risk!' a senior leader observed. 'No one's actually solving the problem.'*

*But the real issue wasn't just conflicting priorities. It was the culture of mistrust that had developed over years of misalignment. Both teams saw the other as an obstacle rather than a partner.*

PART 3  WIN-WIN MINDSET

### Rebuilding Alignment: From 'Me vs. You' to 'We'

*Realising that the dispute was jeopardising a high-profile initiative, the CEO stepped in and assigned Sarah, a senior leader known for cutting through complexity, to realign the teams. Sarah's main role was to break down the silos and help Sales and Underwriting behave like one team.*

*Sarah's first move? Help them see the bigger picture. 'Sales can't hit targets if we're blocking good deals,' she told Underwriting. 'But if we take on too much risk, the whole business suffers.' The message was clear: this wasn't Sales vs. Underwriting, it was about finding a way forward together.*

*Through structured conversations, Sarah created space for both sides to air frustrations in a way that moved the conversation forward. 'This isn't about picking a side between growth and risk, it's about building a strategy that works for both,' she reminded them.*

*Slowly, the teams began shifting from defending their own priorities to solving shared challenges. Sales started involving Underwriting earlier in the process, allowing them to flag high-risk clients before deals got too far. In return, Underwriting worked on streamlining approvals for low-risk policies, giving Sales the speed they needed to close deals without compromising the company's financial stability.*

*As the teams built trust and clarity, their culture shifted. The default question changed from Who's to blame? to How do we fix this together? A senior sales leader summed it up: 'Before, we were stuck in a win-lose mindset. If one side 'won', the other 'lost'. Now, we're actually working toward a win-win.'*

This example highlights how even well-intentioned teams can become misaligned, and the damage that toxic competition can cause. But it also shows that:

- **Shared goals don't guarantee alignment.** If teams have different priorities, they'll pull in opposite directions, even if they're working toward the same big-picture outcome.

- **Culture can be a bigger obstacle than strategy.** Years of frustration had created a default mindset of blame, which kept both teams stuck. Alignment only became possible once they rebuilt trust.

- **Win-win isn't about compromise—it's about co-creation.** The goal wasn't to 'meet in the middle' but to create a solution that worked for both teams without forcing one side to concede.

- **The shift starts with leadership.** Sarah didn't dictate a solution, she modelled collaboration, set the right conversations in motion, and helped both teams see the bigger picture.

Ultimately, this isn't just a story about launching a new policy. It's about transforming how teams work together to drive business success. By embracing a Win-Win Mindset, Sales and Underwriting moved beyond finger-pointing to building a high-trust, high-performance culture, one that didn't just benefit them, but the entire organisation.

## The Power of Win-Win in Personal Relationships

The Win-Win Mindset isn't just for the workplace. It's just as powerful in personal relationships. Whether it's with a partner, child, or co-parent, those who focus on alignment, trust, and shared purpose build stronger, more fulfilling connections. It's not about everyone getting exactly what they want, but finding solutions that prioritise what truly matters in the bigger picture.

### From Power Struggles to Partnership: A Parent-Teen Example

Parents and teenagers often clash, especially when it comes to school, social life, and responsibilities. Picture this: a teenager is juggling school, sport, and a packed social calendar, leaving them overwhelmed. Their parent, frustrated by what looks like a lack of effort, pushes them harder, demanding they 'work more' or 'get organised'. The result? Deadlock. The teen feels controlled, the parent feels ignored, and neither is getting anywhere.

A Win-Win approach breaks the cycle. Instead of doubling down on demands, the parent steps back and acknowledges the bigger goal—helping their child succeed without burning out. They start a conversation: *What are the biggest stress points? How can we work together to manage the load?*

The shift is immediate. The teenager, feeling heard instead of pressured, starts to open up. Together, they adjust commitments, explore better time management, and find ways to reduce stress. Over time, not only does the tension ease, but the teen develops confidence, resilience, and practical skills for managing their responsibilities, knowing their parent is there for support, not just pressure.

**Win-Win Co-Parenting: From Conflict to Collaboration**

Co-parenting after divorce is often challenging, especially when parents have different priorities. One might believe academic tutoring is the best way to support their child, while the other sees sport as a way to build confidence and resilience. If they stay stuck in a 'who's right?' argument, the child loses.

A Win-Win approach shifts the focus to the shared goal: the child's well-being. Instead of debating which activity is more important, they align on what matters most—nurturing their child's growth and happiness. The solution might be taking turns supporting different activities, or finding ways to blend both approaches.

The impact is huge. The child feels supported, rather than caught in the middle. The parents, by working together instead of against each other, lower stress, rebuild mutual respect, and communicate more effectively. Over time, their dynamic moves from tension to cooperation, proving that even difficult relationships can improve when the focus shifts to a shared purpose.

### Partnerships that Last: Moving Beyond 'My Way vs. Your Way'

Even in long-term relationships, the Win-Win Mindset makes a difference. Take a couple debating between saving aggressively for retirement or spending on family holidays. At first, it's a tug of war. One wants security, the other experiences.

Through a Win-Win lens, the conversation shifts: What's the real goal here? Both partners want a stable future and meaningful experiences, so rather than picking sides, they find a balance. Maybe they allocate a set amount to savings while keeping a reduced budget for annual trips.

The immediate benefit is obvious—less conflict, more agreement. The deeper impact is even bigger. When both partners feel heard and valued, trust grows. The relationship becomes stronger, more adaptable, and more resilient, not just in this decision, but in all future challenges.

### More than Conflict Resolution—A Blueprint for Stronger Relationships

At its core, Win-Win isn't about compromise, it's about co-creating better solutions.

By focusing on shared values, alignment, and mutual respect, the Win-Win Mindset doesn't just solve problems, it strengthens relationships. It builds trust, connection, and resilience, creating relationships that are less stressful and deeply fulfilling.

## The Win-Win Blueprint: Understanding the Dynamics that Shape Relationships

This section builds on Stephen R. Covey's concept of the Win-Win

Matrix, as introduced in his book *The 7 Habits of Highly Effective People*.[1] Here, we expand on its principles by incorporating new applications in leadership, teamwork, and personal development. Conflict resolution and negotiation can be broadly categorised into four types of dynamics: outcomes where both parties gain, where one wins at another's expense, where one concedes to avoid conflict, and where both sides suffer losses. In applying these dynamics, we recognise that true success comes from moving beyond individual wins to co-created solutions.

Recognising these dynamics is the first step to creating stronger relationships that are based on trust, healthy conflict, and mutual respect.

**Dominance-Defeat: 'My Way or the Highway'**

The Dominance-Defeat dynamic occurs when one party pushes forward without regard for others, believing success must come at someone else's expense. It's the boss who says, *Just do it my way*, or the parent who shuts down a conversation with, *Because I said so*. In these moments, one person prioritises their needs at the expense of others, using authority, power, or even manipulation to get their way.

At first glance, it looks effective. Decisions get made quickly, and results follow. But the cost is often invisible. People mistake decisiveness for leadership, telling themselves, *We don't have time to debate; we just need to move forward*. But when we push decisions without involvement, we create resentment and disengagement. People might comply in the moment, but their lack of buy-in can lead to poor execution, passive resistance, or even sabotage later on.

Take a manager who ignores their team's concerns about a new process and declares, *This is how we're doing it*. Sure, the change happens, but when problems arise, the team feels zero ownership to fix them. The manager may have won the battle, but the organisation loses the war.

It erodes trust, stifles collaboration, and silences valuable perspectives. Over time, it kills innovation, fractures relationships, and weakens teams. We might get our way today, but at what cost tomorrow?

### Self-Sacrifice: 'Keeping the Peace at any Cost'

The Self-Sacrifice pattern emerges when a person prioritises harmony over their own needs, leading to resentment and disengagement. It's the colleague who nods along with a bad plan to keep the team happy, or the parent who gives in to every demand just to avoid a meltdown. On the surface, it might look like compromise or selflessness, but in reality, it's a trap.

A common excuse is 'being the bigger person'. But when we're always giving way, this isn't about strength or generosity; it's about avoiding discomfort. We might tell ourselves we're keeping things harmonious, but underneath, frustration and resentment start to build. Over time, this can lead to disengagement and a sense of invisibility in the relationship.

Self-sacrificing also skews power dynamics. When we constantly accommodate others, we risk sending the message that our needs, ideas, or contributions don't matter. It's one thing to adjust when it serves the bigger picture, but if it becomes a habit, it teaches others to expect compliance instead of collaboration.

A team member who always backs down might believe they're being flexible, but in reality, they're training colleagues to overlook their input. A parent who never holds their ground may think they're keeping the peace, but they're also reinforcing an imbalance that makes future conflicts harder to resolve.

It doesn't solve conflict; it buries it, creating cracks that only widen over time.

### Mutual Destruction: 'If I Can't Win, Neither Can You'

This is where relationships and outcomes go to die. Mutual Destruction happens when disagreement escalates to the point where neither side is willing to concede, ultimately harming everyone involved. Picture two co-workers who can't agree on how to pitch to a client. Instead of working together, they undermine each other, until the client walks away entirely. In Mutual Destruction, ego and stubbornness replace logic, and the focus shifts from the goal to the conflict itself.

This mindset shows up when we operate in Little Me mode—reactive, defensive, and consumed by being right rather than being effective. It's the colleague who won't back down even when they know they're wrong, or the family feud that escalates until no one's speaking. It thrives in toxic environments where trust is low and people are more interested in winning the argument than in solving the problem.

The damage isn't just short-term losses. It also poisons relationships, makes future collaboration impossible, and corrodes trust. Fixing Mutual Destruction dynamics takes serious effort, not just to resolve the issue, but to rebuild trust, shift perspectives, and realign on shared goals.

Mutual Destruction isn't just a waste of opportunities, it's a roadblock to progress.

### Win-Win: 'What's a Better Way Forward?'

Win-Win is where collaboration thrives. It's not about competing or conceding; it's about co-creating. It's the parent who asks their teenager, *How can we make this work for both of us?* or the manager who genuinely listens to their team's concerns before making a decision. Win-Win prioritises shared goals, mutual respect, and sustainable solutions.

Achieving a Win-Win outcome requires both assertiveness and empathy, the ability to advocate for our needs while genuinely listening to and valuing the other party's perspective. When these elements are balanced, they create space for creative problem-solving, leading to solutions that don't feel like compromises but rather mutually beneficial breakthroughs. Win-Win takes effort. It's often slower at the start than just pushing our own agenda or giving in to someone else's. But the long-term rewards are worth it—stronger relationships, greater trust, and solutions that everyone feels invested in.

Ultimately, Win-Win is a choice, not just to resolve conflict, but to build better relationships. It's about moving past surface-level disagreements to uncover the shared values and goals that bring us together. This is where innovation happens, trust grows, and challenges turn into opportunities.

The Win-Win blueprint isn't just a tool for resolving conflict. It's a framework for growth. By recognising these dynamics, we can break reactive patterns and actively choose the path of connection, progress, and success.

## Beyond Compromise: How BMW and Toyota Drove Innovation Together (Case Study)

A Win-Win outcome isn't just about compromise. It's about co-creating solutions that go beyond what either party could achieve alone. It requires constructive challenge, pushing past limitations to create something bigger and better. In an industry as competitive as the automotive, true collaboration is rare.

Yet, BMW and Toyota, two independent automotive giants, have done just that. Their partnership is a masterclass in Win-Win, proving that when companies pool their strengths, they can accomplish far more together than they ever could alone.

### Competing Strengths, Shared Vision

In 2011, BMW and Toyota joined forces to develop next-generation, environmentally-friendly technologies.[2] At the time, both companies had distinct strengths.

BMW was a leader in engineering precision and high-performance vehicles.[3]

Toyota was ahead of the curve in sustainable mobility and hybrid technology.[4]

Rather than competing, they leveraged each other's expertise, starting with BMW supplying efficient diesel engines to Toyota Motor Europe and quickly expanding into joint research on lithium-ion batteries.[2]

By 2013, their partnership deepened further.[5] They signed binding agreements to co-develop:

- A hydrogen fuel cell system.
- Lightweight materials to improve vehicle efficiency.
- A shared platform for a next-gen sports car.

This partnership meant:

- Toyota gained access to BMW's expertise in vehicle dynamics, enhancing its performance-focused models.
- BMW benefited from Toyota's advancements in sustainability, accelerating its transition to zero-emission vehicles.

### More Than a Deal—A Strategic Edge

The collaboration has delivered real-world advantages. Together, they developed a third-generation hydrogen fuel cell system, set to launch in 2028, positioning both companies as leaders in zero-emission mobility.[6] BMW plans to introduce its first hydrogen-powered vehicle that year, leveraging co-developed technology to meet rising demand for clean energy transport.[6]

Beyond technology, their partnership has worked because of shared values. Both companies emphasise:

- Technology openness, exploring multiple solutions to sustainability challenges
- A long-term vision, investing in future mobility rather than chasing short-term wins
- Mutual respect, maintaining independence while contributing equally to the partnership.

The BMW-Toyota alliance is a perfect example of what makes

a Win-Win partnership so powerful. By leveraging each other's strengths, they've accelerated hydrogen technology, sustainable mobility, and market positioning, all while staying independent yet deeply collaborative.

This isn't just about sharing resources. It's about pushing the boundaries of innovation together and creating solutions that benefit their customers, their businesses, and the planet.

This is the essence of Win-Win: a collaborative search for breakthroughs that neither party could accomplish alone.

## The Power of Constructive Conflict and Challenge

The BMW-Toyota collaboration is a powerful contrast to the toxic competition we saw between the insurance Underwriting and Sales teams. It shows what's possible when teams move beyond silos and turf wars to embrace mutual respect and constructive challenge. Just as Sarah helped Sales and Underwriting see their success as interconnected, BMW and Toyota recognised that their unique strengths—BMW's engineering precision and Toyota's sustainability expertise—could elevate them both.

Constructive challenge isn't easy. Confronting differences and questioning assumptions can feel uncomfortable, but that's where real momentum happens. In both cases, diverse perspectives weren't barriers; they were the key to innovation.

These stories reinforce that Win-Win isn't about compromise or settling. It's about co-creating something better. When different strengths work in harmony, individual contributions turn into game-changing breakthroughs, whether in revolutionising transportation or reshaping how teams collaborate.

## Commitment to True Alignment: Win-Win or Nothing

At the heart of meaningful collaboration is a simple yet powerful principle: Win-Win or Nothing. This mindset encourages us to seek solutions that genuinely benefit all parties involved, without forcing compromises that breed resentment or inefficiency. When alignment isn't possible, it advocates for stepping back and reassessing rather than pushing forward with an unsustainable resolution.

This approach is particularly useful in high-stakes decisions, whether in business negotiations, leadership, or personal relationships. It helps prevent short-sighted compromises that ultimately lead to dissatisfaction. Instead of accepting an outcome that doesn't serve the long-term interests of both sides, it promotes strategic patience, the willingness to walk away until a better path emerges.

However, applying this mindset in practice is not always straightforward. People often resist the idea of no agreement, depending on their personal approach to collaboration. Let's explore the typical objections and how to reframe them for more effective outcomes.

## Overcoming Common Misconceptions

*Sometimes Someone Needs to Take Charge* (Dominance-Defeat Thinking)

Some people push back on Win-Win or Nothing, believing that leadership is about decisiveness. *We don't have time to keep everyone happy,* they argue. *Sometimes a decision just needs to be made.* While urgency and authority have their place, this approach often backfires when people feel excluded or overpowered.

Take a manager who makes unilateral decisions to move things forward. It might seem like an efficient shortcut but without buy-in, the team won't be fully engaged. Execution suffers, resistance builds, and progress slows down in the long run. Win-Win or Nothing, on the other hand, ensures that decisions aren't just made, they're embraced, creating trust, commitment, and follow-through.

Does this mean leaders or parents need unanimous approval before making a call? Of course not. But decisions should be balanced with broader considerations and communicated with both clarity and respect, bringing people on the journey, rather than dragging them along.

### *I'm Just Being the Bigger Person* (Self-Sacrifice Thinking)

Some see their compliance as generosity or emotional maturity. *It's better to give in than to cause tension,* they tell themselves. While flexibility has its place, constantly prioritising others at our own expense isn't sustainable.

'Being the bigger person' becomes a trap when it hides a lack of conviction in our own needs and goals. Over time, this creates unhealthy power dynamics where dominant personalities expect compliance, and those who give in start to feel invisible and undervalued.

Win-Win or Nothing challenges this mindset by reframing compromise. It's fine to adjust to someone else's position if it aligns with our bigger picture goals, but it should be a conscious choice, not a default reaction. When we clearly communicate our reasoning, we set the expectation that collaboration is intentional, not just blind compliance.

### *We'll Never Agree, So Why Bother?* (Mutual Destruction or Loser Thinking)

Some people see Win-Win or Nothing as wishful thinking. *We're too far apart to find common ground,* they argue. Over time, this thinking hardens into resentment, with statements like, *I won't let them get away with this,* or *Under no circumstance will we give in.* It can feel righteous, but in reality, it's blinding.

When conflict turns highly personal, like in a divorce, stepping away from destructive dynamics can be the best choice. It doesn't mean abandoning responsibility, but rather refusing to engage in a downward spiral of conflict. It's saying, *I don't believe our approach is serving our children's needs. We need to step back and find a better way to resolve our differences that puts them first.*

Mutual-Destruction or loser thinking doesn't just sabotage immediate outcomes. It damages relationships and makes future collaboration nearly impossible. Win-Win or Nothing offers an antidote, challenging both sides to step back, realign, and prioritise integrity over pride. Even if no deal is reached, the process of seeking alignment builds trust and keeps the door open for future opportunities.

### *But isn't it Just Giving Up?* (Win-Win Thinkers)

Even those who believe in Win-Win can hesitate when it comes to the 'Nothing' part, seeing it as a failure rather than a strategic choice. But this misunderstands its purpose. 'Nothing' isn't about walking away for the sake of it; it's about preserving integrity when an agreement isn't truly viable.

When interests don't align, but both sides push for a compromise anyway, it often leads to resentment, inefficiency, and poor outcomes. 'Nothing' is a commitment to finding sustainable solutions rather than forcing a compromise that doesn't serve anyone in the long run.

Sometimes, the most respectful and productive choice is to step back, allowing both sides to reassess, realign, and return with clearer priorities. Far from giving up, it is a deliberate choice to prioritise trust, long-term success, and genuine collaboration.

**Reframing Win-Win or Nothing**

At its core, Win-Win or Nothing is about integrity. It challenges us to aim for alignment, resist the temptation of short-term fixes, and prioritise trust and shared success.

This mindset doesn't mean every interaction ends in agreement. Sometimes, interests are simply too different, and walking away is the best option. Other times, it means pausing the conversation to return with fresh eyes. Either way, this commitment strengthens relationships, making them more intentional and resilient.

By embracing Win-Win or Nothing, we elevate every interaction, striving for outcomes where everyone feels valued, respected, and empowered. When alignment isn't possible, we step away with integrity, ready to find a better way forward.

The Win-Win Mindset isn't just an ideal, it's an essential approach for anyone looking to build stronger relationships and drive meaningful progress. Whether in business, family, or community, shifting from competition to collaboration helps us achieve far more than we ever could alone.

When we move beyond 'Me vs. You' and embrace *What is our way?* we unlock new possibilities that benefit everyone involved.

# KEY INSIGHTS
## FOR BETTERMENT

- **A Win-Win Mindset unlocks greater possibilities:** Moving beyond 'Me vs. You' thinking allows us to shift from competition to collaboration, helping us uncover solutions that serve the collective good rather than just individual desires.

- **Shared values create stronger solutions:** Win-Win outcomes are not about everyone getting exactly what they want. Rather, they are about focusing on the deeper values and shared priorities that drive meaningful, sustainable progress.

- **Collaboration requires intentional effort:** Achieving Win-Win outcomes demands a commitment to open dialogue, mutual respect, and a willingness to move beyond surface-level positions to find common ground.

- **Toxic competition erodes trust and progress:** Whether in personal relationships or business settings, a culture of blame and defensiveness leads to stagnation, while collaboration fosters innovation and long-term success.

- **Betterment thrives on trust and alignment:** The Win-Win Mindset builds stronger relationships by promoting trust, mutual respect, and a commitment to finding solutions that benefit everyone involved.

# REFLECTIVE
# QUESTIONS

1. **Where in my life do I tend to approach situations with a 'Me vs. You' mindset?** How might shifting to a *What is our way?* approach change the outcome?
2. **What beliefs have I internalised about competition and collaboration?** Are they helping me create better outcomes, or are they holding me back from seeking shared success?
3. **Which relationship in my life would benefit from a more Win-Win approach?** What small steps can I take to start fostering mutual understanding and cooperation?

**WHAT'S NEXT?** Collaboration and shared success are built on a foundation of trust, safety, and respect. Without these, even the most well-intentioned efforts can break down. Next, we explore how these elements form the bedrock of meaningful relationships and high-performing teams. By understanding how to cultivate trust and create psychological safety, we foster environments where collaboration and Betterment can truly thrive.

# 8

# Beneath the Surface—Why Trust, Safety, and Respect are Non-Negotiable

*'Trust is the lubrication that makes it possible for organisations to work.'* Warren Bennis

## The Hidden Forces Behind High-Performing Teams

Trust, safety, and respect aren't just nice-to-haves. They're the foundation of every successful team and meaningful relationship. Without them, even the best strategies fall flat.

*I don't trust you.*

Four words that can stop progress in its tracks. Whether spoken outright or left unspoken, a lack of trust creates friction, fuels misalignment, and makes collaboration nearly impossible.

We may have the best product, the most brilliant strategy, and even the most talented people, but without trust, progress grinds to a halt. No matter how much effort is poured into planning, execution, or innovation, nothing truly moves forward in an environment where trust, psychological safety, and respect are missing.

You may have even noticed that reading those words—*I don't trust you*—triggered a physical reaction. Perhaps the hairs on the back of your neck stood up, or you felt a sinking sensation in your stomach. That's

## PART 3 WIN-WIN MINDSET

because trust is deeply wired into our sense of security and connection. When it's broken, it shakes us to our core.

High-performing teams and thriving relationships don't happen by chance. Whether in the workplace or in our personal lives, the absence of these foundational pillars leads to defensiveness, miscommunication, and disengagement.

We often focus on strategy and goals as the primary drivers of success, but without trust, safety, and respect, even the clearest goals can fall apart. These three elements form the unseen infrastructure of every meaningful interaction, providing the stability that allows people to engage fully, share openly, and work together without fear of judgement or failure. They create an environment where ideas can flourish, mistakes can be acknowledged, and progress can happen.

> Neglecting these foundations comes at a high cost. When trust is low, people hold back, ideas are stifled, and progress is painfully slow. The fear of failure prevents innovation, and relationships become transactional rather than transformational. However, when trust, safety and respect are established, people feel valued, empowered, and inspired to show their best selves during every interaction.

Although these elements hold significant value, they are frequently taken for granted instead of being actively developed. Building and maintaining them requires conscious effort, clear communication, and a deep understanding of what it takes to create genuine psychological safety and lasting respect.

In this chapter, we explore why trust is the cornerstone of collaboration, how psychological safety enables risk-taking and innovation, and how respect ensures that every voice is valued. We learn practical strategies to diagnose trust breakdowns, foster openness, and create a culture where Betterment thrives.

Without trust, safety, and respect, all efforts toward collaboration, innovation, and growth remain surface-level. It's time to go beneath the surface and lay the foundation for something truly meaningful.

## Trust: The Ultimate Game-Changer

Trust moves the needle from struggling to thriving relationships. The most striking statistic? Employees working in high-trust organisations report 74% lower stress levels.[1] This advantage proves transformative during times of unprecedented burnout and pressure levels. Trust doesn't just create better work environments; it fundamentally improves how we feel and function.

The benefits don't stop there. Research shows that people working in high-trust companies also experience:[1]

- 106% more energy at work
- 76% higher engagement
- 50% greater productivity
- 40% less burnout
- 29% more satisfaction in their lives
- 13% fewer sick days.

These numbers are more than impressive. They're a call to action. Trust transforms how we work, how we connect, and how we sustain energy over time. But its relevance extends far beyond the workplace. Trust is equally vital in our personal lives. The basis of successful partnerships, friendships, and family dynamics lies in relationships where openness and mutual understanding can flourish.

Here's the most important part: trust should not be viewed as an elusive quality requiring years to earn. Trust functions as a skill, which people can develop deliberately and quickly.

By focusing on behaviours like transparency, consistency, and mutual respect, we can create a culture where trust becomes the foundation of every interaction, whether at work or at home.

Respect is often the outward expression of trust. When people feel trusted, they are more likely to treat others with respect, engaging in constructive conversations even during disagreements. Conversely, a lack of respect often signals underlying trust issues, whether it's dismissing someone's ideas or failing to acknowledge contributions.

This chapter begins with trust because it's the gateway to everything else. Trust isn't a leap of faith; it's a choice, and the results speak for themselves.

## When Trust Breaks: The Cost You Can't Afford

The insurance project explored in the previous chapter demonstrated the negative impact of competitive performance and misaligned objectives. Beneath their misaligned priorities lay a deeper issue: trust was non-existent. The absence of trust got in the way of teamwork and intensified existing problems, which led to unnecessary delays and increased expenses and took a heavy toll on team spirit.

Trust, or the lack of it, was at the core of the dysfunction. Both teams approached interactions defensively, more focused on protecting their turf than on working toward shared goals. The team meetings turned into blame games instead of problem-solving sessions. 'The first question after a problem appeared was not, *What's the solution?* but *Who messed up?*' explained a member of the team. The defensive behaviour generated an adversarial environment that made people reluctant to pursue risks or own up to their errors due to concerns about damaging their professional standing.

The impact wasn't just emotional, it had a measurable impact on progress, creating a series of operational inefficiencies.

The lack of trust eroded psychological safety over time.

The biggest expense they faced wasn't wasted time or higher costs but the gradual destruction of their team's well-being. Team members reported exhaustion, lack of appreciation, and demoralisation due to ongoing tension.

This story illustrates a hard truth: trust isn't a soft skill; it's the backbone of any successful collaboration. Without it, even the most talented teams can fall into dysfunction. The cost of low trust isn't just relational, it's financial, operational, and deeply human. In the next section, we explore how trust can be rebuilt and extended, transforming even fractured teams into aligned, high-performing groups.

## It's not You, it's Me... But Really, it's You: The People Side of Trust

When trust breaks down, processes and systems are essential for clarity and consistency. However, they can only go so far if the people involved don't trust one another. People will resist, miscommunicate, and disengage from even the most effective systems and processes when it's absent. That's why, in low-trust environments, the first step must always be to reconnect on a human level.

### Building Trust through Connection

In low-trust environments, I've often drawn inspiration from the principles behind *The New York Times* '36 Questions to Fall in Love'.[2] These questions, designed by psychologist Arthur Aron, leverage mutual vulnerability to foster closeness. While the exact questions may not always fit a professional setting, the core idea—asking open, personal questions to connect on a human level—can be transformational.

> *In one workshop, I gave participants a set of open-ended questions and asked them to pair up with someone they felt they could benefit from building a stronger personal relationship with. This might be someone they didn't know well, someone they needed to collaborate closely with, or even someone they'd had trust challenges with in the past.*
>
> *Two participants, who had been in a combative dynamic with significant trust erosion, took a courageous step and chose to pair up. I was encouraged by their decision, but when I checked on their progress, I found them locked in the same work-based debate they'd been having for months. They were tense, defensive, and each was trying to justify their position. Their body language exuded friction. With a*

## PART 3　WIN-WIN MINDSET

*gentle interruption, I advised them to trust the process. 'Work discussions can wait until later, so you should focus on the questions at hand now. Just give it a go.'*

*Their immediate response was to tell me that they already knew each other well; after all, they had worked together for years. I pushed them, saying, 'What have you got to lose?' They finally agreed to humour me and give it a go. They began going through the broad non-work-related questions, designed to connect on a human level. Starting with something easy, like, What's the best meal you've ever had, and where was it? then going a little deeper with a question like, If you could relive any year of your life, which one would it be and why? Now the barriers were starting to come down, they could really open up with a question like, What's a personal accomplishment that means a lot to you?*

*Incredibly, something shifted. Their body language softened. By the end, they shared a heartfelt hug and rejoined the group, visibly lighter and more connected.*

### The Impact of Reconnection

*What happened next was extraordinary. During the rest of the workshop, these two team members began supporting each other, defending each other's ideas and collaborating more openly. The following morning, I learned they had met for breakfast, where they'd discussed how they'd been relying too heavily on email to communicate. They agreed to prioritise personal connection moving forward, whether in person or over the phone.*

This breakthrough wasn't just about solving a specific workplace issue; it was about rediscovering their shared humanity.

### Strengthening Bonds in High-Trust Teams

Interestingly, it's not just teams experiencing low trust that benefit from intentional connection. Even teams with exceptionally high trust can find new value in building deeper personal bonds. One organisation

I've worked with is a shining example of a high-trust, high-performing culture.

Yet, even within this exemplary team, something was missing. During a two-day offsite focused on leadership and performance, the group, while undeniably cohesive and professional, realised their bonds were largely transactional. They trusted one another to do the job and live the values, but they hadn't truly connected on a personal level. They faced no immediate problems, but we believed their work together could reach new heights with better mutual understanding and stronger connections.

Our solution involved creating an exercise that encouraged team members to express their personal goals. The 'Postcards from the Future' technique required participants to reflect on their future selves in five years and share their professional and personal life projections with others. The exercise brought to light undisclosed truths and personal values, which would not have emerged during regular interactions. When they shared their personal journeys and goals, team members began supporting one another better, helping with both organisational objectives and personal success.

This experience reinforced a powerful lesson: trust is not static. Even teams that function cohesively can still improve their trust levels through intentional connections. When personal aspirations matched organisational goals, the team was able to evolve from a highly functional unit to a purpose-driven, connected leadership group where every individual felt valued.

The Win-Win Mindset embodies the principle of achieving shared goals while making certain every team member develops and succeeds. This is the essence of the Win-Win Mindset—not just meeting shared objectives, but ensuring that everyone grows and thrives along the way.

## Trusting the Process: How Systems Can Build or Break Trust

Processes play a critical role in organisations. They set expectations, highlight interdependencies, and create accountability, key factors in fostering trust. When designed thoughtfully and used with the right intentions, processes can act as a powerful enabler, supporting high performance and collaboration. However, in low-trust environments, the same processes can become weaponised, eroding trust further and deepening divisions.

### Processes as a Tool for High-Trust Teams

Trust is supported when processes establish expectations and accountability while highlighting essential connections between tasks and people. However, the same processes can be weaponised when trust levels are already low, deepening division.

In a high-performing organisation built on trust, accountability is not about blame. It is about learning, adapting, and progressing together.

*One organisation I work with exemplifies this balance beautifully. Each month, cross-functional teams gather for detailed performance reviews. If targets are missed three times in a row, teams are required to present countermeasures, plans for how they will address the gap and move forward. Far from a punitive exercise, this process is grounded in curiosity and support. For example, one team member who had joined from a low-trust environment felt significant anxiety when he saw three red lights (indicating repeated missed targets) against his area. His prior experiences had taught him to expect blame and public criticism in such situations.*

*To his surprise, the meeting took a completely different tone. Senior leaders including the global president posed reflective questions such as, What do we need to move forward? and How can we support this area to overcome the challenges? They directed the conversation toward solutions rather than blame. Leadership quickly implemented resourcing strategies to provide support once they realised the team lacked resources for their ambitious targets. The approach transformed the team member's understanding of the process and showed that trust grows through structured accountability combined with constructive intent.*

## When Processes Are Weaponised

However, not all processes are created, or used, equally. In low-trust environments, the same tools can easily be turned into weapons. This was evident in the ongoing challenges faced by the Sales and Underwriting teams discussed earlier. A team member suggested introducing a process to capture and track ongoing issues, aiming to improve visibility and collaboration. Another team member quickly noted, 'We already have that, it's called the issues log.'

The problem wasn't the process; it was how it was used. Instead of solving issues, the log became a blame game, calling out individuals rather than tackling real challenges. People avoided it, fearing it would be used against them. What should have built trust fuelled mistrust, stalling progress and shutting down collaboration.

## The Intersection of Trust and Process

Processes may seem neutral, but their impact depends on how they're used. In high-trust teams, they bring clarity, alignment, and better collaboration. They ensure that the right people are involved at the right times and that everyone knows what to expect. When teams trust that processes will be used constructively, they can focus on problem-solving rather than self-protection.

On the other hand, when processes are misused, whether to assign blame, consolidate power, or highlight failures, they undermine trust and stifle engagement. The saying 'trust the process' only works when people trust the intentions behind it.

**Designing Processes that Foster Trust**

To design and implement processes that build trust:
1. **Set Clear Intentions**: Communicate the purpose of the process and ensure it is aligned with shared goals rather than individual agendas.
2. **Focus on Solutions, not Faults**: Use processes to uncover challenges and drive collaborative problem-solving, not to assign blame.
3. **Engage Thoughtfully**: Foster a culture of curiosity, where processes are used to ask, *How can we move forward?* or, *Do we have the right assumptions?*
4. **Adapt and Evolve**: Regularly review how processes are working and adjust them to ensure they continue to serve their intended purpose.

When trust in people and process work together, they create a powerful dynamic. Processes provide the structure and consistency needed to sustain performance, while people ensure those structures are embraced with goodwill and collaboration. The key is ensuring that processes are used to support, not replace, the human connections that drive meaningful collaboration.

**Diagnosing Trust Breakdowns: Character vs. Competence**

People often refer to trust as the essential element that binds relationships, but once trust fails, it can cause seemingly permanent damage. The first step to restoring trust involves identifying the fundamental reason behind its collapse. In *The Speed of Trust*, Stephen M. R. Covey outlines a practical model for evaluating personal credibility, built around two fundamental elements: character, which reflects integrity and intent, and competence, which represents capabilities and results.[3] This model offers a structured way to diagnose and strengthen trust in professional and personal relationships.

## Character: Who You Are

Character refers to the personal traits that inspire trust in others. It encompasses:

- **Integrity**: Doing what we say we'll do and being honest, even when it's difficult.

- **Intent**: Acting with genuine motives and prioritising the interests of others, not just our own.

When trust breaks down due to character issues, it often feels personal. Consider a leader who promises transparency yet consistently fails to share essential information with their team. The team members may start to feel disenchanted (or even betrayed) and the leader's effectiveness becomes overshadowed by a lack of integrity that causes distrust, despite their leadership abilities. A team member who consistently puts their personal objectives above collective team targets exhibits self-centred behaviour which harms their relationships, despite their professional skills.

> Understanding character-based trust issues demands reflecting honestly on how others may perceive our behaviours and underlying motivations. Are our words consistent with our behaviour? Are our intentions clear and authentic? A failure in either integrity or intent erodes trust at its core.

## Competence: What You Can Do

Competence refers to the abilities and results that demonstrate trustworthiness. It includes:

- **Capabilities**: Having the skills, knowledge, and expertise to deliver results.

- **Results**: Following through and achieving what we set out to do.

Competence-related trust breakdowns are more situational. For example, a brilliant marketing professional may inspire trust through their character but lose credibility if they fail to adapt to new digital tools, leaving them unable to deliver results. On the other hand, a well-meaning team member with limited experience in a critical area may struggle to gain the trust of others, not because of their intent, but because their capabilities do not align with the task at hand.

> To diagnose competence-related trust issues, ask yourself, *Do I have the necessary skills for this task? Am I delivering the results expected of me?* If the answer is no, building trust may require developing expertise or seeking additional support to meet expectations.

**The Interplay of Character and Competence**

High trust emerges when character combines with competence. A senior manager gains trust by showing integrity and intent through their continuous support for ethical practices. However, if they consistently miss deadlines or fail to deliver results, their competence becomes questionable, which undermines trust. Conversely, someone with exceptional technical skills but questionable intent, such as taking credit for others' work, will struggle to earn lasting trust.

By breaking trust down into these two areas, teams can identify the issue and take action. Whether it's strengthening character or improving competence, rebuilding trust starts with understanding its roots.

The framework of character and competence provides a powerful lens for diagnosing trust breakdowns, whether we're examining why we might not trust someone else or another team, or even assessing our personal credibility. Breaking trust into tangible elements like integrity, intent, capabilities, and results allows us to move beyond vague or accusatory statements like, *I don't trust you*, which can feel unproductive or confrontational.

Instead, we can identify specific areas of concern: is the issue about follow-through on commitments (results)? Or is it about unclear motives (intent)? This clarity enables constructive conversations focused on what is needed to build or rebuild trust, rather than assigning blame. Similarly, using this framework to assess our credibility can help us understand how others perceive our actions and capabilities, so we can address gaps proactively and strengthen our relationships. By embracing this level of transparency, the framework transforms trust from an emotional hurdle into a practical, actionable pathway for growth and alignment.

## *The Trust Contract: Making it Real and Actionable*

Building trust isn't about leaving things to chance. It's about being intentional. This is where developing a Trust Contract can be helpful. This practical tool fosters open dialogue about what trust looks like in action, even in the most challenging contexts. By explicitly defining commitments and expectations, the approach helps build stronger, more resilient relationships.

The idea is simple: each person (or team) describes the specific behaviours that signal trust to them, aligns with the other party on what they can commit to, and establishes a clear baseline for expectations. This contract becomes a visible reminder of high-trust behaviours and a constructive way to address concerns if those behaviours aren't being met.

### How it Works

 **Describe Trust Behaviours.** Each person starts by identifying the behaviours that build trust for them. This is a chance to get specific. What does trust look like in action for you? For example:

*It's okay to miss a deadline if it's flagged early, so I can adjust expectations.*

*I trust you more when you share regular updates, even if there's nothing major to report. It helps me feel connected to the process.*

*If you disagree with me, I appreciate when you bring it up directly rather than venting to others. It shows me you value our relationship enough to be honest.*

2. **Align on Commitments.** After everyone shares their trust behaviours, they align on realistic, shared commitments, setting clear expectations everyone can follow. For instance, one person might say, *I can commit to flagging potential delays early,* while the other might say, *I can commit to providing feedback within forty-eight hours when you send me a draft.*

3. **Establish the Baseline.** The commitments the team agrees on forms the baseline for trust. This is the foundation they'll return to if trust is ever strained. The clarity of a Trust Contract means that when behaviours fall short, it's easier to address them constructively. Instead of vague frustrations or misunderstandings, they can refer back to the specific commitments: *We agreed to flag issues early. Can we talk about what happened here?*

---

A Trust Contract works because it transforms trust from an abstract concept into visible, measurable actions. It creates a shared language for trust, making it easier to spot issues and focus on solutions instead of blame. Instead of assuming bad intent, it sparks curiosity: *What's getting in the way, and how can we fix it?*

It shows that both parties are committed to doing the work to support each other, and sets the tone for mutual respect and accountability. Over time, these small but intentional behaviours reinforce trust, creating a stronger foundation for whatever challenges lie ahead.

Leaders set the tone for respect in their teams. By listening without interruption, acknowledging contributions, and treating every individual with dignity, leaders show that respect isn't conditional, it's a standard that underpins every interaction. When everyone knows what to expect, and knows they can count on each other to follow through, it doesn't just strengthen relationships, it accelerates performance and fosters a culture where trust thrives.

## Psychological Safety: The Gateway to Growth and Innovation

To fully realise the potential of trust, teams also require psychological safety, an environment where people feel secure enough to take risks, share ideas, and acknowledge mistakes without fear of criticism or reprisal. Research from McKinsey highlights the critical role psychological safety plays in fostering Betterment within both individual and collective performance.[4]

Psychological safety acts as the bridge between trust and ongoing performance. It ensures trust is more than just an internal belief, becoming a shared team dynamic where vulnerability is not a liability but a strength. With safety in place, teams are empowered to embrace challenges, engage in constructive conflict, and explore bold ideas, key drivers of the Betterment Mindset.[5]

This concept aligns powerfully with the principles of Betterment. The Responsible Mindset encourages ownership of actions and learning from mistakes, which can only occur if admitting errors is met with support rather than judgement. The Win-Win Mindset thrives in a culture of collaboration, where individuals feel safe to challenge ideas and raise concerns. The Opportunity Mindset depends on psychological safety to fuel the experimentation and innovation needed to reframe challenges as possibilities.

McKinsey's research demonstrates the direct impact of psychological safety on team performance.[4] Teams with high safety levels perform better than others because they show more creativity along with better adaptability and resilience.[5] Members of these environments actively participate in information sharing and feedback-seeking while contributing new perspectives, which drives collective intelligence and innovative outputs.

Leaders are essential in creating environments of psychological safety. When leaders show curiosity toward new ideas, acknowledge their own errors, and solicit different viewpoints, they create an inclusive workplace that values the contributions of all team members. When a leader responds with, *I hadn't considered that, let's explore it further*, they demonstrate their willingness to consider new ideas, which helps to foster participation among their team members. These behaviours generate trust and make safety a common standard, which allows people to participate without worrying about negative consequences.

Without psychological safety, potential development becomes restricted. Settings where individuals worry about blame or criticism prevent people from taking risks and exploring new ideas, which results in lost opportunities and reduced team spirit. Psychological safety is not a luxury. It is essential for Betterment, providing the conditions for teams to connect, perform, and grow.

**Beyond Words: Making Trust and Respect Inclusive for All**

Trust and psychological safety go hand in hand, with respect as the bridge. When people feel trusted and valued, they're more open, engaged, and willing to contribute, creating a culture where safety thrives. However, as critical as trust and respect are, they may not always be sufficient to establish psychological safety for everyone. Safety is deeply personal, shaped by individual experiences and cultural contexts, and it cannot be achieved through a one-size-fits-all approach.

*I had the privilege of leading a six-month Thrive with Change program with the Australian Institute of Aboriginal and Torres Strait Islander Studies (AIATSIS), one of the most diverse organisations I've ever worked with. During the program, I had a conversation with an Indigenous employee that left a lasting impression. She told me that Aboriginal people face a feeling of danger whenever they step outside their homes, which initially shocked me. As she explained, I began to grasp the deep truth embedded in her words. Her daily experiences with micro-aggressions and overt racism required her and her peers to maintain constant vigilance.*

*This was not an expression of victim mentality or an excuse for failing to meet expectations. It was a statement of fact. For her, psychological safety was not just about trust or respect in the workplace; it required acknowledging and addressing the layers of threat she faced simply by existing in a society where systemic discrimination persists. Her perspective was a powerful reminder that safety cannot be assumed. It must be created, intentionally and inclusively, with an understanding that different individuals have different needs.*

*This insight had a direct and profound impact on how I designed and delivered the program. Before every workshop, I held a separate session with two Elders from the organisation, respected role models within their mob. During these sessions, I shared the tools and concepts I planned to introduce and discussed how these might resonate with Indigenous employees. Where appropriate, the Elders would play a more active role during the workshops and share a much-needed layer of perspective from their unique experiences.*

*The benefits were tremendous. Not only did I have the privilege of learning about Indigenous cultures in deeply personal ways, but the process opened up essential conversations about the experiences of Indigenous people in the workplace. Indigenous employees experienced a greater sense of safety and relatability, making it easier for them to embrace the tools from our discussions in a relevant way.*

Similarly, someone who has experienced workplace harassment, discrimination, or trauma may require more nuanced support to feel safe. They may require greater levels of confidentiality or transparency to feel secure. Without acknowledging and accommodating these diverse needs, organisations risk alienating valuable voices and perspectives, inadvertently diminishing the inclusivity and richness of their teams.

This is why safety demands more than just blanket policies or well-meaning platitudes. It requires active listening, cultural competence, and a willingness to ask, *What do you need to feel safe here?* By making space for these conversations, we signal to individuals that their experiences are valid and their contributions valued. In doing so, we create the conditions for true psychological safety, where every person, regardless of background or past experiences, can bring their full selves to the table.

Ultimately, psychological safety isn't just about fostering a sense of comfort; it's about unlocking the full potential of a team by ensuring that no one feels excluded or silenced.

# KEY INSIGHTS
## FOR BETTERMENT

- **Trust is built through consistency and transparency:** Trust isn't automatic; it's built through consistent actions and honest communication, and by following through on commitments. To build trust, we need to focus on being reliable, transparent, and accountable.

- **Psychological safety starts with how we show up:** Creating an environment where people feel safe to share ideas and take risks begins with us. Practising active listening, showing vulnerability, and encouraging open dialogue are key to psychological safety.

- **Respect strengthens relationships and drives collaboration:** Respect builds solid relationships and encourages teamwork. We need to treat every exchange as an opportunity to learn by showing curiosity and appreciation for different perspectives.

- **Building trust, safety, and respect requires daily effort:** These elements aren't one-time achievements; they are ongoing commitments. Proactively seeking feedback, addressing concerns with empathy, and consistently aligning our actions with our values nurtures lasting relationships.

- **Betterment starts with taking responsibility for trust:** Trust is a two-way street. Instead of waiting for others to earn it, we need to take ownership by being trustworthy ourselves through integrity, reliability, and a commitment to shared success.

# REFLECTIVE
# **QUESTIONS**

1. **Where in my life or work do I sense a lack of trust, safety, or respect?** What small actions could I take to start rebuilding these foundations?
2. **How do I personally contribute to building, or breaking, trust in my relationships?** Are there any behaviours I could adjust to foster a more trusting environment?
3. **Thinking of a time when I felt psychologically safe to share an idea or take a risk,** what factors made that possible, and how can I create similar conditions for others?

**WHAT'S NEXT?** Meaningful collaboration starts with trust, safety, and respect. However, the real difficulty emerges in aligning people with different perspectives and priorities. Next, we explore how to bridge differences, overcome roadblocks, and create alignment in even the most complex situations. Through practical strategies and real-world examples, we learn how to turn conflict into cooperation and build momentum toward shared success.

# 9

# The Art of Alignment—Moving Beyond Stalemates to Shared Purpose

*'Coming together is a beginning, staying together is progress, and working together is success.' Attributed to Henry Ford*

## Stalemates and Standstills: Why We Fail to Move Forward

One of the most frustrating dynamics in collaboration is the tug of war, each side pulling firmly on their end of the rope, unwilling to budge. Sometimes, it's about entrenched positions, where neither party is willing to compromise. Other times, it's a quiet refusal to engage or accommodate. Either way, the result is the same: progress stalls, opportunities slip away, and energy that could have been channelled into solutions is wasted in conflict or avoidance.

Stalemates don't always stem from outright disagreement. More often than not, they're the result of misalignment—differing perspectives, unclear expectations, and poor communication. Without the right tools to bridge these gaps, conversations break down into blame, defensiveness, or silence. Meanwhile, the chance to create a better way forward moves further out of reach.

Take the transition to hybrid working, for example. Organisations were required to manage competing needs while also dealing with differing expectations and varying flexibility levels. Many became trapped in a frustrating cycle because they pulled in opposite directions, failing to reach a mutual understanding.

### Pulling in Different Directions: Kylie's Story

*A tight-knit team I worked with felt the strain of hybrid working firsthand. Seeking clarity, they turned to their leader, Kylie, who introduced a three-day in-office policy, quickly labelled 'the mandate'. What was meant to provide structure instead sparked resistance. Frustration grew, and team dynamics suffered. Once part of the group, Kylie suddenly found herself excluded from team lunches, a clear sign something was off.*

*The problem wasn't the policy itself. It was how people felt about it. Kylie thought she'd gathered enough input and assumed the team would be on board. But from their perspective, the decision had been made for them, not with them. They felt unheard, and frustration set in. What they really wanted wasn't just a better policy; they wanted to be part of shaping the solution.*

*Recognising the disconnect, Kylie brought me in to help reset the conversation. Through structured discussions, the team shifted focus from individual preferences to shared purpose—how hybrid work could support both autonomy and collaboration. With that clarity, they co-created a solution that worked for everyone.*

This scenario plays out in workplaces everywhere. When we pull too hard in opposite directions, alignment feels impossible. But with the right approach, we can move from tug of war to teamwork, finding solutions that bring people together.

In this chapter, we explore how to move beyond fixed positions to uncover shared purpose, gain clarity, and negotiate solutions that create win-win outcomes. Whether it's hybrid work, strategic decisions, or personal conflicts, the frameworks in this chapter will help us align faster and more effectively.

# Purpose—What Do You Really Want?

## From Positions to Purpose

At the heart of every misalignment lies a fundamental question: What do we really want?

It's easy to get stuck in positions, surface-level demands that mask deeper needs. Positions create tension and stall progress as people dig in. But when we step back and focus on the purpose behind them, collaboration and progress become possible.

This distinction, explored in *Getting to Yes* by Roger Fisher, William Ury, and Bruce Patton, is a game-changer.[1] Their research at Harvard's Negotiation Project transformed the field by focusing on underlying interests, not rigid demands, providing a powerful framework for shifting from conflict to collaboration.

## People Defend Positions but Strive for Purpose

When conflicts arise, people naturally cling to their positions. Positions are what people say they want:

- *We need more budget.*
- *I want a higher salary.*
- *I refuse to work weekends.*

Positions feel tangible and easy to defend, but they're often rigid. The more they're repeated, the harder they are to let go of, creating an adversarial dynamic that stalls progress.

Purpose, on the other hand, reveals the deeper motivations driving those positions. Behind 'we need more budget' may be a desire to deliver high-quality work without overburdening the team. Understanding purpose allows us to shift from defending demands to exploring solutions that meet shared needs.

Fisher, Ury, and Patton emphasise that when negotiators fixate on their positions, they risk becoming entrenched in conflict rather than seeking mutual solutions.[1]

A purpose-driven approach reduces conflict and fosters collaboration, helping us find common ground, prioritise shared goals, and drive meaningful progress.

**Why Focusing on Positions Fails**

Getting stuck in fixed positions leads to frustration, deadlock, and missed opportunities.

When we focus on what we want, rather than why we want it, problems tend to escalate instead of getting solved. Take this common workplace standoff:

- A manager insists, *We need to hire three more people to hit our targets.*
- The leader managing the budget pushes back, *We can't afford that.*
- Both sides dig in, and progress grinds to a halt.

What's missing? Purpose. The manager is trying to prevent burnout and protect quality, while the leader is focused on financial stability. By shifting the conversation to shared goals, they can explore creative solutions that work for both, like streamlining processes or reprioritising tasks.

**How to Shift from Positions to Purpose**

Shifting from positions to purpose starts by asking the right questions. We need to dig deeper into motivations with questions like:

- *What is the greater impact we are trying to achieve?*
- *What matters most—to me, to the other person, to the team?*

THE ART OF ALIGNMENT **CHAPTER 9**

- *What are we trying to avoid?*

It's equally important to communicate our interests clearly.

When we focus on shared values instead of rigid demands, we open the door to alignment and collaboration.

> Purpose doesn't just resolve conflict, it transforms it. When we focus on why something matters, we unlock creativity, collaboration, and better solutions, the kind that never emerge when we're stuck in fixed positions.

In organisations, this is even more powerful. Teams that align on purpose move faster, innovate better, and stay engaged longer. They don't just solve problems; they create momentum.

The challenge? People tend to think in positions. It's not surprising. Leaders often push for solutions. Over time, people get attached to their position (i.e., their solution), seeing it as the only way forward. But when we ask why that position matters, we find better ways to move forward.

Take a classic parenting standoff:

- One parent walks in, sees the kids playing video games, and declares, *No video games during the week!*

- The other, busy cooking, replies, *I already said they could have thirty minutes.*

- And just like that, the battle lines are drawn.

But if the first parent had led with the deeper purpose, *I want the kids to prioritise schoolwork and family time,* the conversation shifts. The second parent, now seeing common ground, might respond, *I completely agree. I let them play while I finished dinner so I could focus on homework with them afterward.*

Now, instead of butting heads, they can find a solution that works for both:

- Homework first, then video games as a reward.

- A family game later, balancing responsibility and fun.

That small shift, from position to purpose, turns a pointless argument into a win-win solution.

The takeaway? People often focus on what they want, but real progress comes from asking, *What do we really want?* That's where the best solutions live.

**Recognise Positions, Uncover Purpose**

It's easy to get stuck in surface-level demands that create tension and stall progress. But beneath every position is a deeper purpose, the real needs, motivations, and values that matter. When we shift from what someone wants to why they want it, we open the door to collaboration and better solutions.

**Some Common Workplace Examples**

Below are ten examples that illustrate this shift, drawing from both workplace and personal contexts.

> **Position**: *I need three more team members to hit our targets.*
> **Purpose**: *I want to ensure the team isn't overworked and that we maintain quality while meeting deadlines.*
>
> **Position**: *We need to cut costs by 10% this quarter.*
> **Purpose**: *I want the business to remain financially stable during an uncertain period.*
>
> **Position**: *I won't work on this project unless I'm the lead.*
> **Purpose**: *I want my skills and contributions to be recognised and valued.*
>
> **Position**: *The client presentation must be perfect before we share it.*
> **Purpose**: *I want to protect our reputation and ensure we deliver work that reflects our expertise.*

**Position**: *We can't launch until all the product features are ready.*
    **Purpose**: *I want our customers to have a seamless experience that builds trust and satisfaction.*

## Some Common Personal Examples

**Position**: *I don't want the kids to play video games during the week.*
    **Purpose**: *I want to make sure they prioritise schoolwork and family time.*

**Position**: *I want to go to the beach for our holiday this year.*
    **Purpose**: *I need time to relax and recharge somewhere peaceful.*

**Position**: *I need you to call me every day when you're travelling.*
    **Purpose**: *I want to feel connected and reassured when we're apart.*

**Position**: *I'm not hosting Christmas this year.*
    **Purpose**: *I want to enjoy the holiday without the stress of organising everything myself.*

**Position**: *We're not spending money on a new car right now.*
    **Purpose**: *I want us to feel financially secure and prepared for unexpected expenses.*

## From Conflict to Collaboration

Positions often feel rigid or combative, but when we dig into the real purpose—what we want and why—it shifts the conversation. Instead of getting stuck in a battle of 'either-or', we find better dialogue, deeper understanding, and smarter solutions.

Understanding purpose helps us approach conversations with curiosity and empathy, turning potential conflicts into opportunities for collaboration. Instead of attacking each other's ideas as adversaries, we should come together as allies, directing our energy toward solving the problem.

When we focus on shared purpose, we stop seeing differences as roadblocks and start using them to drive better outcomes.

### How to Ask 'Why' Without Asking 'Why'

Understanding why someone holds a position is key to collaboration, but asking *Why?* directly can backfire. It often puts people on the defensive, making them justify rather than explain.

I learned this early in my career as a market researcher. When I asked, *Why did you choose that option?* responses were brief or defensive. But when I reworded it, *What is it about that option that appeals to you?* people opened up and shared real insights.

To keep conversations open, try swapping, *Why do you think that's important?* for:

- *What is it about that's important to you?*
- *If we did that, what difference would it make?*
- *How would that impact your goals or priorities?*

### Shifting from 'Why' to Curiosity-Driven Questions

When tackling misalignment, ask questions that encourage discovery rather than defence:

- *What would success look like for you here?*
- *How would this help your team or the organisation?*
- *What's the bigger picture you're hoping to achieve?*
- *What's at stake if we don't address this?*

Genuine curiosity builds trust, keeps conversations productive, and leads to better problem-solving.

**Understanding Your Own Why**

It's just as important to understand our own motivations as it is to explore others'. Asking the right questions brings clarity and intention to our approach:

- *What's really driving my perspective?*
- *Am I holding onto a position, or have I defined my purpose?*
- *How will my approach impact this conversation or relationship?*

Checking in with ourselves keeps our intent aligned with our actions and helps us show up with the same openness and curiosity we expect from others.

## From Ambiguity to Alignment: The Power of Clarity

Purpose alone isn't enough. Clarity is what turns purpose into action. Without it, even the best intentions can lead to confusion, frustration, and wasted effort. When expectations are vague, people make assumptions, pull in different directions, or focus on the wrong priorities.

Achieving clarity goes beyond just setting goals. It's about aligning on roles, expectations, priorities, and measurable outcomes.[2] Success needs to be clearly defined, along with acceptable trade-offs and progress indicators. Without this, teams and relationships drift apart, making even simple decisions feel complicated and contentious.

When clarity is established upfront, alignment becomes easier, decision-making is faster, and collaboration feels more focused and effective.[3] By looking beyond surface-level demands to the real motivations behind them, we build trust, strengthen relationships, and create better outcomes for everyone involved.

**PART 3** WIN-WIN MINDSET

# The ALIGN Model: A Framework for Negotiating Win-Win Outcomes

The ALIGN Model helps us tackle tough conversations, sort out conflicts, and reach win-win solutions. Instead of getting stuck in a stand-off, it shifts the focus to shared purpose and collaboration. Whether we're negotiating at work, juggling competing priorities, or managing personal challenges, ALIGN gives us a practical way to move from frustration to real progress.

### *The Five Steps of the ALIGN Model*

The ALIGN Model follows five interconnected steps to navigate tough conversations, resolve conflicts, and find win-win solutions.

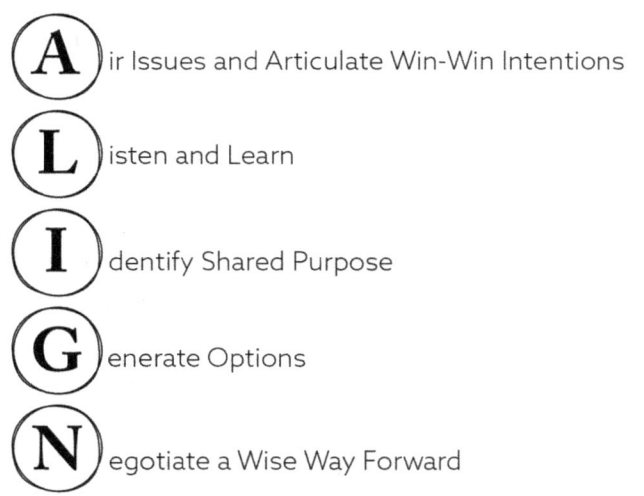

*Figure 5.*

1. **Air Issues and Set a Collaborative Tone**
   Start by acknowledging concerns openly while making it clear you're working toward a solution that benefits everyone. This

reduces defensiveness and sets the stage for a constructive discussion.

**Why it matters:**
- Builds trust and psychological safety
- Shifts the focus from me vs. you to us vs. the problem.

**Example phrases:**
- *I know we see this differently, but I'd love to find a way forward that works for both of us.*
- *Help me understand your concerns so we can agree on a solution together.*

**Checkpoint before moving on:**
- Have you acknowledged key concerns?
- Have you set a collaborative tone?

2. <u>Listen and Learn</u>

Move beyond surface-level disagreements by listening with curiosity. Instead of assuming what matters to the other person, take the time to understand their deeper needs and concerns.

**Why it matters:**
- Makes people feel heard and valued
- Uncovers hidden concerns that could be driving resistance.

**Key actions:**
- Ask open-ended questions: *What's most important to you in this situation?*
- Reflect back to confirm understanding: *It sounds like your biggest concern is workload balance. Is that right?*

**Checkpoint before moving on:**
- Have you identified both individual and bigger-picture needs?
- Does the other person feel heard and understood?

PART 3  WIN-WIN MINDSET

**3.** **Identify Shared Purpose**
Alignment happens when you move beyond individual demands and find the common goal that connects everyone. This step shifts the focus from what you want to why it matters.
**Why it matters:**
- Moves the conversation from conflict to collaboration
- Creates shared commitment to the outcome.

**Key actions:**
- Reframe the discussion around shared priorities: *It sounds like we both want to maintain quality while meeting deadlines. Let's focus on achieving that balance together.*
- Validate alignment before moving forward.

**Checkpoint before moving on:**
- Have you clearly articulated the shared purpose?
- Does everyone agree on the overarching goal?

**4.** **Explore Multiple (Mutually Beneficial) Options**
Rather than getting stuck on a single solution, encourage flexibility and creative problem-solving to find approaches that work for everyone.
**Why it matters:**
- Encourages innovation and shared ownership
- Expands possibilities instead of fuelling defensiveness.

**Key actions:**
- Brainstorm openly before evaluating ideas: *Let's explore all possible solutions, even the unconventional ones.*
- Keep solutions focused on the shared purpose, not just individual preferences.

**Checkpoint before moving on:**
- Have you explored multiple options before narrowing down?
- Do the ideas align with the shared purpose?

## 5. Negotiate a Wise Way Forward

The final step is ensuring the solution makes sense based on your individual and shared goals and priorities. The way forward is clear, practical, and beneficial to everyone involved. This is where alignment turns into action.

**Why it matters:**
- Provides clarity, accountability, and follow-through
- Avoids misalignment or lingering doubts.

**Key actions:**
- Summarise the agreed path forward and confirm commitment: *Based on our discussion, it sounds like the best approach is [solution]. Does everyone feel good about this?*
- Clarify roles, responsibilities, and timelines.

**Checkpoint before concluding:**
- Is the solution clear, practical, and aligned with shared goals?
- Does everyone feel confident moving forward?

## Adapting to Different Situations

The ALIGN Model provides structure for navigating tough conversations, but its real power is in its flexibility. The five steps stay the same, but how we apply them depends on the situation.

For example, ALIGN can be used in structured written exchanges, such as SMS or Teams messages, to ensure clarity and alignment when real-time discussion isn't possible. One client leveraged ALIGN to navigate a difficult customer interaction, carefully structuring a series of emails to acknowledge concerns, clarify shared goals, and propose solutions. In another case, a leadership team used the model in a formal workshop, guiding cross-functional stakeholders through a collaborative discussion to brainstorm solutions that balanced competing priorities.

**PART 3** WIN-WIN MINDSET

Whether in written communication, live conversations, or team discussions, the ALIGN Model helps keep interactions productive, fostering alignment and shared purpose even in challenging situations.

No matter if it's a high-stakes negotiation, a project discussion, or a personal disagreement, ALIGN helps cut through roadblocks, build trust, and create alignment. It's not about following a rigid formula. It's about keeping conversations focused, clear, and productive in a way that works for everyone involved.

Why ALIGN works:

- Keeps conversations on track: Avoids distractions and keeps things moving.

- Builds trust: Encourages openness and mutual respect.

- Sparks creative solutions: Helps find better ways forward.

- Ensures clarity: Aligns everyone on practical next steps.

By adapting ALIGN to different situations, we can navigate challenges with confidence, whether we're in a boardroom discussion or sorting things out at home.

## The ALIGN Model in Action: Balancing Speed and Quality

Let's say you're leading a high-stakes project where two teams are stuck in a standoff.

- **Team A (Sales/Marketing):** *We need to launch in two weeks to align with our campaign and meet the client deadline.*

- **Team B (Product/Operations):** *We need six weeks to ensure quality. Rushing could hurt customer trust and long-term success.*

Both teams feel unheard, frustrated, and locked into their positions—speed vs. quality. It's up to you to guide the conversation using the ALIGN Model.

### 1. Air Issues and Set a Collaborative Tone

Start by acknowledging the tension and setting a collaborative tone:

*I know we're coming at this with different concerns. One team is focused on meeting the deadline, the other is worried about the risks of rushing. But we all want this to succeed, so let's find a solution that works for everyone.*

This signals that the goal isn't about taking sides, it's about working together.

### 2. Listen and Learn

Ask open-ended questions to understand each team's deeper concerns.

To Team A: *What's driving the need for a two-week launch? What happens if we miss that window?*

- The campaign is booked. If we delay, we lose visibility, and it could hurt our credibility with the client.

To Team B: *What risks do you see with launching too soon?*

- If we rush, we risk bugs and customer complaints, which could damage trust and cause bigger problems later.

By reflecting back their concerns, both teams feel heard and the conversation shifts beyond surface-level positions.

### 3. Identify Shared Purpose

Once their concerns are clear, bring them back to a common goal:

*It sounds like both teams care about making this project a success. Team A is focused on delivering for the client, while Team B is committed to quality and long-term trust. So, how do we achieve both?*

Now, instead of being on opposing sides, they're working toward the same outcome.

PART 3  WIN-WIN MINDSET

### 4. Generate Multiple (Mutually Beneficial) Options

With shared purpose established, brainstorm solutions together:

- **Launch a minimum viable product (MVP) in two weeks** to meet the campaign deadline while refining additional features post-launch.
- **Extend the campaign slightly** to allow for more testing.
- **Shift internal priorities** to free up more resources for the project.

This encourages flexibility and shared problem-solving instead of pushing one rigid solution.

### 5. Negotiate a Wise Way Forward

Once options are on the table, align on next steps: *It sounds like launching an MVP in two weeks meets the deadline, while ongoing refinements ensure quality. Does this work for everyone?*

Final responsibilities are set:

- **Team A** manages client communication and expectations.
- **Team B** ensures quality and phased improvements post-launch.

Both teams feel invested in the plan and instead of a standoff, you now have alignment, accountability, and shared ownership.

### From Frustration to Progress

Using the ALIGN Model, the two teams moved from frustration to a solution that worked for everyone, balancing priorities while keeping the project on track.

By following this approach, we:

- Created a space for open, productive dialogue.

THE ART OF ALIGNMENT **CHAPTER 9**

- Uncovered the real concerns behind each team's stance.
- Found creative solutions that met both speed and quality needs.
- Secured clear commitments and accountability.

> ALIGN isn't just a process, it's a way of thinking. Whether we're negotiating a project deadline, managing stakeholders, or navigating personal challenges, it helps us approach tough conversations with clarity, confidence, and collaboration.

## The Positive No Sandwich: Saying No While Strengthening Relationships

Sometimes saying 'no' is necessary, but how we say it matters. The Positive No Sandwich helps us set boundaries while maintaining trust, goodwill, and collaboration.

Inspired by William Ury's framework in *The Power of a Positive No*,[4] the Positive No Sandwich is a structured way to set firm boundaries while maintaining trust and goodwill. Unlike the well-known 'criticism sandwich' (compliment-criticism-compliment), which often feels insincere or confusing, the Positive No Sandwich provides clarity, respect, and a productive way forward.

It consists of three steps. When used effectively, this approach ensures the 'no' is received in a way that fosters collaboration and preserves relationships.

### Step 1: Start with a 'Yes' to the Intention

Saying 'no' can feel like shutting someone down, but when you start with a 'yes', you set the tone for respect and shared understanding. This step is about affirming what matters, your values, priorities, or relationship, before delivering a clear and constructive 'no'.

As William Ury explains in *The Power of a Positive No*, leading with 'yes' reinforces why you're saying 'no'.[5] Before responding, ask yourself:

- Is this a purpose-driven no? Does the request conflict with your values or long-term goals?

- Is this a priority-driven no? Do you support the request but lack the time or resources right now?

Understanding the difference ensures your 'no' is grounded in clear reasoning. A purpose-driven 'no' keeps you aligned with your bigger objectives, while a priority-driven 'no' acknowledges constraints while keeping the door open for future collaboration.

By starting with a 'yes', you shift the conversation from rejection to alignment. The other person feels heard, trust is reinforced, and the discussion stays focused on shared goals rather than conflict. It's not just a technique; it's a mindset that turns 'no' into a conversation, not a roadblock.

**Step 2: Deliver a Clear and Respectful No**

Once you've set a positive foundation, the next step is to say 'no' with clarity, respect, and integrity. A strong 'no' isn't personal or confrontational; it's purposeful.

A vague 'no' leads to confusion and repeated requests, while an overly blunt one can damage trust. The key is to be clear and direct without over-explaining.

A respectful 'no' keeps the conversation open, even when you can't meet the request. It shows appreciation for the other person's perspective while maintaining your boundaries.

A well-framed 'no' might:

- Acknowledge the importance of their request.

- Express appreciation for their perspective.

- Offer a simple, thoughtful explanation without defensiveness.

Saying 'no' clearly and respectfully strengthens relationships, rather than harming them. It allows you to prioritise what matters while preserving trust and keeping future conversations productive.

A well-delivered 'no' isn't just a refusal. It's an opportunity to set boundaries with integrity and thoughtfulness.

## Step 3: Offer a Constructive Path Forward

The final step in the Positive No Sandwich shifts the focus from rejection to collaboration. Saying 'no' doesn't have to shut down the conversation. It can open the door to a solution that works for both sides.

Offering a way forward reassures the other person that your 'no' isn't a dead end, but a pivot toward something more workable. You don't need to have an immediate answer. Sometimes, the next step is revisiting the issue later or brainstorming alternatives together.

**How to Offer a Path Forward**

- **Be realistic:** Only suggest alternatives that fit your capacity.
- **Balance boundaries with flexibility:** Respect your limits while considering their needs.
- **Encourage collaboration:** Frame the conversation as a shared problem to solve.

**Possible Alternatives**

- **Phased approaches:** Breaking the request into manageable steps.
- **Alternative support:** Suggesting other resources or approaches.
- **Timing adjustments:** Revisiting the request when circumstances change.

By offering constructive options, you show that your 'no' is about protecting priorities, not rejecting people. This approach builds trust, keeps communication open, and strengthens relationships, ensuring future collaboration remains possible.

Let's look at a couple of scenarios to see the Positive No Sandwich in action.

## Scenario 1: Saying No Due to Purpose Misalignment

**Context:** You're a senior leader, and your team is being asked to take on a project that doesn't align with your strategic goals.

1. **Start with a Yes to the Intention:** *I really appreciate the opportunity and understand how important this project is to the organisation's growth.*

2. **Deliver a Clear and Respectful No:** *However, after reviewing our current strategic goals, we've determined that this project doesn't align with our long-term priorities and would divert resources away from our core objectives.*

3. **Offer a Constructive Path Forward:** *That said, I'd love to explore ways we can support the initiative in an advisory capacity or revisit it next quarter when our strategic objectives may evolve.*

**Why It Works:**
- It acknowledges the importance of the project without compromising the team's long-term direction.
- It provides an alternative way to stay engaged without taking on full ownership.
- It reinforces alignment with organisational priorities while maintaining goodwill.

THE ART OF ALIGNMENT **CHAPTER 9**

**Scenario 2: Saying No Due to Priorities**

**Context:** A colleague asks you to take on an additional project, but your current workload is at full capacity.

1. **Start with a Yes to the Intention:** *I really appreciate you thinking of me for this project, and I know how important it is to deliver it successfully.*

2. **Deliver a Clear and Respectful No:** *Right now, I'm fully committed to our existing priorities, and taking on additional work would impact my ability to deliver at the level I strive for.*

3. **Offer a Constructive Path Forward:** *I'd be happy to help in other ways, such as reviewing the project plan or offering input at key milestones. Alternatively, we can explore how to redistribute tasks within the team.*

**Why It Works:**
- It reinforces a commitment to delivering quality work.
- It offers alternative ways to contribute without overcommitting.
- It maintains a spirit of collaboration while protecting current priorities.

> Remember, sometimes the best course of action is a Positive No. Setting clear boundaries while maintaining trust and goodwill is essential to long-term success, both professionally and personally. Think about the situations in your life where saying 'yes' has come at the cost of your priorities, energy, or well-being. Could a more thoughtful 'no' have created better outcomes?

Consider where the Positive No Sandwich could be useful in your work and relationships. Whether it's declining additional responsibilities that stretch you too thin, turning down requests that don't align with your values, or simply managing expectations with greater clarity, using this approach can help you stay true to what matters most while keeping relationships strong.

## Troubleshooting and Dealing with Difficult People

Even with the best intentions, difficult conversations can take unexpected turns. Whether facing high emotions or disengagement, navigating conflict effectively requires thoughtful approaches that encourage collaboration rather than division.

### Cool down Hot Conflicts, Warm up Cold Ones

Conflicts generally fall into two categories: hot and cold.[6]

- **Hot conflicts** are emotionally charged and fuelled by frustration, anger, or blame. In these situations, it's important to contain emotions by setting ground rules such as, *Let's take turns talking without interruption.* Acknowledging emotions can also help de-escalate tension. *I can see this is really important to you. Let's work together to find a solution.*

- **Cold conflicts** manifest through avoidance and disengagement, which keeps underlying issues unresolved. To re-engage people in these situations requires open-ended questions such as, *What's been on your mind about this?* or *What would success look like for you?* to stimulate honest dialogue and reveal deeper concerns.

Whether cooling down a heated discussion or warming up a disengaged one, the focus should always be on creating an environment where collaboration can thrive.

## Establish Ground Rules for Engagement

Establishing clear ground rules at the start of discussions helps maintain productive and respectful exchanges when emotions run high. When people follow set rules like speaking one at a time, avoiding interruption, and focusing on solutions rather than blame, they enable an open environment for productive discussions.

A simple guideline like, *Let's focus on what we can control rather than revisiting past mistakes,* ensures that discussions remain solution-oriented. Aligning on an acceptable tone of voice can also help maintain a respectful atmosphere. *Let's both commit to staying constructive, even if we don't see eye to eye.*

By creating mutual expectations, ground rules provide a framework that enables even the toughest conversations to stay on track.

## Pause Before Reacting

In challenging situations, it's easy to let emotions take over and react impulsively. Taking a pause, whether it's a deep breath or a moment of reflection, can prevent reactive responses and allow us to respond from a place of clarity and intention.

Pausing helps shift from Little Me, the defensive and emotionally-driven self, to Big Me, the grounded and thoughtful version of ourselves. Asking reflective questions like, *What do I really want to achieve here?* or *What's the bigger picture?* can help ensure our response aligns with our values and long-term goals.

A simple pause can change the entire tone of a conversation, helping us stay composed and engaged in problem-solving rather than escalating conflict.

## Disarm by Stepping onto Their Side

One of the most effective ways to diffuse tension is by stepping onto the other person's side. This doesn't mean agreeing with them blindly. It's about acknowledging their perspective and demonstrating understanding.

Instead of escalating a disagreement, we might say, *I completely understand why this is frustrating, and I want to make sure we find a solution that works for you.* This approach reduces defensiveness and fosters collaboration by shifting the conversation from 'me vs. you' to 'us vs. the problem'.

Disarming someone with empathy and understanding can transform a combative interaction into a productive discussion.

## Allow the Other Person to Save Face

When someone is wrong or has acted defensively, it's tempting to point it out directly. However, insisting on being right can push them further into defensiveness, making resolution harder. Allowing them to save face is key to preserving relationships and encouraging forward progress.

William Ury refers to this as 'building a golden bridge',[7] offering the other person a way to move forward while maintaining their dignity. Instead of highlighting their mistake, we might say, *Now that we have a clearer picture, let's focus on the best way to move forward together.* This approach keeps the focus on solutions rather than blame.

Giving people the opportunity to correct course without feeling exposed fosters trust, reduces resistance, and paves the way for a more collaborative future.

Remember…

Difficult conversations are part of life, but they don't have to create conflict. By defusing tension, setting clear boundaries, and responding with patience and empathy, we can handle them with confidence and composure. Ultimately, the goal is not to 'win' the conversation but to create an environment where meaningful dialogue can happen, leading to better relationships and stronger outcomes.

# KEY INSIGHTS
## FOR BETTERMENT

- **Alignment is an ongoing process, not a one-time event:** Continuous effort is essential for achieving alignment because our goals and priorities always change, as does the context shaping past decisions. The process involves keeping communication channels open to achieve lasting success.

- **Moving beyond positions to purpose unlocks collaboration:** Focusing on deeper motivations rather than surface-level demands fosters creativity and mutual understanding. When we seek shared purpose instead of rigid positions, we create solutions that truly benefit all parties.

- **Saying 'no' can strengthen relationships when done right:** Using the Positive No Sandwich, affirming shared intent, delivering a clear and respectful 'no', and offering a constructive path forward helps set boundaries without damaging trust or goodwill.

- **Effective conversations require emotional intelligence and structure:** Managing difficult conversations involves setting ground rules, pausing before reacting, and using techniques like stepping onto the other person's side to create a collaborative environment.

- **Clarity and focus drive meaningful progress:** Ensuring clarity in expectations, priorities, and next steps eliminates confusion and helps teams and individuals align their efforts toward shared goals more effectively.

# REFLECTIVE
# QUESTIONS

1. When have I found myself stuck in a position rather than focusing on the bigger purpose? How could I have shifted my approach to uncover shared goals?
2. What patterns do I notice in how I say 'no'? Are there opportunities to apply the Positive No Sandwich to strengthen my boundaries while maintaining relationships?
3. How can I better approach difficult conversations with emotional intelligence, whether by pausing before reacting, setting ground rules, or stepping onto the other person's side?

**WHAT'S NEXT?** In the next section, we transition from alignment and collaboration to Opportunity Mindset, the ability to reframe challenges and see them as catalysts for growth and innovation. In Chapter 10, we explore how shifting our perspective can turn obstacles into opportunities and fuel personal and professional Betterment.

# PART 4

# Opportunity Mindset—From Problem to Possibility

# 10

# Unlocking Potential—Transforming How You See Challenges

*'The real voyage of discovery consists not in seeking new landscapes, but in having new eyes.' Marcel Proust*

## The Power of Perspective

### The Tightrope Walker and the Horizon

*In 1859, a hushed crowd gathered at Niagara Gorge as Charles Blondin prepared to do the unthinkable—walk a tightrope a hundred and sixty feet above the raging waters, with no harness, no safety net, just a balancing pole and sheer focus.[1]*

*What set Blondin apart wasn't just skill or bravery; it was where he placed his focus. He didn't stare at the thin rope beneath him or at the deadly drop below. Instead, he locked his eyes on the far bank—his destination. Every step depended on this wider perspective, keeping him steady despite the risks.*

Tightrope walkers know that looking down throws them off balance. The same applies to us. When we're caught up in immediate pressures, fixating on problems and obstacles, we lose sight of the bigger picture.

Too often, we approach challenges in survival mode, reacting to fires as they flare up. But just like Blondin, stability comes from lifting our gaze, focusing beyond the struggle to see the possibilities ahead. That shift in perspective can make all the difference.

## The Opportunity Ladder: Expanding Your Perspective

Life and work constantly test our resilience. Some days are spent putting out fires, others allow for planning, and sometimes, we get the chance to create something truly innovative. The challenge? Recognising when we're stuck in reactive mode and when to shift our thinking.

This is where the Opportunity Ladder comes in.

The Opportunity Ladder helps us see where we are in the face of challenges and, more importantly, how to move toward growth and transformation. It's not just about climbing higher; it's about knowing when to zoom in on the details and when to step back for the bigger picture.

Think of Blondin on the tightrope. Keeping his gaze on the horizon was crucial, but if he'd ignored the rope beneath him, he wouldn't have made it across. Balance comes from shifting focus between immediate tasks and long-term goals.

The Opportunity Ladder has three levels:

- **React Mode:** Handling urgent, unexpected challenges.
- **Respond Mode:** Regaining balance and thinking strategically.
- **Transform Mode:** Unlocking opportunities and creating real change.

UNLOCKING POTENTIAL **CHAPTER 10**

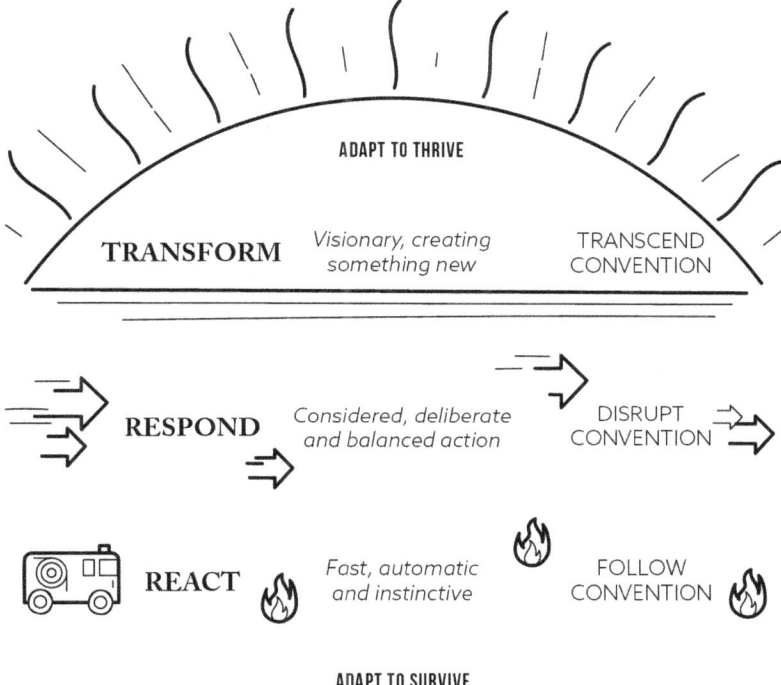

*Figure 6.*

Before diving deeper, let's be clear. All three levels matter.

If our boat suddenly starts leaking, we're not going to plan a new route. We're going to plug the hole, fast. That's React Mode, and it's essential.

Take COVID as an example. When lockdowns hit, businesses had to react immediately, setting up remote teams, adapting on the fly, and doing whatever it took to survive. However, staying in React Mode or survival mode too long means missing the real opportunity to rethink, adapt, and transform.

## Level 1. React: Firefighting for Survival

At the base of the Opportunity Ladder is React Mode where survival

211

takes priority. It's about quick fixes, immediate action, and getting through the crisis. Sometimes, that's exactly what's needed.

Think of moments like:

- A key team member suddenly resigns, leaving us scrambling to fill the gap.
- An unexpected budget cut forces fast adjustments.
- A system failure needs urgent fixing before operations can continue.

React Mode keeps things afloat, but staying here too long leads to burnout, poor decisions, and constantly feeling on the back foot.

**When to React**

- When a crisis demands immediate action.
- When survival is on the line.
- When there's no time to pause and plan.

The goal isn't to avoid React Mode, it's knowing when to move beyond it. We need to ask ourselves, *Am I stuck in reaction mode, or is it time to steady the ship?*

## Level 2. Respond: Steadying the Ship

Moving into Respond Mode, we shift from short-term survival to long-term stability. Instead of just plugging holes, we start steadying the ship, taking deliberate action to prevent future crises and improve how we work.

For example:

- If a resignation forces a rushed hire (React Mode), Respond Mode is where we create a succession plan.

- If a budget cut leads to quick reductions (React Mode), Respond Mode helps us reallocate resources strategically.
- If a system failure needs a patch (React Mode), Respond Mode is where we implement long-term fixes.

Responding moves us from chaos to control, helping us make more sustainable, informed decisions.

**When to Respond**

- When the immediate crisis is under control, and it's time to think ahead.
- When we're ready to prevent future fires, not just put them out.
- When stability is needed before making bigger moves.

We need to ask ourselves, *Where can we anticipate future challenges to create more stability?*

## Level 3. Transform: Raising the Sail

At the top of the ladder is Transform Mode, where we stop reacting and responding and start asking, *What's possible here?*

If React Mode is plugging holes and Respond Mode is steadying the ship, Transform Mode is raising the sail, setting a new course, embracing fresh opportunities, and making bold moves toward the future.

For example:

- Instead of just fixing customer complaints, a company redesigns its entire service model to improve the experience.
- Rather than adjusting to budget cuts, a business creates new revenue streams through partnerships and innovation.
- Instead of treating remote work as a stopgap, leaders embrace

flexible models that boost productivity and engagement long term.

Transform Mode is where we shift from solving problems to seizing opportunities. It's where real growth happens.

**When to Transform**

- When the basics are under control, and it's time to innovate.
- When there's an opportunity to do things differently.
- When we're ready to move beyond business-as-usual and create something better.

We need to ask ourselves, *Are we just getting by, or are we building something better?*

Understanding what's needed and where we are on the ladder allows us to take intentional steps forward and avoid getting stuck in one place for too long.

The Opportunity Ladder isn't about climbing higher as quickly as possible. It's about knowing which level to operate in at the right time. Whether we need to react, respond, or transform, mastering the art of moving between them will set us up for long-term success.

# Mental Cages: The Invisible Barriers Holding Us Back

The Opportunity Ladder helps us recognise when to react, respond, or transform. But what if we feel stuck? More often than not, it's not the challenge itself holding us back, it's the mental cages we've built around our thinking.

Mental cages are invisible barriers, the assumptions, fears, and fixed ideas that limit how we see ourselves, others, and what's possible. They keep us trapped in React or Respond Mode, unable to move forward.

## A Familiar Scenario: When we Feel Stuck

You're in a meeting, facing a big challenge. The pressure's on, the room is tense. Someone sighs, *We've tried everything. There's nothing we can do.* Heads nod. The energy drops. Silence.

Sound familiar?

This is how mental cages work. They are quiet but powerful limits on what we believe is possible. They often creep in as absolutes:

- *We can't pull that off.*
- *There's no way to make this work.*
- *That's just how it is.*

These thoughts might feel reasonable under pressure, but they're not facts; they're stories we tell ourselves about what's achievable. When we buy into them, we get stuck in React Mode, focusing on the immediate problem instead of looking for possibilities.

[ Breaking free isn't about ignoring reality; it's about recognising that many 'truths' are actually assumptions. When we start questioning them, we unlock creativity, growth, and transformation. ]

We need to ask ourselves, *Are we really out of options, or are we just stuck in a way of thinking?*

## How Mental Cages Take Hold

Stressful environments serve as the breeding ground for mental cages to develop. Under pressure, people instinctively concentrate on resolving the immediate problem. However, this strategy, which is necessary in emergency situations, can become a barrier to long-term growth and creativity.

The mental cages we develop eventually function as filters, which subtly modify our perception of the world. They influence our decision-making abilities, restrict our perspective, and keep us trapped at the bottom levels of the Opportunity Ladder.

Let's look at an example.

A small non-profit wants to launch a critical community program but feels trapped by limited funding. The team concludes, *We can't do what bigger organisations can.* Stuck in this mindset, they scale down their ambitions, doing just enough to scrape by.

This reactive thinking blinds them to new possibilities. Instead of asking, *How can we stretch this budget to survive?* they could shift to, *What resources haven't we tapped into yet?* This simple reframing could lead to creative solutions—partnering with others, involving volunteers, or finding new ways to increase impact.

The irony? The biggest limitations are often internal, not external. Mental cages persist because we accept them as truth instead of challenging them. The belief that 'there's no way forward' may feel real, but it's just one way of seeing things, not the whole picture.

## Three Common Types of Mental Cages

Mental cages often feel like truths rather than perspectives. They are subtle, unexamined assumptions that shape how we see ourselves, others, and the world.

What makes them so powerful? They usually contain a kernel of truth. They seem logical, even protective, but over time, they become rigid constraints, boxing in our thinking and limiting new opportunities.

Let's explore three common types.

### Cages About Ourselves

These are the stories we tell ourselves about what we can and can't do, which shapes what we attempt and what we avoid.

We might catch ourselves thinking:

- *I'm not creative enough to solve this.*
- *I don't have the skills for that role.*

- *This is too much for me to handle.*

These thoughts creep in quietly, convincing us we're not capable. While they might feel true, they're often just assumptions, mental barriers that hold us back from reaching our full potential.

**Cages About Other People**

These are the assumptions we make about others; what they'll do or how they'll respond, which often shape our decisions before we've even tested them.

We might think:

- *The team will never agree to this.*
- *My manager won't go for it.*
- *They don't understand our perspective.*

These thoughts might seem practical, but they shut down solutions before they're explored. More often than not, they reflect our own fears of rejection, failure, or conflict, rather than reality.

**Cages About the World or Circumstances**

These are broad assumptions about how things work, often mistaken for immovable truths. They shape our decisions and discourage us from exploring new possibilities.

We might think:

- *There's no budget for that, so it's not worth considering.*
- *That's just how this industry works.*
- *There's no time to rethink the strategy.*

While these beliefs may stem from real constraints, they often harden into rigid rules that stifle creativity. When we accept them without question, we miss opportunities to challenge the status quo and find new solutions.

**Do You Recognise these Mental Cages?**

> Take a moment to think of a current challenge. Write down all the beliefs you have about that challenge. Take notice: are you feeling trapped by mental cages?

Breaking free starts with recognising these cages for what they are: stories, not facts. By questioning them, you begin to widen your perspective, opening the door to creativity, collaboration, and transformation.

**Breaking Free: Widening the Lens**

Breaking free from mental cages doesn't mean ignoring constraints or pretending challenges don't exist. It's not about blind optimism or unrealistic thinking. Instead, it's about widening the lens, acknowledging the constraints while refusing to let them define what's possible.

For example, consider a common reaction to time pressure: *There's no time to rethink this strategy.* This statement feels absolute, but what if someone asked instead, *If time weren't an issue, what's one thing we'd do differently?*

That question doesn't erase the urgency, but it creates space to think creatively. It shifts the mindset from, *This is impossible* to *What might be possible?*

The key here is to recognise that mental cages feel like the whole story, but they're not. They're a snapshot, a narrow way of seeing the situation. By questioning the assumptions that form the bars of the cage, we give ourselves the chance to reimagine what's achievable.

**Challenging the Bars of the Cage**

Think of mental cages as invisible bars made of assumptions. By questioning these assumptions, we begin to bend or even remove the bars altogether.

For example, instead of thinking, *I'm not ready for this role*, try asking, *What skills do I already have, and what can I learn along the way?* Instead of assuming, *The team will never agree*, ask, *How might I present this idea in a way that resonates with them?*

When we start to challenge these stories, we create space for new ideas, perspectives, and possibilities to emerge.

Breaking free from mental cages is the first step to climbing higher on the Opportunity Ladder. By questioning what feels fixed, we open the door to creativity, resilience, and transformation.

## Scarcity vs. Abundance: How Mindset Shapes Possibility

Mental cages often go hand in hand with scarcity thinking, a mindset that narrows our perspective and focuses on what's missing or unavailable. These two forces feed into each other. Scarcity thinking reinforces the bars of the cage, while the cage itself limits our ability to think expansively.

The way we see the world influences the decisions we make, the opportunities we notice, and the solutions we create. When facing challenges, we tend to operate from one of two mindsets: scarcity thinking (focused on limitations) or abundance thinking (focused on possibilities). These perspectives shape how we approach problems, explore solutions, and drive outcomes.

While scarcity and abundance thinking are often discussed alongside fixed and growth mindsets, they differ in focus. Fixed and growth mindsets explore how we perceive our abilities, whether we see ourselves as static or capable of growth. Scarcity and abundance thinking, on the other hand, are about how we perceive the resources and opportunities around us. Are we trapped by what we think is lacking, or inspired by what's possible?

### The Impact of Scarcity Thinking: A Narrow View

Scarcity thinking is a mindset that locks our focus on constraints, convincing us that resources—whether time, money, or energy—are so limited that our options are equally restricted. When we're in scarcity thinking, our attention narrows to immediate problems, and we default to working defensively to preserve what we have. While this approach can help in a true crisis, it limits our ability to think strategically or creatively.[2]

Research backs this up. A 2019 study found that scarcity thinking increases stress, lowers confidence, and reduces activity in parts of the brain responsible for goal-directed decision-making.[3] As a result, we're more likely to make reactive, short-term choices that prioritise immediate needs over long-term opportunities.

Imagine a team facing budget cuts. With a scarcity mindset, they immediately slash initiatives and cut corners, just trying to get by. It may seem practical, but it keeps them stuck in survival mode. By reframing the challenge to *How can we make the most of what we have?* they open the door to innovation and smarter solutions instead of just making do.

### Abundance Thinking: Expanding Possibility

Abundance thinking shifts the focus from what's missing to what's possible. It doesn't ignore constraints; instead, it treats them as starting points for creativity rather than barriers to success.

Imagine Charles Blondin, the tightrope walker, high above Niagara Falls. To succeed, Blondin couldn't afford to focus only on the rope beneath his feet. That narrow view would disrupt his balance and paralyse him. At the same time, he couldn't ignore the rope entirely. Instead, he maintained balance by shifting between the immediate challenge and the horizon ahead. That's what abundance thinking asks of us: to expand our perspective, acknowledge constraints, and use them to build momentum toward what's possible.

Research supports this shift in thinking. The same 2019 study that explored scarcity thinking found that adopting an abundance mindset enhances creative problem-solving and strategic decision-making.[3] Participants with an abundance mindset were more willing to consider broader possibilities and less likely to feel paralysed by constraints.

Abundance thinking is about leveraging what's available, not dwelling on what's missing. Studies show that this mindset reduces stress, fosters optimism, and builds confidence, all of which are crucial for navigating challenges.[4] Unlike scarcity thinking, which narrows our perspective, abundance thinking opens doors to innovation by reframing obstacles as opportunities to learn, grow, and adapt.

Let's go back to the example of a team facing budget cuts. With an abundance mindset, they might ask, *How can we amplify our impact with fewer resources?* This shift opens the door to smarter strategies—simplifying processes, leveraging partnerships, or focusing on high-impact goals. Instead of feeling stuck, they use the constraint as fuel for creativity and innovation, shaping solutions rather than retreating from the challenge.

> At its core, abundance thinking is about constructing possibilities through effort, resourcefulness, and collaboration. It's not about ignoring constraints but rather working within them, using them as scaffolding for new ideas.

## Scarcity vs. Abundance in Action

Scarcity and abundance thinking don't just shape how we approach challenges. They influence how we view the world, interact with others, and pursue opportunities.

**Scarcity thinking** pulls us into a defensive posture, focused on protecting what we have and avoiding risks. Rooted in fear, it narrows our perspective, discourages collaboration, and keeps us stuck in survival mode.

**Abundance thinking**, on the other hand, is expansive and proactive. It encourages possibility, smart risks, and collaboration, shifting focus from limitations to opportunities. Instead of scarcity and constraint, it fosters generosity, optimism, and shared success.

| SCARCITY THINKING | ABUNDANCE THINKING |
| --- | --- |
| **Defensive:** *Protects what's already possessed.* | **Expansive:** *Creates and pursues opportunities.* |
| Believes resources are insufficient. | Believes untapped resources exist. |
| Sceptical and competitive in relationships. | Trusts and collaborates to build partnerships. |
| Pessimistic about the future. | Optimistic and forward-thinking. |
| Resistant to change, stagnant. | Adaptive, dynamic, and growth-oriented. |
| Focuses narrowly on immediate obstacles. | Explores possibilities beyond the obvious. |
| Stingy with time, ideas, and effort. | Generous with time, ideas, and knowledge. |
| Thinks in win/lose dynamics. | Thinks in win/win outcomes. |

*Figure 7.*

The shift from scarcity to abundance thinking unlocks opportunities, fosters innovation, and transforms how we navigate challenges. By moving beyond fear and defensiveness, we reimagine what's possible and approach challenges with creativity and collaboration.

## Mapping Your Mindset: Scarcity or Abundance?

We all approach different areas of life with varying mindsets. You might think abundantly in some situations but lean toward scarcity in others. Recognising these patterns is the first step to shifting your perspective.

Here's a simple exercise:
1. On a blank piece of paper, draw a straight line across the middle.
2. Label the left side 'Scarcity Thinking' and the right side 'Abundance Thinking'.
3. Reflect on the different areas of your life—work, finances, relationships, or personal growth—and plot where your mindset tends to land.

For instance, you might notice scarcity creeping into financial decisions, where you focus on limitations or what's lacking. But when it comes to relationships, you may naturally think abundantly, believing there's always time to nurture connections or explore new opportunities.

This exercise isn't about judgement but awareness. What patterns do you see? Why do you think certain areas feel more expansive, while others feel constrained?

[ Finally, ask yourself, *What can I learn from the areas where I already think* abundantly? Could the same mindset shift how you approach challenges in other parts of your life? This simple reflection can reveal new possibilities and help you apply an expansive mindset more consistently. ]

## Tools to Strengthen Abundance Thinking

An abundance mindset doesn't happen overnight. It's a skill we build through deliberate practice. The good news? Like any skill, it gets easier with repetition. Here are three simple tools to help you think more expansively.

### 1. Gratitude Practices: Seeing what You Have

One of the fastest ways to shift toward abundance is to focus on what's already good in your life. Try starting or ending your day by writing down three things you're grateful for, big or small. It might be a supportive colleague, a small win, or a quiet moment having a coffee. Over time, gratitude helps you shift your focus from what's missing to what's present, creating space for new possibilities.

### 2. Achievement Lists: Celebrating Progress

Traditional to-do lists can feel like constant reminders of what you haven't done. An achievement list flips that perspective by focusing on what you've accomplished. Take a moment to jot down things you're proud of—big wins, creative solutions, or small victories you've had along the way. Recognising progress, however incremental, builds confidence and reminds you of your ability to move forward.

### 3. Aspirations Lists: Expanding Your Vision

If achievements ground you in the past, aspirations pull you toward the future. Ask yourself, *What excites me? What would I love to create, learn, or experience?* Write these down, even if they feel ambitious or far off. These aspirations give you a horizon to work toward, reminding you to look beyond immediate challenges to what's possible.

Together, these tools—gratitude, achievements, and aspirations—help shift our mindset. They retrain our focus: gratitude roots us in the present, achievements celebrate what's behind us, and aspirations open the door to what's ahead. With practice, they create a foundation of abundance, enabling us to see potential instead of limits.

## The Power of Reframing: How We See and Speak Shapes Possibility

### Reframing: A Small Shift with Big Impact

Shifting from scarcity to abundance, or breaking free from mental cages, doesn't always require big moves. Often, it starts with how we choose to see a situation.

Reframing is about looking at challenges differently, turning limitations into opportunities. It's not about ignoring problems but expanding perspective to uncover possibilities that might otherwise stay hidden.

If mental cages keep us stuck and scarcity thinking narrows our focus, reframing is the tool that helps us unlock the door. By shifting our language and perspective, we can break free of limiting patterns and move toward a more abundant, creative way of thinking.

These shifts don't need to be headline-worthy to make an impact. In fact, some of the most profound transformations I've seen come from small, quiet moments of clarity, like when someone decides to reframe a setback as a stepping stone or a constraint as a chance to innovate.

The beauty of reframing is that it's practical, immediate, and accessible. It's a skill you can start using today to create ripples of meaningful change in how you approach your work, relationships, and challenges.

**Redefining Obstacles: A Shift in Perspective**

*Some of the biggest mindset shifts come from how we interpret setbacks. When faced with obstacles, it's easy to focus on what's missing, but that mindset can drain momentum fast.*

*I worked with an executive leading a high-stakes project under tight constraints—a lean budget, limited resources, and growing frustration. The team's conversations revolved around what they lacked. They were saying things like, If only we had more time, or, We just don't have enough people for this.*

*The energy in the room plummeted as the focus on limitations took over.*

*In one session, I encouraged the executive to shift the conversation. Acknowledge the constraints but treat them as a starting point for problem-solving. Instead of, What's missing? the team began asking, What can we control or influence?*

*That subtle shift changed everything. They explored creative ways to repurpose resources, find efficiencies, and build partnerships. Letting go of what was out of their control freed them to focus on what they could impact.*

This is the power of the CIA Model in action, explored in Chapter 6.

The last step is to accept the constraints and adapt. Reframing is part of that adaptation process. Even as challenges continued, this solution-focused approach kept the team engaged. What was once a source of frustration became a driver for resilience and innovation. By reframing the problem, they not only completed the project but did so with a renewed sense of capability and purpose.

**The Simplicity of Reappraisal**

Sometimes, setbacks happen, and there's nothing we can do to change them. Reappraisal is a simple but powerful technique that helps us reinterpret challenges and manage emotions by asking, *What's good about this?* or *How else can I see this?*

Research shows that reframing emotions can boost happiness and resilience, especially in situations beyond our control.[5] However, when we have the power to act, relying only on reappraisal can sometimes increase frustration instead of solving the problem.

Reappraisal works best when progress depends on adapting ourselves, not changing external circumstances. It helps us focus on possibility and growth, even when the next step isn't clear.

**The Power of 'Yet': From Limitation to Progress**

Language doesn't just reflect our mindset, it creates it. One small word can turn a dead end into a stepping stone—'yet'. As Carol Dweck highlights in *Mindset*,[6] the word 'yet' is a powerful tool for fostering growth. It shifts our mindset by reinforcing that learning is an ongoing process, not a fixed state. For example:

- *I don't know how to do this*, transforms possibility when it becomes *I don't know how to do this yet.*

- And, *Our team hasn't figured this out* is motivating when it becomes *Our team hasn't figured this out yet*.

This small tweak reframes challenges as opportunities. We can take it even further by adding a progress reminder:

- *I'm not confident presenting* » *I'm not confident presenting yet, but I'm improving.*

- *I don't have the skills to lead this project* » *I don't have the skills yet, but I can learn with practice and support.*

The power of 'yet' turns obstacles into starting points. It shifts our focus from limitations to progress, encouraging growth, action, and momentum.

Sometimes, the smallest words make the biggest difference. 'Yet' doesn't just change how we think, it opens the door to what's possible.

## How Words Create Worlds: Turning Tasks into Opportunities

While words may not change a situation, they shape how we experience it. The right language can motivate and inspire, while the wrong words can drain energy and keep us stuck.

This is especially true at work, where small shifts in wording change how tasks feel. Compare these phrases:

- *I have to go to work*, vs. *I get to go to work*.

- *I need to write this report*, vs. *I choose to write this report*.

See the difference? 'Get to' reminds us that what feels like a chore is often a privilege. 'Choose to' reinforces ownership and control, moving us from victim mode to intention.

### Reframing Tasks to Boost Engagement

*A manager I worked with applied this concept, shifting from, We need to fix this, to We have the opportunity to improve this. That simple change transformed how the team approached their work.*

*Instead of feeling like tasks were forced on them, team members saw them as contributions they wanted to make. One employee streamlined a routine reporting process, turning a dull task into a valuable improvement. Another felt more motivated and trusted because they had a say in shaping their work.*

*Over time, these subtle shifts reshaped team culture. Work became less about ticking boxes and more about making an impact. This new mindset sparked creativity, collaboration, and a shared sense of purpose.*

By choosing our words carefully, we can turn obligations into opportunities, helping ourselves and others feel more engaged, capable, and empowered.

Just as the power of 'yet' reframes limitations into opportunities, the words we choose in our daily lives can inspire autonomy, purpose, and momentum.

Consider how you might reframe common limiting phrases into empowering ones:

| LIMITING LANGUAGE | | EMPOWERING LANGUAGE |
|---|---|---|
| I have to lead this meeting. | → | I get to lead this meeting. |
| We need to fix this. | → | We have the opportunity to improve this. |
| That's not possible. | → | What might be possible if we tried? |
| We don't have the resources. | → | How can we make the most of what we have? |

*Figure 8.*

These small shifts remind us that we are not powerless in the face of challenges. We have choices and opportunities to approach our work, our language, and our lives with intention and curiosity.

## Reframing Beyond Work: Words in Relationships and Parenting

The way we speak doesn't just shape our work, it influences our relationships, parenting, and daily interactions. Choosing language that fosters choice and collaboration helps create an environment where others feel empowered to grow.

### Parenting: Encouraging Independence

My three-year-old daughter, Charlotte, is strong-willed and endlessly curious. Like most toddlers, she loves testing boundaries. I want to nurture that independence, not overpower it, and I've found that language plays a key role.

Saying, 'You need to pick up your toys,' often leads to resistance (as any parent knows!). But when I reframe it as a choice, 'Would you like to pick up your toys before dinner or after?' she feels a sense of control within clear boundaries.

It doesn't eliminate every battle, but it plants seeds of independence and confidence, helping her learn to make decisions and take ownership of her actions.

### Relationships: Shifting Focus to Appreciation

In close relationships, it's easy to focus on what hasn't been done. *Why didn't they clean up?* or *Why don't they do this my way?* These small frustrations can snowball into resentment.

A simple shift in perspective can break the cycle:

- *What have they done that I appreciate?*
- *What am I grateful for in this relationship?*

**PART 4** OPPORTUNITY MINDSET

A genuine 'thank you' or a moment of appreciation doesn't just feel good for them, it changes how we experience the relationship. It makes them more open to feedback, less defensive, and more likely to contribute positively.

The words we choose, whether with a partner, child, or friend, can either create barriers or encourage trust and connection. Prioritising gratitude and choice fosters collaboration, respect, and lasting positivity.

# KEY INSIGHTS
# FOR BETTERMENT

- **Perspective shapes possibility:** Challenges are not just obstacles, they are opportunities to learn, grow, and innovate. Shifting from a reactive mindset to a more expansive one allows us to climb higher on the Opportunity Ladder, embracing creativity and transformation.

- **The power of reframing:** Small shifts in how we frame problems can transform limitations into stepping stones. Language tools like 'yet' and empowering phrasing create space for optimism, collaboration, and growth.

- **Mental cages are invisible barriers:** Mental cages often feel like unchangeable truths, but they're assumptions that limit perspective. By challenging these beliefs, we can expand our thinking and unlock new opportunities.

- **Scarcity vs. abundance thinking:** Scarcity thinking narrows focus to what's missing, keeping us stuck in survival mode. Abundance thinking shifts focus to what's possible, encouraging resourcefulness, collaboration, and optimism.

- **Language creates worlds:** Subtle changes in how we speak at work, with loved ones, or even in self-talk, can energise and inspire. Choosing words that foster ownership, gratitude, and possibility has a ripple effect, shaping the culture around us.

# REFLECTIVE **QUESTIONS**

1. **Expanding Perspective:** Think of a recent challenge you faced. How did your mindset shape your response? Could you have viewed the situation differently? Are there areas where you find yourself stuck in React Mode? How might you shift toward Respond or Transform Mode?
2. **Recognising Mental Cages:** What 'truths' about yourself, others, or your circumstances might actually be assumptions? How could questioning these beliefs open up new possibilities?
3. **Scarcity and Abundance Thinking:** Where in your life do you tend to think in terms of scarcity? Are there areas where you already think abundantly? What small shifts could help you reframe a current limitation as an opportunity?
4. **The Power of Language:** Reflect on how you speak to yourself or others when facing challenges. Are your words energising or limiting? How might you replace 'I have to' with 'I get to' or 'I choose to' in your daily life?

**WHAT'S NEXT?** In the next chapter, we take language and reframing to a new level by exploring optimism, not as a personality trait but as an explanatory style that can be learned. Optimism fuels performance, persistence, and creativity, helping us turn setbacks into stepping stones, maintaining momentum even in the face of challenges.

# 11

# **Optimism**—Opening New Doors to Opportunity and Momentum

*'A pessimist sees the difficulty in every opportunity; an optimist sees the opportunity in every difficulty.'*
*Winston Churchill*

*When I was a teenager, I tried out for the state basketball team. I made it all the way to the final round, one step away from selection, only to miss out.*

*I was devastated, but I wasn't the only one. Another girl who had also been cut shook her head and said, 'They always pick the same people. There's no point even trying out again.' And with competition like Lauren Jackson in the mix, she wasn't wrong. It was tough.*

*But I saw it differently. Yes, the competition was fierce, but that just meant one thing: I needed to train harder.*

*Here's what happened next.*

*That girl continued playing the way she always had. She was a good player, but she never cracked the next level. Meanwhile, I went to the basketball stadium every day after school to train on my own. I worked harder than ever, and my effort got noticed. Local coaches offered extra one-on-one training sessions, helping me refine my game beyond the regular team practices. My skills improved dramatically.*

*The next year, I tried out again, against the same tough competition. This time, I didn't just make the team, I made the starting five.*

Same setback. Different explanation. Different actions. Different results.

This is the power of optimism. Not blind faith. Not wishful thinking. But a way of explaining setbacks that drives persistence, performance, and improvement.

Psychologist Martin Seligman, known for his research on Learned Optimism[1], highlights that our explanatory style, the way we interpret setbacks, plays a crucial role in resilience. It shapes whether we see obstacles as insurmountable or as opportunities for growth.

## Why Optimism Fuels Betterment

Optimism isn't just a feel-good mindset, it's deeply practical and measurable. Decades of research reveal that optimism has a tangible impact on how we live, work, and perform.

First, optimistic people achieve more. They're more resilient in the face of challenges, more action-oriented, and better equipped to persevere when others give up. This isn't just a nice idea. It's been tested and proven over and over, especially in industries where resilience is the name of the game.

Take sales, for example. It's a job built on rejection. Salespeople hear 'no' way more than 'yes', and if they can't shake off the setbacks, they won't last long. Seligman's studies in Learned Optimism found that optimistic salespeople outperformed their pessimistic peers by 20%–300%, largely due to their ability to reframe rejection.[1]

This difference in mindset has real consequences. In insurance sales, for instance, Seligman found that pessimistic agents were twice as likely to quit as their optimistic counterparts.[2] Imagine the impact of that: quitting too soon means we miss out on every future opportunity, whereas sticking with it, even after setbacks, gives us a chance to succeed. It's not that optimistic people face fewer challenges. They just interpret those challenges differently. Instead of seeing a door slam shut forever, they look for another one to open.

Optimism isn't just for sales or business. It's useful in pretty much any part of life where persistence matters. Whether we're leading a team through a rough patch, dealing with personal challenges, or working toward a big goal, optimism helps us push forward. It stops us from getting stuck in frustration or blame and keeps us looking for solutions instead.

And it's not just about mindset. It actually affects our health. Studies show that optimistic people have lower stress, stronger immune systems, and even a lower risk of heart disease.[3] They also tend to look after themselves better—eating well, staying active, and reaching out for support when they need it—because they believe their actions make a difference. While pessimism can weigh us down physically and emotionally, optimism lightens the load, helping us adapt better to stress and navigate life's inevitable challenges.

Most importantly, optimism encourages us to take action. When pessimists encounter setbacks, they're more likely to fall into learned helplessness, the belief that no matter what they do, nothing will change. Optimists see setbacks as problems to solve, not dead ends. Instead of throwing their hands up, they zero in on what they can control. That shift in focus is what keeps them moving forward, finding solutions and building momentum.

Imagine a corporate leader whose company is facing severe market disruption. Targets have been missed, pressure is mounting, and the team's morale is low. A pessimistic leader might spiral into blame, see the crisis as insurmountable, and lose confidence in their ability to turn things around. An optimistic leader approaches the same situation differently. They reframe the crisis as a temporary setback, a challenge that, while difficult, can be addressed. They focus on where they can adapt and take action, bringing the team together to rethink their approach and find new opportunities. Instead of shutting down, they push through, tweaking, problem-solving, and eventually landing on a better way forward.

**PART 4** OPPORTUNITY MINDSET

> Optimism is at the heart of the Opportunity Mindset. It's what helps people turn obstacles into chances to grow. It's the belief that even in tough times, there's something to learn, something to improve, and a way forward. This perspective keeps momentum going, sparking resilience, creativity, and better results.

When we build optimism, setbacks stop feeling like roadblocks, and new possibilities start to open up. We begin to ask, *What can we do with this? Where's the opportunity* here? That's when real Betterment happens, when challenges become stepping stones to something even stronger.

## The Three Elements of Explanatory Style

When something happens, good or bad, how we explain it to ourselves can make all the difference. Seligman identified three core elements that shape how we interpret events. Together, these factors form what's known as our explanatory style:[1]

### 1. Permanent vs. Temporary

This is about time. Do we see what happened as a one-off moment, or do we believe it will last forever?

- A **permanent explanation** assumes the situation will never change. It's here to stay.
- A **temporary explanation** sees it as just a moment in time, something that can improve or pass.

### 2. Pervasive vs. Specific

This is about scope. Do we let the event define everything, or do we keep it contained to one area?

- A **pervasive explanation** believes the event impacts every part of life or work.
- A **specific explanation** keeps the event focused on one particular area, without letting it spread.

### 3. Situational Weight

This is about influence. Do we recognise the role of external factors, or do we overlook them entirely?

- **Situational recognition** acknowledges that outside influences may have contributed to what happened. For example, a difficult outcome might be seen as influenced by unexpected circumstances, like poor weather, changing markets, or timing. Similarly, a good outcome might include favourable conditions, such as an easy competition or lucky timing.

- **Situational absence** gives little or no consideration to external factors, focusing instead on personal explanations. This might mean overlooking situational challenges and placing all the weight on personal failure or skill or luck.

How much weight we give to situational factors shapes how we see the outcome and its causes. Do we focus entirely on ourselves, or do we consider the context surrounding what happened?

These three factors—time, scope, and influence—work together to determine how we respond to what happens in our lives. They shape whether we feel motivated to take action or whether we feel overwhelmed and stuck.

Next, we explore how these elements play out through two distinct patterns: optimistic and pessimistic explanatory styles.

## Explanatory Style in Action

Now that we've unpacked the three elements time, scope, and influence, let's explore how they come together to shape our outlook in moments of success and failure. The difference between an optimistic and pessimistic explanatory style can be profound, influencing our energy, motivation, and ability to keep moving forward.

**PART 4** OPPORTUNITY MINDSET

### When Things Go Wrong: Negative Events

Let's start with setbacks—missed opportunities, project failures, losing a client, or struggling to meet expectations. Here's where the two styles look very different:

**A pessimistic style** interprets the setback as:

- **Permanent:** *This will always happen. Things will never change.*
- **Pervasive:** *This failure ruins everything. Nothing we do works.*
- **Absent Situational Weight:** This could be simply not considering situational factors or feeling a sense of fault or blame, *This is all my fault,* or *We're not good enough.*

These explanations make problems feel immovable. If failure is forever, it infects everything, and it is all our fault, what's the point of trying again? We're left feeling stuck, helpless, and drained of energy.

Now, let's contrast that with an optimistic style. In the face of the same challenge, the explanations shift:

- **Temporary:** *This is a tough spot, but it won't last forever.*
- **Specific:** *This problem is limited to this project, not to everything we're doing.*
- **Situational Recognition:** *The client pulled out because their budgets changed, not because our work wasn't strong.*

See how different that feels? An optimistic style keeps the setback contained and allows us to move forward. It doesn't ignore the problem, it looks at what's fixable. Instead of getting stuck in blame or despair, we're more likely to regroup, stay motivated, and look for solutions.

**Examples in Action**

**1. A Supplier Delay Threatens a Product Launch**

Imagine you're leading a team on a critical product launch. A key supplier calls with bad news: they can't deliver the part you need, on time or within budget. This threatens to delay the entire launch and risks missing a huge market opportunity.

Pessimistic Explanatory Style:

- Permanent: *This always happens.*

- Pervasive: *The whole project is a disaster.*

- Absent Situational Weight: *Suppliers are unreliable.*

When we see the situation this way, it feels immovable. If delays always happen, if the project is now a 'disaster' and if we can't see the factors contributing to the outcome, it's easy to freeze. We might lose motivation, give up on finding a solution, or let the stress ripple through our team.

Optimistic Explanatory Style:

- Temporary: *This is a critical challenge right now.*

- Specific: *What aspects of the project are unaffected? Can we make up time elsewhere?*

- Situational Recognition: *Major supply chain issues are hitting the whole industry. What alternatives do we have?*

Optimistic explanatory style is not about being positive; it's about being pragmatic and productive in thinking. We might call a backup supplier, adjust timelines, or tweak the design to work with an alternative part. This mindset keeps energy high, encouraging resourcefulness and perseverance.

PART 4 OPPORTUNITY MINDSET

### 2. Being Overlooked for a Promotion

You've worked hard all year, delivered strong results, and set your sights on a promotion. Then the news comes: someone else got the role.

Pessimistic Explanatory Style:

- Permanent: *I'll never move up in this company. I never get recognised for my work.*

- Pervasive: *It's a bad culture.*

- Absent Situational Weight: *It's hopeless. I don't belong here.*

This way of thinking makes the rejection feel like a dead end. If it's permanent, pervasive, and entirely personal, why bother trying again? Your energy tanks, and resentment or self-doubt takes hold, making it harder to step up for future opportunities.

Optimistic Explanatory Style:

- Temporary: *I didn't get this promotion, but that doesn't mean I won't in the future.*

- Specific: *This decision was about this role at this time. It doesn't mean my work isn't valued.*

- Situational Recognition: *They might have needed someone with a very specific skill set for this position. What can I learn to be ready for the next opportunity?*

With this mindset, you keep things in perspective. You focus on what you can control—seeking feedback, building new skills, or looking for other growth opportunities. You might not have got this role, but there's no reason you can't succeed in the next one. This thinking keeps your confidence intact and helps you keep moving forward.

### 3. A Disagreement with an Ex-Partner

Let's say you argue with an ex-partner about shared finances for the children's education. It ends badly, and you leave the conversation feeling frustrated and hurt.

Pessimistic Explanatory Style:

- Permanent: *They're always difficult and never consider my perspective.*

- Pervasive: *Why am I the one who is forced to compromise on everything.*

- Absent Situational Weight: *I can't co-parent effectively with them.*

Thinking this way leaves you feeling powerless and stuck. If the problem feels permanent and pervasive, it's hard to believe things could ever get better. The lack of consideration for what's making this particular issue so challenging creates helplessness, making it even harder to see a path forward or engage constructively in future conversations.

Optimistic Explanatory Style:

- Temporary: *This was a tough conversation.*

- Specific: *We're finding financial matters difficult. There are still plenty of things we're handling well.*

- Situational Recognition: *Both of our bills have gone up significantly, making us both extra-stressed about finances. That probably made it harder to communicate clearly.*

With this explanation, the disagreement feels less overwhelming. It becomes something you can learn from and improve on, rather than a reason to feel defeated. Maybe you decide to revisit the conversation when emotions aren't so high, or you focus on what's working well to build a more constructive relationship moving forward.

These examples show how the same situation, whether it's a supplier delay, missing out on a promotion, or a personal disagreement, can be interpreted in radically different ways.

- A pessimistic explanatory style makes problems feel permanent, pervasive, and hopeless. It drains energy, crushes motivation, and leaves you feeling stuck.
- An optimistic explanatory style keeps problems temporary, specific, and grounded in situational factors. It creates space for action, encourages resourcefulness, and helps you focus on what you can do next.

When setbacks happen, and they always do, it's your explanatory style that determines whether you'll spiral into helplessness or pick yourself up, learn, and move forward.

**When Things Go Right: Positive Events**

Now, let's flip to success. This is where the two styles behave in exactly the opposite way. A pessimistic style explains the win as:

- Temporary: *We got lucky this time.*
- Specific: *So this part worked out; it doesn't mean much for the rest of our work.*
- Situational Weight Overemphasised: *The conditions were easy. Anyone could've done it.*

The problem with this approach? It steals confidence. If you dismiss success as luck or circumstance, it doesn't feel repeatable. You're left feeling unworthy or that your success won't last, and instead of building momentum, you hesitate, feel pessimistic about the next challenge that comes along, or simply wait for things to go wrong to prove you right.

On the other hand, an optimistic style owns the success, explaining it as:

- Permanent: *This win shows we're on the right track. It's something we can build on.*

- Pervasive: *This success proves we're capable of solving any challenge we're faced with.*

- Situational Weight Minimised: *This happened because of our preparation, effort, and skill.*

This mindset creates confidence. You see success as earned, not accidental, and that belief propels you forward.

**Examples in Action**

**1. A Supplier Delivers Ahead of Schedule**

You're leading a critical product launch, and a key supplier calls with great news: they've sourced the part faster than expected, and under budget. This puts you ahead of schedule and creates an opportunity to bring the product to market sooner.

Pessimistic Explanatory Style:

- Temporary: *This is a first. Let's see how long it lasts.*

- Specific: *Even if we get that part earlier, nothing else is ready.*

- Situational Weight Overemphasised: *We got lucky. Another company cancelled their order.*

With this mindset, you dismiss the win as a fluke. The team doesn't get credit for their role in managing the supplier relationship or coordinating the project. The success feels fleeting, and confidence in future wins remains low.

Optimistic Explanatory Style:

- Permanent: *This shows we've built a strong partnership with the supplier that we can rely on.*

- Pervasive: *This success highlights the efficiency of our planning and execution across the project.*

- Situational Weight Minimised: *We delivered early because we stayed on top of timelines and communicated well.*

Here, the success feels real, something the team earned and can build on. They see the part they played in making it happen, which lifts their confidence, motivation, and trust in the process. That energy carries into the next project, pushing them to step up and keep improving.

### 2. You Get Promoted

After a year of hard work, strong results, and dedication, you're promoted to a leadership position. It's an achievement you've been striving toward for a while.

Pessimistic Explanatory Style:

- Temporary: *I was just in the right place at the right time. This won't last.*

- Specific: *This was about one project going well; it doesn't mean I'm good at everything.*

- Situational Weight Overemphasised: *They probably had no one else to promote, so I got lucky.*

This way of thinking undercuts the accomplishment. Instead of feeling capable, you feel like an imposter who's stumbled into success. It erodes your confidence and makes it harder to step into the role with conviction.

Optimistic Explanatory Style:

- Permanent: *This promotion reflects my hard work and consistent results over time.*

- Pervasive: *This shows I'm ready to step up and lead across different areas of the business.*

- Situational Weight Minimised: *I earned this by delivering results, learning new skills, and showing initiative.*

With this mindset, the promotion feels like proof of your hard work and growth. You own it, and that confidence pushes you to take on new challenges and opportunities with even more conviction.

### 3. A Positive Conversation with an Ex-Partner

You and your ex-partner have a calm and constructive discussion about parenting responsibilities. You both agree on a plan that works well, and it feels like real progress.

Pessimistic Explanatory Style:

- Temporary: *This was a one-off. Things will go back to being difficult soon.*

- Specific: *This only worked because they happened to be in a good mood today.*

- Situational Weight Overemphasised: *The only reason this happened is because the issue was simple, not because we can actually communicate well.*

With this outlook, the success feels fragile. It doesn't build confidence that future conversations can be constructive. You're left waiting for things to fall apart again.

Optimistic Explanatory Style:

- Permanent: *This shows we're capable of having calm, productive conversations when we focus on what's best for everyone.*

- Pervasive: *This progress reflects the effort we've both put into improving how we communicate.*

- Situational Weight Minimised: *We're finding ways to work together because we're both showing up constructively.*

## PART 4  OPPORTUNITY MINDSET

Here, the success feels significant and repeatable. It reinforces the belief that progress is possible and encourages us to keep approaching conversations with the same patience, care, and focus.

These examples show how success can feel either earned and repeatable or fleeting and fragile, depending on our explanatory style.

- A pessimistic style makes success feel like a fluke. By attributing it to temporary, isolated, and situational factors, we strip away confidence and momentum.

- An optimistic style makes success feel like a natural outcome of effort and capability. By seeing it as permanent, pervasive, and influenced by our contribution, we build confidence, motivation, and the belief that good outcomes can and should happen.

Our ability to celebrate and own success is just as important as how we handle setbacks. It's what allows us to keep growing, taking risks, and believing that our hard work will pay off, again and again.

### The Impact on Behaviour and Outcomes

The way we explain setbacks and successes isn't just about perspective; it's about what happens next. When things go wrong, optimism helps us see problems as temporary and manageable, making it easier to adapt and try again. We stay resourceful, motivated, and focused on solutions.

When things go right, optimism allows us to own our success. It feels earned, lasting, and proof of our ability. That confidence fuels energy and momentum for whatever comes next. Pessimism, on the other hand, does the exact opposite. It makes setbacks feel permanent, pervasive, and personal, leaving us stuck and disheartened. When things go well, it downplays the win as temporary or situational, stripping away confidence and belief.

Every day, we face wins and losses, challenges and opportunities. Start listening to the way you explain these moments to yourself. Do you let setbacks feel bigger than they are, or do you keep them in perspective? When something good happens, do you own the win, or do you dismiss it as luck?

Our explanatory style is a powerful tool. When we learn to shift it, making setbacks smaller and success bigger, we find ourselves more motivated, confident, and resilient. It's not about ignoring reality; it's about focusing on what we can learn, own, and do next.

When we believe things can get better, and that we have what it takes to make it happen, we unlock energy, creativity, and momentum. And that's when real progress begins.

**Recognising Your Beliefs through the Consequences**

Sometimes, it's easier to notice how you're feeling or acting—the consequence—before you're even aware of the belief driving it. Take the example of missing out on a promotion. You might feel deflated, withdrawn, or start doubting your abilities. Maybe you stop putting your hand up for new opportunities, or lose the motivation to keep performing at your best.

When you pause and ask yourself, *What belief is driving this?* you might uncover thoughts like, *This proves I'm not good enough. I'll never get ahead.* The problem is that this belief makes the setback feel permanent, pervasive, and personal, turning it into a roadblock rather than a bump in the road. But what if you challenged it? What if you asked yourself, *Is this really a permanent failure, or just one outcome? What specific feedback can I learn from? Are there situational factors I might be overlooking?*

By reframing the belief, *I didn't get this role, but I can ask for feedback, improve, and try again,* you shift the consequence. Instead of staying stuck, you feel determined, motivated, and ready to take action, putting yourself in a stronger position for next time.

**How to Adopt an Optimistic Explanatory Style**

When setbacks happen, shifting the way you interpret the situation can make all the difference. Here are some practical tips to guide you:

DO:
- **Identify situational factors:** Brainstorm realistic reasons outside your direct control that might have contributed to the outcome. This helps you keep things in perspective.
- **Be specific about the impact:** Pinpoint the exact areas affected by the setback and recognise what remained unaffected. Keeping it contained prevents problems from spreading unnecessarily.
- **Seek out trusted voices:** Talk to people whose opinions you trust, those who will give you constructive, realistic feedback and help reaffirm your strengths.

DON'T:
- **Generalise or use permanent language:** Avoid statements like, *This will never work* or *This always happens*. They make setbacks feel bigger and more permanent than they are.
- **Spread the disappointment:** Don't transfer the negative consequences to unrelated areas of your life, or fall into blanket statements like, *Everything is messed up* or *nobody cares*.
- **Turn to negativity for validation:** Avoid people who encourage a pessimistic mindset or who reinforce helplessness, no matter how validating it might feel in the moment.

Adopting an optimistic explanatory style doesn't mean ignoring the problem or sugarcoating reality. It's about seeing setbacks for what they are—specific, temporary, and influenced by factors you can learn from. By shifting the way you think, you maintain your energy, resourcefulness, and confidence to tackle what comes next.

# KEY INSIGHTS
## FOR BETTERMENT

- **Optimism is a learned skill, not a personality trait:** Optimism isn't about being naturally positive. It's a habit of thinking that can be developed. By shifting how we explain setbacks, we can increase persistence, performance, and creativity.

- **Our explanatory style shapes our outcomes:** How we interpret challenges determines how we respond. Optimistic thinkers see setbacks as temporary, specific, and influenced by external factors, which keeps them moving forward. Pessimists see them as permanent, pervasive, and personal, which often leads to stagnation.

- **Reframing fuels momentum:** The difference between giving up and improving often comes down to perspective. Small shifts in explanation, such as focusing on what we can control, or seeking learning opportunities, can dramatically impact long-term success.

- **Optimism drives action, not denial:** Optimistic explanatory style doesn't ignore reality. It helps us see challenges as stepping stones rather than dead ends. This mindset fuels resilience, problem-solving, and continuous improvement.

- **Optimism expands our imagination:** Optimism opens the door to creativity and visionary thinking. We become more willing to challenge assumptions, ask bolder questions, and explore possibilities we wouldn't otherwise consider. Optimism fuels innovation by shifting our mindset from *What is?* to *What could be?*

# REFLECTIVE
# QUESTIONS

1. **Recognising Your Explanatory Style:** Think about a recent setback. Did you view it as temporary or permanent? Specific or pervasive? Did you consider external factors, or did you take full personal blame? How might shifting your explanation change the way you respond to similar challenges in the future?
2. **Building Optimism as a Habit:** Are there specific situations where you tend to think more pessimistically? How might you practise an optimistic explanatory style in those moments?
3. **What opportunity might be hiding within your current frustration?:** Think of a recent moment where you felt stuck or discouraged—what might that experience be inviting you to rethink, learn, or do differently?

**WHAT'S NEXT?** Now that we've explored how optimism fuels persistence and momentum, we turn to the next essential step: taking inspired action. The final chapter of Opportunity Mindset focuses on how powerful questions and creative problem-solving help unlock new possibilities. By learning to ask better questions, challenge assumptions, and explore unconventional solutions, we can expand our potential and turn obstacles into breakthroughs.

# 12

# **Inspired Action**—Expanding Possibility Through Questions and Creative Problem-Solving

*'Logic will get you from A to B. Imagination will take you everywhere.' Albert Einstein*

## Possibilities Don't Create Themselves

When I was a kid, anytime I complained about having nothing to do, my mum would say, 'Only boring people get bored.' At the time, I rolled my eyes. But as I got older, I realised what she really meant. We don't have to wait for something interesting to happen; we create it.

The same is true for opportunities. Possibilities don't create themselves. We create them, not by waiting for the perfect moment or the right circumstances, but by learning to think differently, ask better questions, and challenge the limits of conventional problem-solving.

Some people seem to have a natural ability to spot opportunities, where others see dead ends. They ask questions that unlock new ideas, challenge assumptions that hold others back, and take creative action to move forward, even in uncertain situations.

But here's the secret: this isn't just intuition or talent. It's a skill, and like any skill, it can be learned.

This chapter is designed to stretch our thinking. It's not about finding the 'right' answer but about exploring new ways to approach challenges, ones that push us beyond obvious solutions. The best thinkers don't just have more ideas; they ask better questions, reframe problems, and explore possibilities others overlook.

In this final chapter on the Opportunity Mindset, we move from seeing possibilities to creating them. We learn practical tools to define challenges in a way that inspires possibility, generates creative solutions, and has us taking meaningful action, not by waiting for inspiration to strike, but by thinking differently, questioning deeply, and creative problem-solving.

## Opportunity Statements: Turning Roadblocks into Springboards

Some challenges push us forward, while others hold us back. Every problem has the potential to be either a roadblock or a springboard, a dead end or the beginning of something better. The key lies in how we frame it.

Most challenges start with a problem; declining sales, disengaged teams, budget constraints. But problems, on their own, don't create solutions. A powerful opportunity statement opens the door to what's possible. It shifts our focus from what's wrong to what's possible, and great questions usually offer the best springboards.

When we intentionally reframe a challenge as an opportunity, we move from limitation to possibility, from reactive thinking to creative problem-solving. To move from problem-driven to possibility-driven thinking, we need to reframe challenges as opportunity statements.

A well-crafted opportunity statement doesn't just describe a problem; it opens the door to new ways of thinking and problem-solving. It shifts focus from what's wrong to what's possible, sparking creativity and forward momentum.

A strong opportunity statement has four key qualities:
1. **It's people-focused**: Centres on those impacted rather than just the issue itself.

2. **It's specific**: Defines the challenge clearly without being too broad or vague.
3. **It's generative**: Encourages new ideas rather than limiting options.
4. **It's aspirational**: Frames the challenge as something worth solving, making it engaging and motivating.

Let's apply this to a real-world example.

## Reinventing a Category: Beyond the Problem

*I once worked on a global innovation project for a major air freshener brand. The brand was known for its beautiful fragrances, but its approach to innovation was broken. They kept producing fragrances in different forms—candles, plug-ins, sprays, and diffusers. The problem? People only needed so many fragrance products, and every new launch cannibalised existing sales. They were stuck in a cycle of incremental innovation rather than true reinvention.*

*Eventually, we stepped back and asked a different question. Is our only role fragrance, or could we be more? If we could invent a new category, what would we create?*

*Instead of seeing themselves solely as a fragrance brand, we explored the broader role of air in people's lives. What if air wasn't just about scent but about well-being, energy, focus, relaxation, and entertainment?*

*This shift in perspective led to a more expansive opportunity statement. How might we empower people to enhance their mood, well-being, and personal spaces through air?*

*This opened up entirely new avenues:*

- *Air that helps people relax or sleep better.*
- *Air that boosts energy or focus.*
- *Air that creates immersive environments for entertainment.*

- *Air that purifies and enhances health.*

*This wasn't just about selling more fragrance product. It was about rethinking the category itself.*

## Beyond Product Innovation: Expanding Possibility in any Challenge

Opportunity statements aren't just for product development. They apply to any challenge where a shift in perspective can unlock better solutions.

For example:

- Instead of, *How do we make meetings more productive?* we can ask *How might we design meetings that energise and engage people?*
- Instead of, *How do we improve customer service?* we can ask *How might we create an experience that makes customers feel valued and understood?*
- Instead of, *How do we get employees to adopt this new system?* we can ask *How might we make this system so intuitive that people love using it?*

A great opportunity statement is typically framed as a question, as questions by nature are generative. Great questions lead to great solutions. When we move from problem-solving to possibility-creating, we unlock new ways of thinking and new opportunities that might never have surfaced otherwise.

# The Power of Questions

Have you ever noticed how a single, well-timed question can shift everything?

It can spark curiosity, get a team talking, or unlock a solution that's been hiding in plain sight. As we explored in the last section, defining a great opportunity statement is an important first step. But the truth is, real possibilities emerge when we keep asking great questions.

Questions aren't just tools for gathering information. They shape the way we engage with challenges, people, and ideas.

- **Questions drive engagement.** Leaders who ask questions instead of just giving answers invite teams into the conversation, increasing performance and buy-in.[1]

- **Questions build trust.** Asking someone's perspective shows we value their voice, building connection and psychological safety.

- **Questions fuel innovation.** Great questions spark 'aha' moments, helping us see new possibilities and solutions.

- **Questions improve decisions.** Questions encourage critical thinking and problem-solving, helping teams focus on what really matters.

A simple truth for complex challenges is that any challenge can be solved with enough of the right questions. It's why I always say, great results begin with great questions.

This is where Question Thinking, as explored by Marilee Adams in *Change Your Questions, Change Your Life*, comes in.[2] It is a mindset and approach that helps us become more intentional about the questions we ask, shaping how we think, collaborate, and solve problems.

## What is Question Thinking?

The concept of Question Thinking highlights how shifting from judgemental questions to learning-focused ones can reshape our thinking.

It's about being intentional, choosing questions that open up thinking rather than shutting it down. Instead of asking, *Why is this failing?* which assumes failure is inevitable, try asking, *What's one thing we could try differently?* which encourages learning and action. By making a simple shift in the questions we ask, we expand our ability to solve problems, uncover new opportunities, and create better outcomes.

## Four Types of Powerful Questions

Different challenges require different types of thinking. The right question at the right time can shift perspective, uncover new opportunities, and act as a springboard for creative problem-solving. Here are four types of possibility-driven questions that help expand thinking in different ways.

### 1. Reflective Questions: Learning from the Past

Sometimes, the best way forward starts with looking back. Reflective questions help us extract valuable insights from past experiences, whether successes or setbacks. They allow us to identify patterns, build on what has worked, and avoid repeating mistakes.

Consider these questions:

- *What has worked well before that we can build on?*
- *What patterns do we notice from past successes and failures?*
- *What is this challenge teaching us?*

These questions are especially useful when:

- We're trying to improve an existing approach rather than starting from scratch.
- We've encountered similar challenges before and want to learn from experience.
- We need to turn a setback into a learning opportunity.

Example: A marketing team launching a new campaign might ask, *What made our most successful past campaigns work?* instead of simply reinventing the wheel.

## 2. Hypothetical Questions: Pushing Boundaries

When teams get stuck in conventional thinking, hypothetical questions can help break free from assumed limitations. These questions push us to explore big, bold ideas by temporarily removing constraints and considering alternative perspectives.

Try asking:

- *What would we do if there were no constraints?*
- *If we had unlimited budget, time, or talent, how would we approach this?*
- *What would a completely different industry do in our situation?*

These questions are powerful when:

- A team feels stuck, and ideas seem limited.
- We need fresh, unconventional solutions instead of incremental improvements.
- We're working in a competitive market and need to rethink our approach.

Example: City planners working to reduce traffic congestion might ask, *What if traffic laws didn't exist. How would we design seamless ways for people to move?*

This question removes the assumption that rules are the only way to create order, pushing teams to consider self-organising traffic systems, AI-driven coordination, or pedestrian-first city planning. Instead of just optimising existing roads, it challenges them to reimagine urban mobility entirely.

## 3. Future-Oriented Questions: Defining Success

When faced with a challenge, it's easy to get caught up in the details of what's not working. But what does success actually look like?

Future-oriented questions help teams create a clear vision, align priorities, and define what they're working toward.

Consider these:

- *What does great look like?*
- *If we solved this challenge completely, what would be different?*
- *How will we measure success beyond just the numbers?*

These questions are helpful when:

- There's no clear end goal, and decisions feel scattered.
- A project is in the early stages, and we need alignment on what success looks like.
- We want to ensure short-term wins align with long-term goals.

Example: A company trying to improve customer service might ask, *If we were the most customer-centric brand in our industry, what would that look like?* This question expands the scope of solutions and helps teams aim for meaningful, lasting improvements.

### 4. Pragmatic Questions: Taking Action

Big ideas are great but without action, they're just ideas. Pragmatic questions help shift thinking from possibility to progress by identifying immediate, practical steps that move things forward.

Ask:

- *What's one step we can take right now?*
- *What's within our control today that moves us forward?*
- *What resources do we already have that we're not fully using?*

These questions are most useful when:

- A project feels overwhelming and we need to create momentum.

- A team is stuck in analysis paralysis and needs to start executing.
- We have a big goal but need to break it into smaller, achievable steps.

Example: Instead of feeling stuck on a stalled initiative, a team might ask, *What's one small action we can take this week to make progress?* This helps shift the focus from what's blocking the project to what's possible right now.

## Asking the Right Questions Opens Opportunity

Every challenge presents a different kind of opportunity, whether it's to learn, innovate, grow, or solve a problem. The key is to match the question to the challenge so that it unlocks the right kind of thinking.

- **Opportunity for Learning » Reflective Questions:** This help us draw insights from the past, so we can build on what works and avoid repeating mistakes.

- **Opportunity for Innovation » Hypothetical Questions:** This challenges assumptions and pushes creative boundaries, helping us think beyond existing limitations.

- **Opportunity for Growth » Future-Oriented Questions:** This defines what success looks like, ensuring we stay focused on what really matters.

- **Opportunity for Problem-Solving » Pragmatic Questions:** This drives action and builds momentum, shifting us from ideas to implementation.

## Q-Storming: A Process Generating Better Questions for Better Solutions

If brainstorming is about generating ideas, then Q-Storming, coined by Marilee Adams, is about generating questions, because better questions lead to better answers.[3] Instead of jumping straight to solutions, Q-Storming helps us step back and explore the challenge from multiple angles. It expands our thinking, challenges assumptions, and uncovers insights we might otherwise miss.

**How to Run a Q-Storming Session**

A Q-Storming session follows a simple but powerful process:

1. **Start with your opportunity statement.**
   Write it clearly where everyone can see it. A well-defined opportunity statement focuses the conversation and ensures the right challenge is being explored.

2. **Generate as many questions as possible.**
   No filtering, no judging, just pure curiosity. Encourage people to push past their first instincts and explore the challenge from different perspectives. If the group gets stuck, creative techniques (which we'll explore in the next section) can help inspire fresh thinking.

3. **Group into themes and highlight the most powerful questions.**
   Once you've captured a broad set of questions, group them into themes and identify the ones that challenge assumptions, spark ideas, or point to clear next steps. By the end of a Q-Storming session, you'll have a roadmap of thought-provoking questions, ones that help you think beyond the obvious and uncover powerful new solutions.

## Generating Questions at Every Level of the Opportunity Ladder

No matter where we are on the Opportunity Ladder, questions give us momentum. They help us navigate challenges, uncover possibilities, and keep climbing toward better outcomes. Q-Storming works best when you generate questions across all three levels of the Opportunity Ladder, explored in chapter 10:

- **React:** Questions to understand and address the immediate challenge.

- **Respond:** Questions to improve and balance the current situation.

- **Transform:** Questions to explore bold, future-focused possibilities.

To bring this to life, let's say our opportunity statement is, *How can we improve customer satisfaction with service installation?*

### 1. React Questions—Addressing Immediate Challenges

At the React level, the focus is on clarity: identifying pain points, diagnosing issues, and addressing urgent concerns. These questions help stop the bleeding before moving into long-term improvements.

- *What are the biggest complaints customers have about service installation today?*

- *Where are delays or errors happening most often?*

- *What's frustrating customers in their first interaction with us?*

- *How many issues are we seeing each week, and what's causing them?*

React questions ensure we're solving the right problem before we start improving the process.

## 2. Respond Questions—Improving and Balancing the Current Situation

At the Respond level, the focus is on progress, identifying small wins, improving efficiency, and making thoughtful adjustments. These questions help stabilise and optimise performance.

- *Which customers are most satisfied, and what's working well for them?*
- *What are the key drivers of customer satisfaction in the installation process?*
- *How can we better set and manage customer expectations upfront?*
- *What quick wins could we implement immediately to improve the experience?*

Respond questions help us shift from firefighting to steady improvement, ensuring we're not just fixing problems but actively making things better.

## 3. Transform Questions—Exploring Bold, Future-Focused Possibilities

At the Transform level, the focus is on breakthroughs: challenging assumptions, rethinking the status quo, and exploring entirely new ways of doing things. These questions drive innovation and long-term impact.

- *If we were starting fresh, what would an ideal installation experience look like?*
- *What are the best examples of customer satisfaction in other industries that we can learn from?*
- *What trends are emerging in customer expectations, and how can we get ahead of them?*

- *If we had no constraints—unlimited time, budget, and resources—how would we redesign this process?*

- *What would it take for customers to say this was the best service they've ever experienced?*

Transform questions move us beyond incremental improvements and into the realm of game-changing possibilities.

When we generate questions across all three levels, we see the full picture, from short-term fixes to long-term breakthroughs, allowing us to uncover far more powerful solutions.

But what if we're struggling to generate new questions? That's where SCAMPER, a technique developed in the 1970s by educator Bob Eberle, may come in.[4]

## SCAMPER: A Tool for Creative Problem-Solving and Ideation

Creativity isn't about waiting for inspiration. Often, it's about looking at challenges from new angles. The SCAMPER technique provides a simple yet powerful way to do just that. SCAMPER builds on the foundational work of Alex Osborn, the father of brainstorming.[5] Osborn believed that structured questioning could spark innovative thinking, and Eberle took that idea further by creating a systematic way to challenge assumptions and explore new possibilities.

One of the biggest barriers to innovation is that we tend to approach problems the same way we always have. We default to familiar patterns, applying past solutions to new challenges, even when they no longer fit. SCAMPER disrupts this pattern by providing a structured way to question the status quo and consider alternatives we might not have explored otherwise.

Think of it like turning a puzzle piece in different directions until you find the angle that fits. By systematically applying SCAMPER, we move beyond obvious solutions and uncover new opportunities.

SCAMPER is built around seven actions, each designed to push thinking beyond the obvious:

- **Substitute:** *What can we replace to make this better?*
- **Combine:** *What elements could work together in a new way?*
- **Adapt:** *How can we borrow or apply something from another area?*
- **Modify (or Magnify/Minimise):** *What happens if we change the size, structure, or focus?*
- **Put to Another Use:** *Can we repurpose something innovatively?*
- **Eliminate:** *What can we remove to simplify or improve efficiency?*
- **Reverse:** *What happens if we flip the order, approach, or perspective?*

Each action provides a fresh way of looking at a problem, helping to break habitual thinking and spark new ideas.

This technique works across industries and problem types, whether we're designing a new product, improving a process, or tackling a business challenge. To see SCAMPER in action, let's apply it to something most people can relate to: unproductive team meetings.

## SCAMPER in Action: Redesigning Team Meetings

Imagine our challenge is, *How might we make team meetings more engaging, collaborative, and results-driven?*

Using SCAMPER, we can explore the challenge from multiple angles:

- **Substitute:** Instead of having the same person run every meeting, could facilitators rotate to bring fresh perspectives? Could lengthy verbal updates be replaced with short, written summaries so meetings focus on discussion rather than information-sharing?

- **Combine:** What if meetings were merged with brainstorming sessions, using a tool like Q-Storming to generate ideas? Could asynchronous tools like shared documents be combined with live meetings to make discussions more efficient?

- **Adapt:** What makes TED Talks or workshops engaging? Could elements like timed discussions, storytelling, or interactive exercises be incorporated into meetings to keep energy levels high?

- **Modify:** What if meetings were shortened to twenty-five minutes instead of an hour? Could participation be magnified by asking each attendee to contribute just one insight or question before wrapping up?

- **Put to Another Use:** Could meetings include a team learning segment, where members share skills or industry insights? What if part of the meeting was dedicated to celebrating team wins and contributions?

- **Eliminate:** Are there agenda items that no longer add value and could be removed? Could lengthy verbal reports be eliminated in favour of pre-meeting summaries?

- **Reverse:** What if meetings started with decisions and action items first, instead of updates, so the most important points were prioritised? Instead of a top-down structure, could team members set the agenda and drive the discussion?

It's like wearing different thinking hats to explore an opportunity. By applying SCAMPER, a once-routine process like team meetings can be completely reimagined. Instead of small, incremental fixes, it helps unlock unexpected, high-impact changes.

[ Take a moment to think about any area of your work and life that feels in need of a shake-up and apply SCAMPER. See what comes up. ]

PART 4 OPPORTUNITY MINDSET

### SCAMPER as a Tool for Innovation

The real power of SCAMPER lies in its ability to push thinking beyond surface-level improvements. It works not just for optimising existing processes but for reimagining entire categories and industries.

My stepson is obsessed with transport and town planning, so for a bit of fun, let's look at how SCAMPER might apply to rethinking urban transportation:

- **Substitute:** What if bike lanes replaced certain car lanes to improve congestion and sustainability?

- **Combine:** Could ride-sharing be combined with public transport to create a more seamless experience?

- **Adapt:** What innovations from air travel or logistics could be adapted to improve city transport?

- **Modify:** How would cities function if roads were designed for self-driving cars from the start?

- **Put to Another Use:** Could parking spaces be repurposed into community spaces, micro-hubs, or green areas?

- **Eliminate:** What if we removed traffic lights and instead relied on AI-driven coordination?

- **Reverse:** What if we designed cities where pedestrians, not cars, had priority everywhere?

SCAMPER forces us to step outside conventional thinking and explore what's possible, often leading to ideas that wouldn't have surfaced otherwise.

SCAMPER is one of those tools that becomes more powerful the more you use it. It's simple, but it can completely change the way you approach challenges. Next time you're feeling stuck, ask yourself, *What could I substitute, combine, adapt, modify, put to another use, eliminate, or reverse*? Sometimes, all it takes to find a breakthrough is to look at a challenge with fresh eyes.

## Expanding Our View: The Circle of Possibility

If SCAMPER helps us look at challenges with fresh eyes, the Circle of Possibility,[6] inspired by William Ury's work in *Possible: How We Survive (and Thrive) in an Age of Conflict*, helps us see beyond the challenge entirely. One of the biggest traps in problem-solving is getting stuck inside the problem itself, focusing only on what's missing, broken, or seemingly impossible. That's why we're ending this chapter with a tool designed to stretch our thinking even further.

The Circle of Possibility shifts our focus from what's probable to what's possible. It helps us zoom out, challenge assumptions, and uncover bold new opportunities that might not have been visible before.

It's the perfect tool to end this chapter on Opportunity Mindset, because it's not just about solving problems, it's about visualising the best possible outcomes that can pull us forward.

### *How the Circle of Possibility Works*

The Circle of Possibility is a structured way to shift from limitation to expansive thinking. It follows four simple steps:

1. **Define the Challenge (But don't Dwell on it)**
   Start by clearly stating the challenge you're facing. Acknowledge the difficulty, but don't let it become the focus. The goal here is to frame the situation objectively, not to get lost in frustration or roadblocks.

2. **Draw a Big Circle**
   Imagine a large circle encompassing the problem. This circle should represent all the possible positive outcomes that

could emerge. The problem sits at the centre, but the circle expands our perspective, pushing us to think beyond immediate barriers and constraints.

3. **Brainstorm Possible Positive Outcomes**

    Now comes the key question, *What is possible here?* Don't limit yourself to what seems likely or achievable. This is the time to think boldly, and it works best when engaging others in brainstorming to surface new perspectives.

    Write down every possible outcome, no matter how unconventional it seems. Importantly, this stage is about the outcomes you want to create, not the actions you may take. It isn't about finding the 'right' answer; it's about opening doors to ideas that might not have been visible at first.

4. **Identify Actionable Steps**

    Once the circle has been filled with possibilities, identify one or two outcomes that feel most inspiring or energising. Then, explore practical steps to turn these possibilities into reality. To see this tool in action, let's explore a real-world workplace challenge and how the Circle of Possibility can help generate new opportunities. A familiar challenge many can relate to is a team resisting changes caused by a restructure and where morale is low.

    When stuck in this problem, it's easy to focus on frustration, resistance, and what isn't working. Instead, we use the Circle of Possibility to shift the conversation.

Some positive possible outcomes could be:
- *The restructure creates opportunities for team members to develop new skills and take on leadership roles.*
- *The team becomes energised as they align around a clear new vision and purpose.*

- *Collaboration improves as silos break down and communication strengthens.*
- *The restructure simplifies workflows and eliminates inefficiencies.*
- *Morale improves as people see how the restructure benefits them personally and professionally.*
- *The team emerges stronger, more innovative, and ready to tackle bigger challenges.*

Let's say that, *The team emerges stronger, more innovative, and ready to tackle bigger challenges* feels most inspiring. The next question becomes, *What small, practical steps can we take to make this possibility a reality?*

Here are a few actionable steps to start moving toward this outcome:

- Facilitate an Innovation Session: Run a team workshop to explore ways to improve workflows, innovate, and embrace change.
- Celebrate Small Wins: Recognise progress toward adapting to the restructure, building energy, and reinforcing a positive mindset.
- Offer Development Opportunities: Provide chances for learning, mentoring, and leadership roles.
- Create a Shared Vision: Ask the team, *What could we achieve if we fully embraced this change?*
- Foster a Culture of Collaboration: Break down silos by encouraging cross-team brainstorming, problem-solving, and open dialogue.

### Possibility Drives Momentum

The Circle of Possibility doesn't stop at brainstorming. It inspires action.

**PART 4** OPPORTUNITY MINDSET

By identifying an energising outcome and taking small, practical steps toward it, we create momentum, build trust, and open up pathways for growth and innovation.

When we start with possibility, we don't just solve problems, we create new opportunities. And that's where the real transformation begins.

# KEY INSIGHTS
## FOR BETTERMENT

- **Opportunities don't create themselves—we create them:** Expanding possibility isn't about waiting for the right moment; it's about shifting perspective, asking better questions, and actively exploring new solutions.

- **How we frame a challenge determines the solutions we find:** A problem can be either a roadblock or a springboard. It all depends on whether we define it in terms of limitations or possibilities.

- **Better questions unlock better answers:** The most effective problem-solvers don't just seek solutions; they ask questions that challenge assumptions, push thinking further, and open up new opportunities.

- **Creative problem-solving requires structure:** Tools like SCAMPER, Q-Storming, and the Circle of Possibility help move beyond conventional thinking, making it easier to reframe challenges, generate fresh ideas, and take meaningful action.

# REFLECTIVE **QUESTIONS**

1. **Recognising Thinking Patterns:** Consider a recent challenge where you felt stuck. What was your initial reaction? Did you focus on barriers and limitations, or did you naturally look for possibilities? Were the questions you asked expansive or restrictive?
2. **Expanding Possibility Through New Tools:** Think about a problem or decision you're currently facing. Are you exploring it from different angles, or are you approaching it the same way you always have? What thinking tools—Opportunity Statements, Question Thinking, SCAMPER, or the Circle of Possibility—could help you see new solutions?
3. **Noticing the Impact of a Mindset Shift:** Reflect on a time when you changed the way you thought about a challenge. How did it shift your energy or perspective? What happened when you moved from limiting assumptions to expansive thinking? How can you apply this shift more often in your work and personal life?

**WHAT'S NEXT?** We explore Betterment Mastery—how to lead with ownership, create high-performing cultures, and build a life that thrives on continuous growth. Whether we're guiding a team, shaping relationships, or inspiring others, these final chapters help us embed Betterment into everything we do.

# PART 5

# Betterment Mastery—From Leadership to Lifelong Impact

# 13

# **Betterment Leadership**—Building Cultures of Ownership and High Performance

*'Culture eats strategy for breakfast.'* Peter Drucker

## The Harsh Truth About Transformation—And Why Most Efforts Fail

Change is a given in leadership. Whether it's a merger, digital transformation, restructuring, or a strategic shift, leaders are constantly navigating it. Yet, despite billions poured into transformation efforts each year, the numbers tell a brutal story:

- 73% of enterprises fail to gain real business value from digital transformation.[1]

- Up to 90% of acquisitions don't deliver the expected results.[2]

- IT projects routinely run over budget by 27%, with one in six blowing out by 200% and facing delays of up to 70%.[3]

The reality? Transformation is one of the biggest drivers of success, but also one of the biggest sources of failure and frustration.

So far, we've explored the power of mindset—how ownership, collaboration, and opportunity thinking fuel high performance.

Now, we turn to embedding these principles into teams, cultures, and organisations.

No matter how well it is planned, transformation won't succeed unless people at every level take ownership and move in the same direction. We can have a brilliant strategy or cutting-edge technology, but if people don't embrace it, or aren't willing to adapt and troubleshoot, it won't get far.

Does this mean we shouldn't try? Absolutely not. According to a McKinsey study, playing it safe with small, incremental changes often leads to stagnation.[4] While they may feel less risky, they increase the chances of an organisation slipping into mediocrity. To truly shift a company's trajectory, bold, decisive moves are needed.

This chapter is about leading change differently. It's about shifting transformation from something that happens to people to something they actively drive. But first, let's look at why most transformations fail, and what leaders can do differently.

**It's not the Strategy—It's the People**

From what I've seen working across industries, transformation rarely fails because of a bad strategy, the wrong tech, or a flawed process. The real issue? People pulling in different directions, resisting change, or already burnt out before they begin. I've never seen a transformation go exactly to plan. There's always a need to pivot, adapt, and troubleshoot. If only a handful of leaders are making those calls while everyone else waits for direction, it's destined to fail. For change to stick, we need energy, ownership, collaboration, and resourcefulness at every level.

When transformations fall apart, it's usually because:

- Teams don't understand why the change is happening or what it means for them.
- Employees follow new directives but don't fully commit.
- Managers micromanage instead of fostering ownership.

- Leaders talk strategy but fail to embed it in day-to-day work.
- People are running on empty before they even start.

A common mistake? Thinking that once a decision is made, execution will follow. However, transformation isn't a single decision; it's a series of daily behaviours, interactions, and adjustments that shape the culture. Change only works when it's owned at every level.

That's where Betterment Leadership comes in.

## Betterment Leadership—The People Side of Transformation

The Betterment Mindset isn't just about personal growth. It's about embedding a way of thinking that transforms teams, cultures, and organisations.

What makes it different?

- It doesn't rely on top-down control but fosters shared ownership.
- It doesn't just set goals but ensures people are aligned, empowered, and accountable.
- It doesn't view resistance as a problem but as a sign that deeper engagement is needed.

Instead of forcing compliance, Betterment Leadership creates an environment where people want to take ownership, where they don't just execute change but actively shape it.

To drive this shift, leaders must focus on three interconnected principles:

1. **Alignment**: Creating clarity and shared purpose.
2. **Ownership**: Moving beyond accountability to real commitment.
3. **Empowerment**: Providing the tools and autonomy to take action.

Each of these is essential. Without alignment, people pull in different directions. Without ownership, they wait for direction rather than driving change themselves. Without empowerment, even motivated teams will lack the tools or confidence to sustain high performance.

When leaders work on all three, simultaneously and at every level, they can accelerate successful transformation.

## 1. Alignment

*'Building a visionary company requires 1% vision and 99% alignment'*—James C. Collins[5]

Alignment is the first interconnected principle of creating people-based transformation. We've already explored the power of trust and shared purpose in driving a Win-Win Mindset. In Chapter 9, we looked at alignment on an interpersonal level. How to resolve conflicts, bridge differences, and find shared purpose when people are pulling in opposite directions. That was about negotiation.

Now, we're taking it one step further. For transformation to succeed, alignment can't just happen in isolated conversations. It has to be embedded in how leaders and teams operate every day. This is about ensuring people move together without friction, bottlenecks, or competing priorities.

This is where leadership and team alignment come in.

Alignment enables collaboration, creative problem-solving, and high trust. It ensures teams don't just function well within their own silos but work seamlessly across functions, levels, and priorities to drive real impact. Without it, even the most well-intentioned teams can end up working at cross-purposes.

But alignment isn't about getting everyone to agree on every detail. It's about making sure people:

- Are clear on the direction, priorities, and success measures

- Understand how their role connects to the bigger picture

- Have the right structures, conversations, and ways of working to execute effectively.

We've covered how a Win-Win Mindset fuels better decisions and how high-trust environments allow for healthy conflict and creative tension. Now, we go further; embedding alignment as an ongoing discipline so that Betterment isn't just an individual mindset, but the foundation of how leaders and teams work together to create real change.

**Alignment is where High Performance Starts**

High performance is about more than just a shared vision. It's the synergy of values, goals, actions, and ways of working that ensures people are moving in the same direction. And it all starts with the leadership team.

Alignment (or misalignment) can happen at multiple levels. See Figure 9.

- At the top, alignment is about clarity on strategic goals—where the organisation is heading, why, and the key priorities for success.

- At the foundation, it's about execution—defining roles, interdependencies, and the behaviours, systems, and processes that support strategic priorities.

When alignment is strong, teams don't just understand the vision, they have the structure and clarity to turn it into real results.

## PART 5 BETTERMENT MASTERY

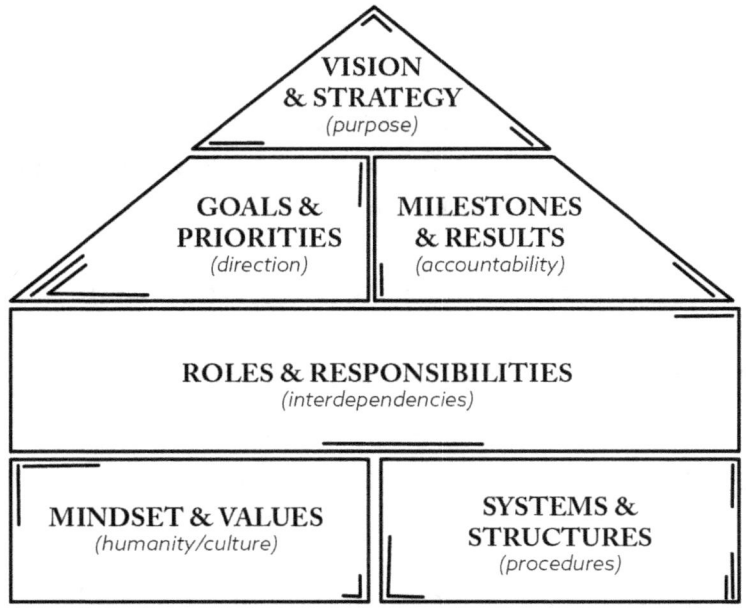

*Figure 9.*

**Types of Alignment**

**Vertical alignment** ensures teams are working toward the organisation's strategic priorities. Leaders must translate big-picture goals into clear objectives at every level so people understand how their role contributes to success. Yet, research shows only 55% of middle managers can name even one of their company's top priorities, a major issue given their influence.[6]

**Horizontal alignment** comes down to cross-functional collaboration, and that's where things often get messy. Even when teams are working toward the same big-picture goals, their day-to-day priorities can pull them in different directions. Finance is focused on cutting costs, while sales is pushing for growth. One wants tighter budgets, the other needs investment. These tensions aren't unusual, but when left unchecked, they create silos, slow down execution, and lead to missed opportunities.

The numbers back this up. While 84% of managers say they trust their direct teams, only 9% feel they can consistently rely on colleagues in other departments.[6] That's a big problem when success depends on functions working together, not just alongside each other. Leaders need to bridge these gaps, helping teams navigate competing priorities and build a culture where shared accountability beats internal competition.

**Where Alignment Breaks Down**

Even when organisations cascade goals from the top down, alignment often falls apart along the way because:

- Just half of the C-Suite have a clear sense of how key priorities fit together.[6]

- Less than a third of senior executives' direct reports understand how corporate priorities connect.[6]

- That number drops to 16% for frontline supervisors, even in organisations with strong communication.[6]

- Only 29% of employees feel their leader's vision aligns with the organisation.[7]

Alignment isn't just a leadership issue. It needs to be embedded across executive teams, functional groups, and cross-functional collaborations. The larger the organisation, the harder this becomes, making it critical for leaders to pinpoint the highest-priority gaps and address them head-on.

**The Three Pillars of Leadership Team Alignment**

Leadership team alignment has three core pillars: trust, focus, and action.
Trust builds the necessary bonds. Focus provides the strategic

**PART 5** BETTERMENT MASTERY

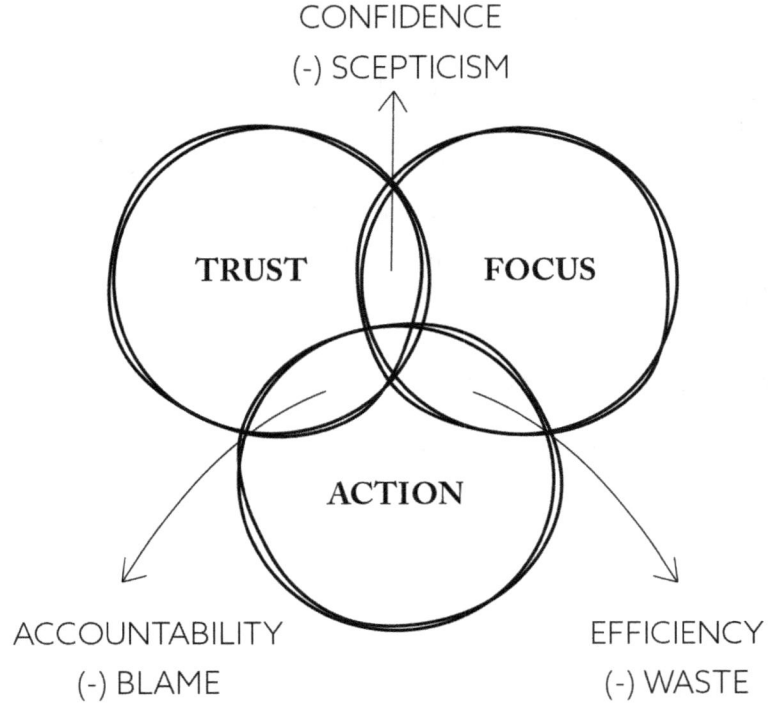

*Figure 10.*

direction. Action turns aspirations into reality, creating a robust framework for sustained organisational alignment and success.

Trust in each other, coupled with an inspiring and clear focus, delivers confidence within a team. When there is no trust or the focus is murky, the team is likely to feel sceptical and to resist change.

Focus and action, also known as operating rhythm, deliver optimal efficiency, helping people make faster decisions and deliver the results that really matter to the overall success of the business. When there is no clear focus or core actions aren't in service of these priorities, people can waste resources and slow down momentum.

Greater accountability and ownership result from trust and behaviours being in service of core priorities. If trust is low or actions aren't clearly aligned with priorities, blame and finger-pointing creep in.

## How to Build Leadership Team Alignment

The alignment process should start with senior leadership and cascade throughout the organisation, with an emphasis on interdependent cross-functional groups or areas of strategic priority.

### Step one: Assess the current situation

Before driving alignment, leaders need a clear picture of where things stand. This means defining priorities, setting expectations, and identifying what's working, and what's not. A strong assessment should include:

- **Reviewing performance data:** Are targets being met? Is engagement high or declining? What do turnover and tenure trends reveal?

- **Observing behaviours:** Are leadership meetings focused on strategy? Are teams collaborating effectively? Is there healthy debate or passive agreement?

- **Asking the right questions:** Surveys give data, but one-on-one conversations reveal the why. Honest discussions, ideally facilitated by a neutral party, uncover the unspoken barriers to alignment.

By understanding the reality, not just assumptions, leaders can pinpoint the biggest gaps and focus on what truly needs to change.

### Step two: Build the core foundations of alignment

How do we build the three core pillars through the alignment process?

**Alignment pillar #1—Trust**

Trust is the foundation of leadership alignment. Without it, collaboration, communication, and commitment fall apart. Leaders who prioritise trust build stronger teams, drive alignment, and create high-performance cultures.

When trust is high, teams experience:

- Open communication: People feel safe to share ideas, concerns, and perspectives.

- Authenticity and vulnerability: Leaders lead with honesty, setting the tone for transparency.

- Stronger collaboration: Teams work cohesively, sharing skills and information freely.

- Innovation and risk-taking: People feel empowered to experiment without fear of blame.

- Healthy conflict resolution: Disagreements turn into productive discussions, not roadblocks.

- Greater accountability: Trust reinforces ownership, ensuring people follow through.

Most importantly, trust creates space for constructive challenge, the kind that sparks bold ideas and drives real breakthroughs.

The most critical areas for a leadership team to align on include:

- **Values and behaviours:** What are the core behaviours that reflect what's important to us?

- **Aspirations and intentions:** What are our hopes for the future, and what do we believe is critical to making it happen?

- **Strategic dualities:** How do we all contribute, and how should we manage the natural tensions that exist?

- **Strengths:** What are our strengths, and how can we leverage them to achieve optimal results?

- **Ways of working:** How should we collaborate, discuss challenges, resolve conflicts, and show up together in a unified way?

**Alignment pillar # 2—Focus**

Focus is about clarity on strategic priorities, ensuring teams know what matters most and how their work contributes to success. The challenge for leaders is balancing big-picture vision with clear, actionable goals that guide daily decisions.

When focus is strong, teams experience:

- Clear communication: Everyone understands expectations, priorities, and strategies.

- Goal alignment: Teams know what they're working toward and how their contributions fit.

- Smart resource allocation: Time, talent, and budgets are directed toward what truly matters.

- Adaptability: A clear vision allows for flexibility without losing direction.

- Faster decision-making: Leaders and teams make informed choices without second-guessing.

- Measurable progress: Clear KPIs and success metrics keep teams accountable.

A focused organisation moves with intention, speed, and impact, avoiding wasted effort on distractions that don't serve the bigger goal.

The most important areas for a leadership team to align on include:

- **Vision and strategy:** Where are we heading, and what will it take to get there? Is it inspiring enough to motivate progress, especially when times are tough?

- **Goals and priorities:** What are the most important areas of focus, and what are the trade-offs we need to make?

- **Desired results:** How will we measure our success?

- **Interdependencies:** What do we need from each other to deliver?

**Alignment pillar #3—Action**

Action is about turning strategy into execution, ensuring the right people connect at the right time to drive key priorities. It's the operating rhythm of a business, where everyone knows what needs to happen, when, and with whom.

Research from McKinsey shows that successful transformations often come down to how well an organisation adapts its planning and operating rhythms.[8] When action is structured and deliberate, we see:

- Vision put into motion: Leaders translate big goals into tangible steps and daily behaviours.

- Consistent decision-making: Clear processes ensure choices align with strategy.

- Accountability and ownership: Teams understand their roles and take responsibility.

- Cultural reinforcement: Daily practices embed company values into how work gets done.

- Agility and adaptability: Strong processes help teams pivot and respond to change effectively.

- Efficiency and impact: Focused execution minimises wasted effort and maximises results.

- Continuous learning: Regular feedback loops drive ongoing improvement and alignment.

With a strong operating rhythm, strategy doesn't sit on a presentation, it drives real outcomes.

The most critical areas for a leadership team to align on include:

- **Core activities:** What are the core behaviours that are most important to achieving strategic priorities?

- **Key meetings:** Based on strategic priorities, what are the critical areas needed for consistent collaboration and alignment?

- **Interdependencies:** For priority areas, who are the right people to collaborate with at the right times to drive optimal outcomes?

- **Milestones:** How should we phase initiatives and what results do leaders expect to see and by when?

- **Systems and process:** How can leaders minimise the pressure and burden on individuals to ensure we stay focused and effective on the things that matter?

- **Incentives:** Do the incentives line up with strategic and behavioural priorities?

## Step three: Commit to a cadence for ongoing alignment

Alignment isn't a one-off event. It needs to be built into the rhythm of how teams operate. With the pace of change in business today, leaders must continuously check in, adjust, and realign to stay on track.

This means setting regular, structured touchpoints to ensure priorities remain clear and teams are moving in sync. The right cadence depends on the context.

- During major change (restructures, mergers, digital transformations), more frequent check-ins keep alignment on track.

- For new teams or leaders, regular alignment sessions accelerate trust and cohesion.

- For established teams, periodic reviews help refine processes, build on strengths, and stay ahead of shifting priorities.

By making alignment an ongoing practice, leaders create agility, clarity, and momentum, ensuring teams don't just set goals but keep delivering on them.

## 2. Ownership

Ownership is the second interconnected principle of creating people-based transformation. The entire premise of this book has been about driving ownership, but the real power happens when we go beyond an individual level to teams and organisations. A Betterment organisation isn't built on top-down directives or rigid accountability structures; it thrives when people at every level take ownership, even when they don't have direct control over strategic decisions or resources.

In this section, we focus on how to embed a culture of ownership, particularly among the critical layer of leaders responsible for executing goals in fast-moving, high-pressure environments. These leaders are often the ones who feel the greatest tension between big strategic ambitions and the day-to-day operational constraints that can make execution feel overwhelming.

Ownership doesn't just happen because we ask people to be accountable. It's built on three transformational shifts:

- **From Overwhelm to Ownership:** Moving from blaming external factors to focusing on what we can control.

- **From Competition to Collaboration:** Instead of individuals working in silos, teams actively shape outcomes together.

- **From Frustration to Problem-Solving:** People use structured tools to navigate challenges productively rather than feeling stuck in limitations.

> When leaders successfully embed these shifts, transformation efforts don't just survive, they thrive. It's the people transformations that drive business transformation.

**Leveraging Tools to Embed Ownership in Culture**

The key to embedding ownership isn't just talking about it, it's in using structured tools that shape thinking and behaviour in real time. This is how we shift from intellectual understanding to real-world application.

To truly embed ownership, teams need a way to connect these tools to their daily challenges. The most effective way to do this is by anchoring ownership tools to specific, high-impact problems.

For example, in a recent leadership program I led, teams were asked to define the biggest ownership barriers they were facing. Some of the most common challenges included:

- **Funding constraints:** How do we secure the right resources while staying agile?

- **Unrealistic client expectations:** How do we navigate boundaries and still deliver value?

- **Under-resourced teams:** How do we make the most of what we have?

- **Lack of clarity:** How do we ensure we understand client and stakeholder needs?

- **Difficult stakeholders:** How do we move past frustration and drive alignment?

By selecting a real-world challenge, teams were able to apply ownership tools in a way that immediately improved their performance.

For example:
- Teams used the CIA Model to focus energy on what they could control, rather than getting stuck in frustration.
- The Align Model helped teams reframe difficult stakeholder relationships, turning roadblocks into collaboration opportunities.
- Question Thinking and the Circle of Possibility unlocked new solutions that weren't previously considered.

By embedding these tools in real scenarios, ownership didn't simply feel like a leadership philosophy. It became an organisational habit. The real power of these tools is that they don't just shift how people think, they change how people act. As a result, they achieved better outcomes. This is how new behaviours are formed and how they stick.

**Embedding Ownership into Ways of Working**

To drive ownership at scale, leaders must ensure that these tools are not just individual practices, but that they are embedded into how teams operate.

A successful approach follows three key stages:
1. **Learn**: Teach teams the principles and introduce key tools.
2. **Apply**: Provide opportunities for teams to use tools in real-world challenges.
3. **Embed**: Build these tools into daily routines, meetings, and team rituals to make ownership sustainable.

For example, one organisation I worked with embedded ownership tools into its dispute resolution processes. They took the core Betterment tools and personalised them into their own 'Resolution Mindset' framework. Every new team member was onboarded into this approach, ensuring that ownership was not just encouraged, but fully integrated into their culture.

**Ownership as a Cultural Shift**

Ownership is not a box to be ticked. It's a fundamental shift in how people engage with their work, their challenges, and each other. It's built when:

- Teams are given the tools to navigate complexity effectively.
- Leaders encourage commitment over compliance.
- Individuals feel personally responsible for driving progress rather than feeling they're just following instructions.

By embedding Betterment Mindsets and structured tools into everyday problem-solving, organisations can create a culture where ownership isn't an aspiration, it's the norm.

## 3. Empowerment

Empowerment is the third interconnected principle of creating people-based transformation. It is the foundation of alignment and ownership, ensuring that individuals and teams are not just expected to take ownership but are equipped to succeed. However, empowerment isn't about giving people free rein. It's about creating the right balance between performance and well-being, so people can thrive rather than just survive.

In many organisations, leaders focus heavily on driving high performance, but when this comes at the expense of well-being, it creates a burnout culture, one fuelled by adrenaline but ultimately unsustainable. On the other hand, focusing solely on well-being without achievement can lead to disengagement, where people feel comfortable but unfulfilled.

A Betterment organisation strikes the right balance, ensuring that:

- Performance without well-being doesn't push people into exhaustion.
- Well-being without performance doesn't lead to stagnation.

## PART 5  BETTERMENT MASTERY

- Empowerment is embedded at every level, so people feel in control of their experience and capable of contributing to results.

> When performance and well-being coexist, people feel both energised and effective, leading to higher engagement, resilience, and sustainable success.

### Personal Empowerment—Helping People Take Control of Their Experience

While leaders play a critical role in shaping culture, no leader can accommodate the full spectrum of personal needs within a team. It's impossible for leaders to tailor their approach to every individual's unique challenges while also delivering strategic results. This is why personal empowerment is essential. Leaders need to equip people with the tools to take responsibility for their own experience.

One of the most powerful frameworks for this is the Betterment Surviving-to-Thriving Ladder, which offers a structured way for leaders and teams to:

- **Recognise where they are**, whether they're in survival mode, coping, managing, leveraging, or thriving.

- **Identify what they need** to move forward, rather than expecting the organisation to 'fix' their challenges.

- **Take personal response-ability**, making intentional choices to shift their mindset and actions.

This ladder reflects a fundamental truth: people experience stress, change, and uncertainty differently, but by providing them with the right tools, they can take ownership of their energy, focus, and decision-making.

## What People Need at Each Level of the Ladder

Not everyone needs the same kind of support at the same time. What helps someone struggling to cope is very different from someone in a high-performance state needing to sustain their momentum.

That's why empowerment isn't about a one-size-fits-all approach. It's about giving people the right tools at the right time, based on where they are.

The Betterment Surviving-to-Thriving Ladder is invaluable for this. Leaders and teams can use this framework to recognise where they are and what they need so they're able to move forward.

Here's how the focus of empowerment shifts across the different levels.

### Surviving and Coping—Recognising Burnout and Rebuilding Resilience

At these levels, people are in survival mode, just trying to get through the day. They often feel overwhelmed, reactive, and emotionally drained. Their thinking is narrow, and long-term goals feel irrelevant compared to immediate pressures.

What they need most is to:

- Recognise signs of burnout early: Spot the warning signs before exhaustion takes hold.

- Overcome resilience fatigue: Sustain their energy rather than just 'push through'.

- Rebuild a sense of control: Use small, practical actions to shift out of helplessness.

This is not the time for big-picture visioning or high-performance strategies. It's about stabilising and regaining energy first. Leaders can support their teams by ensuring there is awareness, open dialogue, and space for individuals to take personal action based on their needs.

### Managing—Moving from Stress to Sustainable Performance

In the managing zone, people are functional but they often feel stretched too thin. They're keeping up, but barely. This is where leaders start to see chronic stress patterns, where people are working hard but not necessarily working smart.

What they need most:

- Energy management: Understanding how to balance high-output periods with proper recovery.

- Time scarcity management: Learning how to make time work for them, rather than feeling like there's never enough.

- Reactive cycle breaking: Moving beyond constant firefighting to proactive problem-solving.

At this stage, empowerment is about optimising performance without pushing toward burnout. Leaders play an essential role ensuring the team is focused on the right things at the right time and all effort is goal directed.

### Leveraging—Transforming Stress into a Driver of Growth

Once people are in leveraging mode, they're not just keeping up, they're actively improving. This is when stress shifts from something that needs managing to something they can use.

What they need most:

- Become stress-positive: Reframe stress as a fuel for performance, connection, and creativity.

- Achieve flow states: Learn how to harness focus, deep work, and momentum to unlock their best work.

- Expand their impact: Move beyond individual contribution to drive collective success.

At this level, empowerment isn't about fixing problems. It's about maximising strengths. When people are in this stage, it's time for leaders to introduce new growth opportunities, rally their teams around a big challenge, and seek opportunities to level up performance.

### Thriving—Sustaining Meaning and Purpose at Every Level

The final shift is from high performance to lasting fulfilment. People in thriving mode need more than just productivity strategies. They need a strong sense of meaning and contribution.

What they need most:

- Deep personal purpose: Ensuring that their work aligns with what matters to them.

- Understanding their contribution to the bigger picture: Connecting daily efforts to the organisation's mission and impact.

- How to sustain momentum over time: Keeping engagement high by continuously evolving and learning.

At this stage, the focus is on legacy and long-term impact, ensuring that every person, at every level, has a strong sense of why their work matters. To help people reach thriving, leaders must ensure that each person's role and contribution is clearly aligned with the overall purpose and accomplishments of the organisation and the team. Understanding personal motivations of their team can also help unlock intrinsic motivation and commitment.

### Empowerment is about Progress, not Perfection

The goal isn't to get everyone thriving all the time. That's not realistic. People will move up and down the ladder based on their circumstances, challenges, and growth stages.

What matters is that no one feels stuck, that they always have the tools, mindset, and support to take the next step forward.

By understanding what empowerment looks like at each level, leaders can meet people where they are, helping them shift from survival

PART 5  BETTERMENT MASTERY

to strength, from stress to momentum, and from high performance to deep fulfilment.

And that's how Betterment becomes a way of life; not just an initiative, but a culture where people are constantly growing, adapting, and thriving.

### From Dependency to Capability—Embedding Empowerment into Culture

The final step in embedding empowerment is ensuring it's not reliant on individual leaders but is instead woven into the fabric of the organisation. This means:

- **Shifting from leader-led solutions to self-directed problem-solving:** Ensuring people don't always escalate challenges but instead feel confident making decisions.

- **Building structured empowerment into ways of working:** Through team rituals, coaching conversations, and embedded decision-making frameworks.

- **Reinforcing ownership and responsibility at all levels:** So people don't just wait for leadership to set the direction but contribute to shaping it.

A Betterment culture is not one where leaders have to constantly motivate and manage their teams. Instead, it's one where individuals and teams feel empowered to take action, solve problems, and thrive, no matter what challenges arise.

Empowerment isn't about removing leadership. It's about creating conditions where people don't need constant intervention to succeed. It's the difference between a culture of dependency and a culture of capability.

When leaders embed empowerment:

- Teams become more resilient and adaptable.

- They avoid burnout because they're not constantly solving problems for others.

- Organisations achieve higher, more sustainable performance.

By balancing performance and well-being, embedding personal empowerment tools, and ensuring empowerment is structurally embedded, leaders create a culture where people don't just work hard; they thrive.

# KEY INSIGHTS
## FOR BETTERMENT

- **Transformation is essential, but success depends on people:** While organisations invest heavily in transformation, failure rates remain high, not because of poor strategy, but because execution depends on the people who bring it to life. Leaders who engage and equip their teams effectively can accelerate change and ensure lasting impact.

- **Alignment, ownership, and empowerment are the cornerstones of successful transformation:** Without these three pillars, even the best plans fall apart. Alignment ensures clarity, ownership drives commitment, and empowerment enables action. Together, they create cultures where change helps them thrive.

- **Alignment must exist at every level to ensure teams are pulling in the same direction:** True alignment starts at the executive level, extends through functional teams, and strengthens cross-functional collaboration. It is built through trust, focus, and ways of working that create clarity and consistency across an organisation.

- **Ownership is the key to engaging the people responsible for execution:** Most employees don't set strategy, but they determine its success. When frontline teams and middle managers feel accountable and invested, rather than that they're simply following directives, transformation gains momentum and resilience.

- **Empowerment helps people take control of their experience of stress, change, and uncertainty:** No leader can tailor their approach to every individual's needs, which is why organisations must equip people with a personal toolbox for resilience and adaptability. The Surviving-to-Thriving Ladder provides a framework for recognising where people are and taking responsibility for their growth and performance.

# REFLECTIVE QUESTIONS

1. **How aligned is my team?** Thinking about the three pillars of alignment—trust, focus, and action—where is my team strongest, and why? Where do misalignments show up, and how could I improve these as a team to ensure everyone is pulling in the same direction?
2. **How well is my team navigating the uncontrollable?** When faced with challenges outside of their control, do they shift into a responsible mindset, lean into collaboration through Win-Win, or apply abundance thinking with an Opportunity Mindset? What tools could I introduce to help them build ownership?
3. **What problems are my team expecting me to solve that they could be empowered to own?** How can I compassionately shift ownership back to them while providing the guidance and tools they need to succeed?

**WHAT'S NEXT?** Betterment isn't just a leadership philosophy. It's a way of being. It shapes how we approach decisions, relationships, and personal growth, guiding us toward a life of greater alignment, authenticity, and impact. In the next chapter, we explore Betterment as a lifelong mindset, one that bridges the gap between work, life, and self. Ultimately, Betterment isn't just about what we achieve. It's about how we show up every day, the legacy we build, and the ripple effect we create.

# 14

# A Betterment Life—A Philosophy for Thriving in Life and Relationships

*'What you do every day matters more than what you do once in a while.'* Gretchen Rubin

We spend much of our lives striving—to lead, to succeed, to improve. But Betterment isn't just about what we do; it's about how we live.

At its core, Betterment is a philosophy, a way of engaging with life that extends beyond work or leadership into every decision, relationship, and challenge we encounter. It's not about fixing what's broken or chasing perfection; it's about approaching life with intentionality, growth, and purpose.

Earlier in this book, we explored how Betterment transforms teams, leadership, and organisations. Now, we step beyond the professional realm and into something deeper; Betterment as a way of being. This chapter is about integration, not balance; about living in alignment with what truly matters.

Betterment provides a compass for navigating complexity and uncertainty, helping us make decisions rooted in our values rather than in external pressures. It fosters resilience, fuels curiosity, and encourages a mindset where progress matters more than perfection.

Rather than rigid rules, this chapter introduces guiding philosophies, principles that shape how we think, act, and grow. These philosophies build upon the four fundamental shifts of Betterment:

- **From Management to Betterment**: Living intentionally, not just reacting.
- **From Overwhelm to Ownership**: Taking responsibility for our experience.
- **From Competition to Collaboration**: Building trust and creating better outcomes together.
- **From Problem to Possibility**: Seeing opportunity where others see limitation.

Each section offers five guiding philosophies that help us apply Betterment to our everyday lives, shaping how we think, act, and grow.

## Shift One: The Mindset Evolution—From Management to Betterment

*Life isn't just something to get through. It's something to shape into what truly fulfils you.*

A Betterment life isn't about just keeping up, it's about stepping up. Managing is necessary at times, but if we stay in that mode too long, we waste our potential.

Mindset shapes everything. It's not just about how we handle work stress or big life decisions; it's how we experience all of life. We don't have separate mindsets for different domains; we're one person. The way we navigate career pressure, relationships, personal challenges, and even self-doubt comes from the same place. That's why recognising where we are as a whole person—whether we're surviving, coping, managing, leveraging, or thriving—is essential.

Self-awareness is freedom. When we understand our state of mind, we gain the power to respond with intention rather than defaulting to habit. And in a world that's moving faster than ever, we can't afford to wait for stress to disappear before we start living fully. Stress is a natural part of modern life, and more than that, it's a sign that something matters. Instead of trying to escape it, we need to learn how to channel it, using it to drive performance, connection, and growth.

The five philosophies below help us move beyond managing and into Betterment, shaping our experience rather than simply reacting to it.

## Philosophy 1. Live by design, not by default

Often, we don't consciously design our lives. We simply react to what happens. We follow routines, respond to immediate demands, and make choices based on habit or external pressure rather than personal intent. Days become weeks, weeks become years, and before we know it, we've built a life we never intentionally chose.

A Betterment life is different. It's not about waiting for clarity but about creating it. Just as we have explored throughout this book, Betterment isn't about passively managing what already exists; it's about actively shaping what's possible. This means deciding what kind of person we want to be, what values we want to embody, and what impact we want to have, then making choices that align with that vision. We don't need to have everything figured out. If we live with intention, even small, deliberate actions compound into a life of meaning and purpose.

This applies to everything—our career, relationships, and personal growth.

Instead of letting circumstances dictate your direction, ask yourself, *Am I creating this life, or am I just reacting to it?* In the end, you either design your life, or it gets designed for you.

## Philosophy 2. Progress is always better than perfection

Perfectionism convinces us to wait, for the perfect conditions, the perfect plan, the perfect confidence before we act. But waiting for perfection is just another form of avoidance. It keeps us safe, but it also keeps us stuck.

Betterment isn't about perfection; it's about progress. High performers aren't the ones who have everything figured out before they begin. They're the ones who start, adapt, and keep moving forward. Small, consistent improvements compound over time, leading to the transformation that perfectionism never allows.

Ask yourself: *Where am I waiting for perfect conditions when I should be taking imperfect action?*

## Philosophy 3. Growth begins where comfort ends

We are wired to seek safety. We avoid difficult conversations, hesitate to take risks, and gravitate toward what feels familiar. But growth never happens inside the comfort zone. The moments that challenge us the most are the moments that shape us the most.

Earlier in the book, we explored how leaders who embrace discomfort build more resilient teams. The same applies in our personal lives. Whether it's learning something new, stepping into a different phase of life, or confronting a long-standing fear, breakthroughs only come when we stretch beyond what we already know.

If we're waiting for growth to feel easy, we'll wait forever. Instead, let's seek the stretch. Lean into the discomfort of learning, evolving, and becoming.

Ask yourself: *Where am I holding back because it feels safer to stay the same?*

## Philosophy 4. What you nurture grows

Our mindset, relationships, and well-being all respond to what we give them. If we focus on stress, worry, and negativity, they expand. If we focus on gratitude, possibility, and learning, they grow.

We've seen this play out in leadership. Teams that nurture blame and competition become toxic, while teams that reinforce trust and shared success create something stronger together. The same principle applies in life. If we want deeper relationships, we must invest in them. If we want confidence, we need to reinforce it with action. If we want to feel more in control, we must direct our energy toward what we can influence.

Looking at where our attention goes, are we reinforcing fear or courage? Scarcity or opportunity? Avoidance or action? Whatever we choose to nurture today will determine the reality we live in tomorrow.

Ask yourself: *What's one thing I want to see grow in my life, and how can I nurture it more intentionally?*

### Philosophy 5. Big change comes from small, daily actions

Betterment isn't a single decision, it's a way of showing up, day after day, in the small moments that shape who we become. We often think transformation happens in bold, sweeping changes, but in reality, it's the little things we do consistently that determine the direction of our lives.

We've already explored how progress matters more than perfection and how what we nurture grows. This is the same principle in action. A small shift in how we communicate can strengthen relationships over time. A single daily habit can change how we feel, think, and perform. Every choice we make reinforces the kind of person we're becoming.

Ask yourself: *What small, daily action, if repeated consistently, would create the biggest positive shift in my life?*

## Shift Two: The Responsible Mindset—From Overwhelm to Ownership

*A Betterment life is built from the inside out. You may not have been the problem, but you are the solution.*

The Responsible Mindset is about owning our experience, even in the face of uncertainty and adversity. It's easy to fixate on external challenges—difficult people, unexpected financial stress, frustrating work situations, family tensions. But while we can't always control what happens to us, we can always control how we respond.

Ownership isn't about blame; it's about agency. It's the difference between feeling stuck and choosing to act, between being at the mercy of circumstances and finding our power within them. When we stop waiting for the world to change and start taking responsibility for what we can influence, we reclaim control over our lives.

The Responsible Mindset isn't about controlling everything; it's about owning what we can and letting go of what we can't. When we embrace responsibility, we:

- Stop waiting and start acting.
- Focus on what moves us forward.
- Take back control of our experience.

Betterment starts when we stop looking outside for change and start choosing it within.

The five philosophies below help us shift from reacting to leading, not just at work, but in every aspect of life.

## Philosophy 6. Lead with empathy—everyone is carrying something you can't see

It's easy to judge people based on their actions, but we rarely know the full story behind them. The colleague who seems disengaged may be struggling with personal stress. The friend who hasn't reached out may be battling self-doubt. The stranger who cuts you off in traffic may have just received bad news.

Taking responsibility for our lives doesn't mean ignoring what others are going through. It means choosing to respond with empathy instead of assumption. A moment of patience, a kind word, or simply choosing to withhold judgement can completely change a situation.

This applies in relationships, parenting, and leadership. When we approach people with curiosity rather than criticism, we create space for understanding, trust, and connection. Compassion doesn't mean tolerating toxic behaviour; it means leading with grace while maintaining boundaries. Most importantly, we should extend the same empathy and compassion to ourselves.

Ask yourself: *Where can I replace judgement with curiosity? How would responding with empathy change the outcome?*

## Philosophy 7. Focus on what you can control, influence what you can, and let go of the rest

We waste so much energy on things beyond our control—our partner's moods, the economy, what other people think, the past. This fixation leads to frustration, resentment, and feeling powerless.

Instead, apply the CIA Model: Control, Influence, Accept. Ask yourself:

- **What can I directly control**? (My actions, my attitude, my habits.)

- **What can I influence**? (My relationships, my finances, my parenting approach.)

- **What must I accept**? (Other people's choices, external circumstances, the past.)

Think about parenting. You can't control your child's personality, but you can control how you guide them. In a marriage, you can't control your partner's reactions, but you can control how you communicate. The key is directing your energy toward what actually makes a difference.

Ask yourself: *Where am I pouring energy into something I can't control? What's one action I can take within my control instead?*

### Philosophy 8. Stop waiting for things to get easier—build the capacity to handle hard things

Many people live as if life will 'settle down' eventually, that the right time will come to start saving money, set boundaries, or pursue a dream. But waiting doesn't create progress; building capacity does.

Our financial situation may not be ideal, but are we developing the discipline to manage what we have? Our relationship may be strained, but are we working on how to communicate under stress? Our job may not be fulfilling, but are we developing the skills and mindset that will open doors?

Ownership means acknowledging that life will always be unpredictable. Instead of waiting for fewer challenges, we can work on becoming stronger, more adaptable, and more resilient in the face of them.

Ask yourself: *What hard thing am I avoiding because I'm waiting for the 'right time'? What would it look like to start now?*

### Philosophy 9. Your emotions are real, but they don't have to rule you

Stress, anger, disappointment—these emotions are real, but they don't have to control our decisions. Many people either suppress their emotions (*I shouldn't feel this way*) or let emotions dictate their actions (*I feel this way, so I must act on it*). Neither leads to better outcomes.

Think about conflict, whether in parenting, marriage, or at work. If we react emotionally in the moment, we often make things worse. If we step back, regulate our emotions, and respond with intention, we get a different result.

The Responsible Mindset means learning to pause between feeling and acting. Instead of reacting impulsively, ask:

- What is this emotion telling me?

- What response aligns with the person I want to be?

A moment of emotional discipline can change the trajectory of a conversation, a relationship, or even a career.

Ask yourself: *When was the last time I reacted in a way I later regretted? What would my Big Me have done instead?*

## Philosophy 10. Responsibility isn't just about results—it's about how you show up

We often think of responsibility as delivering outcomes, hitting targets, or keeping commitments. But at its core, responsibility is about who we are in the process.

- Are we showing up with integrity, even when it's inconvenient?
- Are we responding with patience, even when others aren't?
- Are we choosing to learn, even when it's easier to stay the same?

In parenting, responsibility isn't just about providing, but about how present and engaged we are. In marriage, it's not just about keeping commitments, it's about fostering connection and respect. In finances, responsibility isn't just about making money, but about managing it wisely.

Ownership isn't just about what we do. It's about who we are in the process.

Ask yourself, *How do I want to show up in my hardest moments? What does responsibility look like for me today?*

# Shift Three: The Win-Win Mindset—From Competition to Collaboration

*Relationships thrive when we build trust, move beyond positions, and create better outcomes together.*

The Win-Win Mindset challenges the idea that success is a zero-sum game. Whether at work, in relationships, or in everyday decisions, we often get stuck in 'Me vs. You' thinking, competing for resources, recognition, or control. But when we move beyond individual positions and focus on shared purpose, we unlock ways forward that serve the whole rather than just the parts.

A Betterment life is not about avoiding conflict, forcing agreement, or compromising our values just to keep the peace. It is about creating outcomes that work for everyone involved, whether in a team, a marriage, a friendship, or a community. It is about finding a better way forward together.

When we embrace Win-Win, we:

- Stop seeing others as obstacles and start finding shared solutions.

- Replace conflict with collaboration, building trust, and stronger relationships.

- Create outcomes that are bigger and better than what we could have achieved alone.

Betterment is not about getting *our way*; it is about creating *a better way*.

The five philosophies below help us build stronger relationships, navigate conflicts with integrity, and create more collaborative, fulfilling outcomes.

## Philosophy 11. Seek shared success, not personal wins

In many situations, whether in business, relationships, or parenting, we default to fighting for our own way. We focus on what we want and assume that if someone else gets what they want, we lose. This is Dominance-Defeat thinking, and it breeds defensiveness, competition, and resentment.

A Win-Win approach shifts the focus. Instead of asking, *How do I get what I want?* we ask, *How do we create success together?* This mindset builds trust and strengthens relationships because people feel valued, heard, and invested in the outcome.

This is especially true in long-term relationships—with partners, children, or colleagues. The goal is not to 'win' an argument, but to align on what truly matters. When we redefine success as something we achieve together, we create outcomes that serve everyone, not just ourselves.

Ask yourself: *Where in my life am I treating a situation as a competition to win when I could seek shared success instead?*

## Philosophy 12. Focus on what really matters, not just on proving a point

So many arguments in life, whether in marriages, friendships, or families, are not about what they seem. We get caught up in the small details of a disagreement, defending our position, proving we are right, or refusing to back down. But what if we stepped back and asked, *Does this really matter in the bigger picture?*

Win-Win thinking is about elevating the conversation beyond the moment. It is about recognising when we are clinging to a position that ultimately does not serve the relationship, the family, or the shared vision.

- In parenting, this means choosing long-term connection over winning a single argument.

- In relationships, it is about prioritising respect over being right.

- In friendships, it is recognising that some things are worth letting go of for the sake of trust and longevity.

When we focus on what truly matters, we free ourselves from unnecessary battles and invest in what creates stronger, more meaningful connections.

Ask yourself: *In my relationships, am I prioritising what really matters, or am I just trying to prove a point?*

## Philosophy 13. Start with trust—because trust unlocks everything else

The strongest relationships, whether personal or professional, are not built on constant verification, scepticism, or micromanagement. They are built on trust.

Too often, we wait for people to earn our trust, holding back until they prove themselves. But the best leaders, partners, and collaborators do not just expect trust, they extend it. They lead with trust, creating an environment where others rise to meet it.

This does not mean being naïve or ignoring red flags. It means recognising that trust is built through both character and competence, then showing up with integrity and following through with action.

- In marriage, this means assuming goodwill rather than suspicion.
- In parenting, it is giving children responsibility and letting them grow into it.
- In leadership, it is trusting people to step up, rather than controlling every detail.

When we trust and show up as trustworthy, we create the conditions for deeper connection, collaboration, and shared success.

Ask yourself: *Am I waiting for trust, or am I creating it?*

## Philosophy 14. Be tough on the challenge, and respectful of people

Conflict is inevitable, but how we approach it determines whether it strengthens or weakens our relationships. Too often, people either avoid conflict altogether or handle it in a way that damages trust.

A Win-Win Mindset means separating the challenge from the

person. It means addressing difficult topics with honesty and clarity without making it personal.

- In friendships, this means being direct about issues while maintaining kindness and respect.

- In family, it means not allowing disagreements to erode love and connection.

- In marriage, it means facing problems as a team, rather than as opponents.

Being 'tough' on the challenge means staying committed to finding the best way forward. Being 'respectful' of people means valuing relationships over being right. The strongest relationships are not ones without conflict; they are ones where conflict is handled with care.

Ask yourself: *Do I approach conflict with the goal of solving the problem, or do I make it personal?*

## Philosophy 15. The best outcomes are created together

We often think that we need to figure things out alone, that we must have all the answers, the plan, or the solution. But real, lasting progress rarely happens in isolation.

A Win-Win approach means co-creating the way forward, rather than dictating it. Whether it is in a family, a partnership, or a community, the best outcomes happen when people feel heard, engaged, and invested in the path forward.

- In parenting, this means involving children in decisions that affect them, helping them develop responsibility.

- In relationships, it is about navigating challenges together rather than dictating the terms of compromise.

- In communities, it is about finding shared paths forward, rather than assuming one person has the right answer.

The strongest relationships and the most fulfilling experiences are not created through individual solutions. They are shaped by collaborative, intentional choices.

Ask yourself: *Am I making decisions in isolation, or am I creating better outcomes with the people involved?*

## Shift Four: The Opportunity Mindset—From Problem to Possibility

*Opportunities don't create themselves, we create them.*

The Opportunity Mindset is about how we meet life's challenges. It is not about blind optimism or pretending difficulties do not exist. It is about choosing how we respond, whether we get stuck in limitation or open ourselves to new possibilities.

When life throws an unexpected challenge our way, it is natural to feel disheartened. But if we stay in that place, we limit our potential moving forward. A Betterment life is about looking beyond the problem to the future we want to create, and working backwards from there.

When we embrace the Opportunity Mindset, we:

- See possibilities where others see dead ends.
- Turn obstacles into stepping stones.
- Create a life that is not just reactive, but intentionally designed.

Betterment is not about waiting for the perfect moment. It is about expanding what is possible through action, creativity, and mindset.

The following five philosophies help us live each day with an expansive mindset, transforming obstacles into stepping stones and unlocking the opportunities hidden in plain sight.

## Philosophy 16. Expand your perspective to expand your possibilities

When something does not go as planned, whether it is a career setback, a financial strain, or a personal disappointment, it is easy to dwell on what went wrong. Feeling disheartened is normal. But if we stay in that mindset, we get stuck. The longer we focus on the problem, the smaller our world becomes.

The key to creating new opportunities is to lift our gaze beyond the challenge and toward a future we want to build. Instead of asking, *What went wrong?* we can ask, *What could be next?* starting with the possibility and working backwards from there.

- A job loss could be a chance to pivot toward work that excites us.

- A financial challenge could be the moment that teaches us how to build long-term security.

- A personal setback could be the push to re-evaluate and create a life more aligned with our values.

Ask yourself: *Am I fixating on what is lost, or am I looking for what is possible?*

## Philosophy 17. Use constraints to fuel creativity

We often believe we need more—more money, more time, more resources—to create something meaningful. But some of life's best experiences, solutions, and breakthroughs are born from working with what we already have.

Think about a family on a tight budget. Instead of lamenting what they cannot afford, they turn it into a challenge: *What is the best adventure we can create for under* $50? The result? A memorable road trip, a themed home movie night, or a hike with a picnic, experiences richer than anything money could buy.

Creativity flourishes when we shift from 'I don't have enough' to 'What can I do with what I have?'

Ask yourself: *Where in my life am I seeing limitation instead of possibility? How can I turn a constraint into a creative challenge?*

## Philosophy 18. Ask springboard questions, not roadblock questions

The questions we ask shape our lives. Some questions keep us stuck, while others propel us forward. A roadblock question focuses on limitation and reinforces the problem: *Why is this happening to me? What is wrong? Who is to blame?*

A springboard question, on the other hand, launches us into possibility. *What does this challenge make possible? What strengths can I bring to this situation? How could this be the start of something better?*

Every breakthrough, whether in personal growth, relationships, or decision-making, begins with a better question.

Ask yourself: *Are my questions leading me toward action and possibility, or are they keeping me stuck in frustration?*

## Philosophy 19. Think abundantly—there is more than enough for everyone

Scarcity thinking tells us that success, opportunities, and resources are limited, that if someone else gets ahead, we fall behind. But in reality, the more we give, the more we create.

- Sharing our knowledge does not diminish our expertise. It amplifies it.

- Celebrating someone else's success does not take away from ours. It strengthens relationships and opportunities.

- Being generous with time, advice, and encouragement does

not leave us with less. It makes us a magnet for collaboration and growth.

When we operate with an abundance mindset, we see opportunities not just for ourselves, but for those around us. The more we contribute to others' success, the more we open doors for our own.

Ask yourself: *Where in my life am I holding back because of scarcity thinking? How can I be more generous with my time, knowledge, or support?*

## Philosophy 20. Opportunities don't create themselves—we create them

People often wait for the right opportunity to appear—the perfect job, the right relationship, the ideal conditions. But Betterment is not about waiting; it is about creating.

- The best careers are not stumbled upon. They are built through action and learning.

- The best relationships are not found. They are shaped through connection and effort.

- The most fulfilling lives do not happen by chance. They are designed, moment by moment, through choices.

Opportunities are not given. They are made.

Ask yourself: *Where am I waiting for an opportunity instead of taking steps to create it?*

These philosophies aren't rules to follow. They're guiding principles to help us navigate life with more clarity, confidence, and intention. They aren't about adding more to our plate or about striving for perfection; they're about shifting how we think, so that Betterment becomes a natural way of being rather than another thing to manage.

They apply everywhere. Whether we're leading a team, raising a family, building a career, interacting with a stranger, or working toward personal growth, these mindsets are just as relevant in small, everyday choices as they are in major life decisions. When we find ourselves stuck, overwhelmed, or uncertain, we can come back to them. We can use them as a lens to reframe challenges, create new opportunities, and take ownership of what we can control. Betterment isn't about getting everything right. It's about consistently choosing to learn, grow, and get a bit better every day.

# KEY INSIGHTS
## FOR BETTERMENT

- **Betterment is a way of being, not just something we do:** It's not about achieving perfection but about embracing growth, purpose, and intentionality in every aspect of life.

- **Life can be shaped, not just managed:** Many people live in a reactive state, handling responsibilities but rarely designing their lives with intention. Betterment shifts us from passive management to active creation.

- **Progress matters more than perfection:** Small, consistent improvements over time lead to profound transformation, both personally and professionally.

- **Betterment acts as a compass:** In a world of complexity and uncertainty, adopting a Betterment mindset provides clarity, which helps guide decisions that align with personal values and long-term growth.

- **Legacy is built through daily actions:** The impact we leave on others isn't determined by grand gestures but by the small, everyday choices we make to show up with purpose and authenticity.

# REFLECTIVE QUESTIONS

1. **Which of the twenty philosophies resonated with you the most?** Why did it stand out, and how might applying it shift how you experience challenges, decisions, or relationships?
2. **Which philosophy do you find the hardest to live by?** What gets in the way—old habits, external pressures, fear of change? What would it take to integrate this more fully into your life?
3. **Where do you notice inconsistencies in how you apply these philosophies across different areas of your life?** Do you show up with more intentionality at work than in your personal life? Do you embrace growth in some areas but avoid discomfort in others? What would it look like to bring more alignment across all aspects of life?

**WHAT'S NEXT?** Betterment isn't just a personal pursuit. It's a force for change. In the final chapter, we explore how Betterment extends beyond the self, shaping the teams, families, communities, and organisations we are part of. True Betterment doesn't stop at personal success; it creates ripple effects that influence the world around us. We discover how small shifts in mindset and action can drive meaningful impact and define our mission for Betterment, one that turns growth into contribution and intention into lasting change.

# 15

# Betterment Beyond the Self—A Mission for a Better World

*'Do your little bit of good where you are; it's those little bits of good put together that overwhelm the world.' Desmond Tutu*

## The Shift from Personal Growth to Collective Impact

What if one small shift in perspective could change not just your life, but the lives of millions? What if a single idea, acted on with conviction, could transform entire systems, proving that Betterment isn't just personal, but deeply collective?

Most people begin the journey of Betterment focused on themselves—their goals, growth, and personal success. That's a natural starting point. We all want to improve our lives, find fulfilment, and feel like we are making progress.

But something profound happens when we expand our focus beyond ourselves.

The real power of Betterment isn't found in personal success alone. It's found when we direct our energy from our own needs to something bigger. When we stop asking, *How can I improve?* and start asking, *How can I contribute?* is when we step into something truly transformational.

Betterment, at its core, is a force for creating something better, not just for us, but for the world around us. The way we approach challenges, relationships, and opportunities doesn't just influence our outcomes. It shapes the environments we are part of.

This shift—from personal growth to collective impact—is what turns Betterment from a mindset into a movement. Few stories illustrate this better than the journey of Muhammad Yunus and the birth of microfinance.

### The Story of Muhammad Yunus: A Single Act that Transformed Millions of Lives[1] (Case Study)

In the 1970s, Muhammad Yunus, an economics professor in Bangladesh, faced a realisation that changed everything. He had spent years teaching theories about economic growth, yet outside his university walls, poverty was an inescapable cycle.

One day, he met a group of women who made bamboo stools and who were permanently trapped in financial struggle. The reason? They had to borrow money at exploitative rates just to buy materials, meaning they never made enough profit to escape debt.

Traditional banks refused to lend to them. They were considered 'too risky' for even the smallest loans.

Yunus could have stopped there. He could have focused on his own career, continued publishing research, and carried on with his life. However, instead of accepting the broken system, he made a simple yet transformational decision. He personally loaned $27 to forty-two women, just enough for them to buy materials without predatory lending conditions.

The results were astonishing.

They paid the loans back in full. They reinvested in their businesses. They gained financial independence. And, perhaps most importantly, they proved that the poor were not unreliable borrowers, but capable entrepreneurs in their own right.

That small shift, from self to service, from individual to impact, became something far greater.

Yunus founded Grameen Bank, which pioneered microfinance, the practice of giving small, accessible loans to individuals who lacked traditional credit. Since its creation, microfinance has helped millions of people build businesses, escape poverty, and change their futures.

By 2006, Yunus and Grameen Bank were awarded the Nobel Peace Prize for their impact on global poverty. His belief in a better way didn't just change banking. It changed lives, industries, and entire financial systems worldwide.

## Betterment as a Movement: The True Power of Going Beyond the Self

The story of Muhammad Yunus shows us something essential: Betterment reaches its full power only when it extends beyond personal success. His success wasn't about personal wealth, fame, or achievement. It was about choosing to see a broken system differently, and acting to make it better.

This is the fundamental shift of Betterment at scale:

- From self-improvement to service. Instead of just growing for himself, Yunus used his knowledge to lift others.

- From winning alone to winning together. He didn't just prove a personal theory; he created a model where millions of people could thrive.

- From problem to possibility. He didn't see poverty as an unfixable problem. He saw a system that needed to be reimagined.

This is why Betterment is so much more than self-improvement. The real breakthrough comes when we redirect our energy outward, when we take everything we've learned and ask, *How can I use this to create something better beyond myself?*

During the COVID-19 pandemic, an Australian woman named

Dr Catherine Barrett demonstrated this shift in action when she founded 'The Kindness Pandemic'.[2] What started as a simple idea, encouraging people to share and celebrate acts of kindness, quickly became a movement, attracting hundreds of thousands of people who wanted to make a difference. In a time of fear and uncertainty, these small acts—paying for a stranger's groceries, writing letters to aged care residents, leaving flowers on a neighbour's doorstep—created a ripple effect, lifting the spirits of entire communities.

Dr Barrett didn't set out to build a global initiative. She simply saw an opportunity to bring more compassion into the world and took action. In doing so, she proved that Betterment doesn't require wealth, status, or influence. It begins with everyday choices—choosing to contribute, to support, to uplift others in whatever way we can. When enough people make that choice, Betterment shifts from being a personal practice to a shared movement, one that has the power to transform communities, cultures, and even entire systems.

## From Individual Growth to Collective Impact

Betterment begins with personal growth, but it finds its greatest impact in contribution.

When we apply this lesson to our own lives, we start to see new possibilities:

- **In leadership**: The best leaders don't just improve their skills; they empower others to grow, thrive, and succeed.

- **In business**: The most successful companies don't just maximise profits; they create lasting value for employees, customers, and communities.

- **In daily life**: The moments we remember most are rarely about personal wins. They're about the impact we had on others.

Betterment isn't just about success. It's about significance.

Muhammad Yunus didn't wait for permission. He didn't need a grand plan to start. He just saw a better way, took action, and let that action create ripples.

[ And that's the challenge for all of us. Where in our life do we see an opportunity to create a better way? What small action could set off a ripple effect that goes beyond us? ]

Betterment isn't just a philosophy. It's a movement. Every movement begins with one person who chooses to shift their focus from self to service, and acts.

## The Ripple Effect—How Small Shifts Create Big Change

### Betterment is contagious

When we embody ownership, collaboration, and possibility, we inspire others to do the same. A single shift in mindset, behaviour, or leadership doesn't only improve our own experience. It has the power to shape the culture of our teams, families, and communities.

Think about it.

- A leader who shifts from micromanagement to empowerment doesn't just lighten their own workload. They create an environment where people feel trusted, motivated, and able to do their best work.

- A parent who models resilience and curiosity teaches their children to navigate challenges with confidence, rather than avoidance or fear.

- A business that embraces the Betterment Mindset doesn't just improve its results. It sets a new standard, shaping its industry and the way people work.

These are the ripple effects of Betterment in action, small shifts that, over time, create profound change.

One company that has demonstrated this ripple effect on a global scale is Patagonia.

**Patagonia: A Business with a Ripple Effect Beyond Profit[3]**
**Case Study**

Few companies have embraced the Betterment Mindset as completely as Patagonia. From the beginning, it was never just about selling outdoor gear. It was about redefining how business could be done.

When founder Yvon Chouinard started making climbing equipment, he wasn't thinking about building an empire. He simply wanted better gear. But as the business grew, he began to ask a bigger question: What if a company can prioritise people and the planet as much as profit?

This shift in thinking changed everything.

Patagonia took responsibility for its impact on the environment long before sustainability was a mainstream concern. It pioneered the use of recycled materials, made an early commitment to organic cotton, and openly shared its supply chain challenges, setting a precedent that influenced an entire industry.

The company also challenged traditional business thinking. Instead of pushing for constant consumerism, it ran a now-famous campaign urging customers not to buy its products unless they genuinely needed them. It created a repair and resale program to extend the lifespan of its gear. It redirected profits toward climate action, going so far as to transfer company ownership to a trust dedicated to protecting the planet.

These decisions went against conventional business logic, yet Patagonia thrived. And more importantly, it inspired a shift across industries. Companies that once focused solely on profit began to see the value of sustainability, transparency, and long-term thinking.

This is the ripple effect of Betterment in action. One company, committed to a better way of doing business, set a new benchmark that others were compelled to follow.

## Small Shifts, Big Change

Patagonia's story is an example of how one shift, one decision to do things differently, can have an impact far beyond the individual or organisation that makes it. This concept isn't limited to global brands or industry leaders. In everyday life, the smallest changes can create meaningful ripple effects.

### The Train Conductor Spreading Joy

*Sometimes, the most powerful ripple effects come from the smallest moments. I was on a train heading to North Sydney when something unexpected happened.*

*The train conductor came over the intercom, delivering the usual announcements—'mind the gap' and the like—but there was something different about her tone. She wasn't just reading a script; she was having a chat with all of us.*

*Sprinkled between the standard safety messages were little moments of warmth.*

*'I hope you're enjoying the sunshine today.'*

*'Don't forget to smile.'*

*It was positively infectious.*

*People who had been glued to their phones or lost in thought started looking up. They made eye contact, smiled, and silently shared a moment together. The entire carriage felt lighter, no small feat for a morning commuter train.*

*Then, as we pulled into North Sydney, she delivered her final message.*

*'We are now arriving at our final destination. Please don't forget anything that's important to you. It's been my pleasure to bring you to your destination today. Now go forth and conquer the world.'*

*Yes, she actually said, 'Go forth and conquer the world.'*

*I can't speak for everyone, but I certainly had a bounce in my step as I alighted the train. That energy stayed with me. I took it into my first meeting of the day, and the energy in the room lifted too.*

*The impact was exponential, and it all started with one person choosing to show up differently and make the world around her better.*

*This train conductor wasn't leading a global movement. She wasn't setting out to change the world. She was simply bringing her values into her work and in doing so, she changed the experience of hundreds of people, even if only for a moment.*

That's the thing about Betterment; it doesn't have to be grand to be powerful.

We often think of influence in terms of major achievements—leading companies, launching initiatives, making headlines. But more often, it's the small, everyday choices that make the biggest difference.

- A teacher who takes a moment to encourage a struggling student could change the course of their education.

- A colleague who consistently acknowledges the work of others could shift an entire workplace culture.

- A stranger who offers kindness at the right moment could turn someone's day around.

Betterment isn't about being on a crusade. It's about recognising that we are all creating ripples, every day, whether we realise it or not.

That train conductor may never know the impact she had that day. But she didn't need to. She simply chose to bring a little more energy, warmth, and humanity into her role. Because of that, she changed the experience of everyone who stepped onto her train.

Even the smallest shift can change everything.

### What Ripple Effect are You Creating?

We often underestimate the influence we have on those around us. Every day, whether we realise it or not, we are setting a tone, through the way we communicate, the way we handle challenges, and the way we engage with others.

The question is: What kind of ripple effect do you want to create?

Are you reinforcing old habits and patterns, or are you modelling the mindset you want to see in those around you?

Are you waiting for change to happen, or are you willing to be the one who starts it?

Betterment isn't about waiting for permission. It's about choosing to create something better, one decision, one action, one conversation at a time.

## Living by a Betterment Mission

### From Personal Growth to Purposeful Impact

We've explored how Betterment isn't just about improving ourselves. It's about the ripple effect we create in the world around us. We've seen how small shifts in mindset and behaviour can transform teams, families, and communities. We've seen how companies like Patagonia and movements like The Kindness Pandemic started with simple actions but grew into something much bigger.

Now, it's time to bring Betterment closer to home.

This isn't about waiting for the right opportunity or finding a grand purpose. It's about recognising the way we already make things better and choosing to do it with more intention.

This is your Betterment Mission.

A Betterment Mission is the way you choose to make the world better through your everyday actions.

It's not a title or a career path. It's not something you need to achieve. It's simply the way you show up, the impact you want to have, and the contribution you want to make, no matter where you are or what you do.

It can be big or small, direct or subtle, professional or personal.

- The train conductor's Betterment Mission might be to bring more joy into the world, one lighthearted announcement at a time.

- A parent or teacher's Betterment Mission might be to help people see their potential, so they believe in themselves a little more.

- A business leader's Betterment Mission might be to create environments where people thrive by fostering trust, collaboration, and purpose.

It's not about a job or a role. It's about the energy you bring to the world and the impact you make.

## Discovering Your Betterment Mission

Your Betterment Mission isn't something to force. It's something you already live, in small ways, every day. It's simply about uncovering it and ensuring it drives how you show up each day.

To uncover it, reflect on these three simple questions:

**1. What do you naturally bring into the world?** Think about the qualities, energy, or strengths that feel natural to you. Are you someone who lifts others up? Do you bring clarity, creativity, or connection into spaces? When people walk away from interacting with you, what do you hope they feel?

*Example: I love making people laugh and lightening the mood.*

**2. What moments feel the most meaningful?** Think about times when you've felt truly connected, fulfilled, or that you've made a difference. Was it when you helped someone? When you solved a problem? When you created something that inspired others?

*Example: I feel most fulfilled when I see someone's confidence grow because of something I said or did.*

**3. What's one small way you can live this, every day?** Your Betterment Mission isn't about a single big moment. It's about choosing to bring it into daily life. If your strength is encouragement, can you find small ways to uplift people? If your strength is problem-solving, can you help make things simpler or better for others?

*Example: I can make the world better by making people feel seen, valued, and encouraged in everyday interactions.*

**4. Putting it Together**

Once you've reflected on these questions, you don't need a perfect statement, just something that feels right to you. Here's a simple way to express it:

*I make the world better by [how you naturally contribute] so that [the impact it has on others].*

Examples:

- I make the world better by bringing warmth and humour so that people feel lighter and more connected.

- I make the world better by helping others see their strengths so that they feel more confident in themselves.

- I make the world better by creating spaces of trust and inclusion so that people feel safe to be themselves.

You can shape it however you like. It just needs to feel true to you.

## Living Your Betterment Mission

Your Betterment Mission isn't a statement you write down and forget. It's something you live through small, intentional moments.

Each day, ask yourself:

- How can I bring this to life today?
- Who might benefit from this in a small way?
- Where am I already doing this, even without realising?

There's no pressure to get it perfect. Betterment isn't about perfection. It's about presence. It's about choosing to bring more of what matters into the world, in whatever way you can.

## Betterment in Action

Living your Betterment Mission involves bringing it into your choices, conversations, and daily interactions. The true power of Betterment lies in how it's applied, not just in leadership, but in the way you show up in your teams, families, and communities.

## Lead by Example

Betterment starts with how you show up. The most powerful way to inspire change isn't through words, it's through action.

- If you want more trust in your team, be the one who builds it.
- If you want a more collaborative culture, model generosity and shared success.
- If you want a more supportive community, be the first to extend a hand.

People don't adopt Betterment because they are told to. They adopt it because they see it working.

When you live Betterment consistently, it becomes contagious.

## Create Win-Win Impact

A Betterment Mindset isn't just about self-improvement. It's about elevating others alongside yourself.

- A leader who empowers their team doesn't just achieve better results, they also create an environment where everyone thrives.
- A business that prioritises ethical decisions builds long-term trust, benefiting both people and profits.
- A friend who supports and encourages lifts not just one person, but the people that person goes on to influence.

Betterment isn't about choosing between success and service. It's about finding ways to make both possible.

## Turn Problems into Possibilities

One of the simplest ways to practise Betterment daily is to shift from seeing obstacles to seeing opportunities.

- Instead of frustration, ask, *What's another way to approach this?*
- Instead of blame, ask, *How can we solve this together?*
- Instead of resistance to change, ask, *What's possible here?*

Betterment thrives in curiosity, creativity, and optimism. The more you challenge yourself and others to think this way, the more it becomes the norm.

## Expand the Conversation

Betterment isn't meant to stay personal. It's something you bring into the spaces you influence.

- In teams, introduce a culture of learning, ownership, and shared wins.

- In families, model resilience, kindness, and open conversations.
- In communities, support initiatives that create meaningful impact.

Betterment spreads when you share what you learn, not as a lesson, but as a way of being.

**Commit to Continuous Growth**

Betterment isn't about having all the answers. It's about always asking better questions.

- How can I show up with more intention today?
- What is one small thing I can improve?
- Where can I challenge myself to grow?

Betterment isn't a destination, it's a practice. The more you engage with it, the more natural it becomes.

**Betterment Becomes a Movement When it's Lived**

Betterment is not something you do once. It's something you choose every day.
It's in the way you lead.
The way you contribute.
The way you challenge the status quo.
The more you live it, the more it expands, first in you, then in others, and eventually, into something much bigger.
The only question is, How will you bring Betterment to life today?

# Imagine a World Built on Betterment

Imagine a world where more people embrace ownership, collaboration, and possibility.

# BETTERMENT BEYOND THE SELF CHAPTER 15

A world where, instead of defaulting to frustration or limitation, the consistent question is, *What's the better way?*

> What if workplaces weren't just about productivity, but about helping people grow and thrive?
> 
> What if leadership wasn't about control, but about creating trust and shared success?

What if communities weren't built on competition, but on connection and contribution?

This is the world Betterment creates, not through grand, sweeping changes, but through daily choices, lived consistently, by ordinary people who choose to make things better in whatever way they can.

## Betterment Starts with a Choice

Betterment isn't just a concept, it's a way of being that starts with a single choice.

- A choice to see possibility instead of obstacles.
- A choice to take ownership, rather than waiting for change to happen.
- A choice to lead with intention, in whatever space you influence.

The impact of this choice is bigger than you. It extends to every person you interact with, every decision you make, every culture you help shape.

When enough people choose Betterment, not just for themselves, but for the world around them, it becomes a movement.

## What's Your Next Step?

Now, it's over to you.

How will you take Betterment forward, from a mindset to a mission?

You don't need a perfect plan. You don't need to start a movement.

**PART 5** BETTERMENT MASTERY

You simply need to ask:

- Where can I bring more intention into how I show up?
- How can I create a ripple effect through small, daily actions?
- What's one thing I can do today to bring Betterment to life?

The world doesn't change in a single moment.

It changes in the small, daily decisions of people who choose to live with purpose, integrity, and impact.

So, the question is, What role will you play?

# KEY INSIGHTS
## FOR BETTERMENT

- **Betterment reaches its full potential when it extends beyond the self:** Personal growth is just the starting point. The real impact happens when we shift from *How can I improve?* to *How can I contribute?* turning Betterment from a mindset into a movement.

- **Small actions can create extraordinary ripple effects:** Whether it's a $27 loan, a message of kindness, or a shift in business values, the most powerful changes often start small. What matters is taking action.

- **Contribution is not about wealth, status, or position, it's about intention:** We don't need to be a global leader to make a difference. Our daily choices—how we lead, support, and uplift others—shape the world around us.

- **Betterment is contagious:** When we lead with ownership, optimism, and generosity, we inspire others to do the same. A single shift in mindset or behaviour can change the culture of a workplace, community, or even an industry.

- **The best leaders, businesses, and communities prioritise shared success:** True Betterment isn't about individual wins. It's about creating value that benefits everyone, from sustainable business practices to empowering those around us.

# REFLECTIVE
# QUESTIONS

1. **Where in your life can you shift from self-improvement to contribution?** Think about a skill, experience, or insight you have. How could you use it to positively impact others?
2. **What small action could create a ripple effect?** Reflect on a moment when someone's words or actions uplifted you. How could you pay that forward in your daily life?
3. **What legacy are you creating through your everyday choices?** If someone observed how you show up at work, in relationships, or in your community, what message would they take from it? Is it the impact you want to leave?

# A Final Word

Betterment isn't a destination, it's a practice. A way of thinking, leading, and showing up that evolves as you do. The work of mindset never stops, because growth never stops. There will always be new challenges to navigate, new opportunities to explore, and new ways to stretch beyond what you thought was possible.

Some days, progress will feel easy. Other days, it won't. The real power lies in showing up anyway, choosing, again and again, to take ownership, to collaborate, to see possibility where others see limitation. That's what sets those who thrive apart from those who stay stuck.

The question isn't if you'll face challenges. You will. The question is how you'll meet them. And that choice, every time, is yours.

# Notes and References

## Chapter 1: Mindset as Your Greatest Asset—Thriving in a World of Change and Uncertainty

1. **Justin Trudeau quote:** Trudeau, J. 2018, Keynote remarks for World Economic Forum 2018, World Economic Forum, https://www.weforum.org/stories/2018/01/pm-keynote-remarks-for-world-economic-forum-2018/.
2. **Groundbreaking Study:** Keller, A., Litzelman, K., Wisk, L.E., Maddox, T., Cheng, E.R., Creswell, P.D. & Witt, W.P. 2012, 'Does the perception that stress affects health matter? The association with health and mortality', *Health Psychology*, vol. 32, no. 5, pp. 677-684.
3. **Stress study:** Crum, A.J., Salovey, P. & Achor, S. 2013, 'Rethinking stress: The role of mindsets in determining the stress response', *Journal of Personality and Social Psychology*, vol. 104, no. 4, pp. 716-733.
4. **Exercise and mindset study:** Crum, A.J. & Langer, E.J. 2007, 'Mind-set matters: Exercise and the placebo effect', *Psychological Science*, vol. 18, no. 2, pp. 165-171.
5. **Role in healthy aging:** Levy, B.R., Slade, M.D., Kunkel, S.R. & Kasl, S.V. 2002, 'Longevity increased by positive self-perceptions of aging', *Journal of Personality and Social Psychology*, vol. 83, no. 2, pp. 261-270.
6. **Bryan Cranston's breakthrough:** Cranston, B. 2016, *Bryan Cranston's Advice to Aspiring Actors*, Youtube, https://www.youtube.com/watch?v=v1WiCGq-PcY.
7. **Toyota case study:** Liker, J.K. 2004, *The Toyota Way: 14 Management Principles from the World's Greatest Manufacturer*, McGraw-Hill, New York.

8. **NUMMI Transformation:** Shook, J. 2010, 'How to change a culture: Lessons from NUMMI', *MIT Sloan Management Review*, vol. 51, no. 2, pp. 63-68.
9. **Kaizen principles:** Bennett, D., Blackburn, R., Demirbas, D. 2019, *Kaizen Philosophy in a Modern Day Business*, Istanbul University Press, DOI: 10.26650/B/SS05.2019.001.
10. **Absenteeism and idea implementation:** Adler, P.S. (1992) 'The learning bureaucracy: New United Motor Manufacturing, Inc.', *Research in Organizational Behavior*, 15, pp. 111–194.
11. **Studies about perceived control and stress**
    a. Georgescu, D. and Duiu, A. (2019) 'The relationship between locus of control, personal behavior, self-efficacy, and resilience', *Romanian Journal of Cognitive Behavioral Therapy and Hypnosis*, 6(1-2), pp. 1-10.
    b. Sharma, S. and Sharma, M. (2014) 'The relationship between locus of control and perceived stress among college students', *Indian Journal of Mental Health*, 1(1), pp. 38-45.
    c. Ivanov, L. (2023) 'A study of the relationship between locus of control and self-monitoring to psychological resilience', *European Scientific Journal*, 19(6), pp. 32-45. Available at: https://eujournal.org/index.php/esj/article/view/15864
12. **Opportunity-focused outlook: McKinsey & Company** (2023) *Developing a resilient, adaptable workforce for an uncertain future*. Available at: https://www.mckinsey.com/capabilities/people-and-organizational-performance/our-insights/developing-a-resilient-adaptable-workforce-for-an-uncertain-future

## Chapter 2: The Betterment Ladder—Steps from Surviving to Thriving

1. **Impact of surviving and coping:** Psychology Today 2020, *Why Survival Mode Isn't the Best Way to Live*, https://www.psychologytoday.com/us/blog/lifting-the-veil-trauma/202006/why-survival-mode-isnt-the-best-way-live.
2. Feel Good Psychology 2024, *Survival Mode Part 1: How Stress Impacts Your Well-Being*, https://feelgoodpsychology.com.au/survival-mode-part-1/.
3. **Chronic Stress and Creativity:** Liu, S., Erkkilä, M.M. and Pakarinen, E. (2020) 'Neural mechanisms underlying creativity: The effects of stress on large-scale brain networks', *Frontiers in Psychology*, 11, p. 585969. Available at: https://www.frontiersin.org/articles/10.3389/fpsyg.2020.585969/full
4. **Prioritise urgency over importance**: Zhu, M., Yang, A.X. and Hsee, C.K. (2018) 'The mere urgency effect', *Journal of Consumer Research*, 45(3), pp. 673–690. Available at: https://academic.oup.com/jcr/article-abstract/45/3/673/4847790
5. **Goal-Setting Theory and Performance:** Locke, E.A. and Latham, G.P. (2002) 'Building a practically useful theory of goal setting and task motivation: A 35-year odyssey', *American Psychologist*, 57(9), pp. 705–717.
6. **Stretch Goals and Organizational Performance**: Sitkin, S.B., See, K.E., Miller, C.C., Lawless, M.W. and Carton, A.M. (2011) 'The paradox of stretch goals: Organizations in pursuit of the seemingly impossible', *Academy of Management Review*, 36(3), pp. 544–566.
7. **Flow state:** Alameda, C., Sanabria, D., and Ciria, L.F. (2022) 'The brain in flow: a systematic review on the neural basis of the flow state', *Cortex*, 154, pp. 348–364. Available at: https://doi.org/10.1016/j.cortex.2022.06.005

8. **Self-efficacy and performance**
   a. Honicke, T. and Broadbent, J. (2016) 'The influence of academic self-efficacy on academic performance: A systematic review', *Learning and Individual Differences*, 49, pp. 149–162. Available at: https://www.sciencedirect.com/science/article/pii/S1747938X15000639
   b. Burić, I. and Soric, I. (2017) 'The role of academic self-efficacy in self-regulated learning: The relationship with motivation, metacognition, and achievement', *Learning and Individual Differences*, 55, pp. 29–37. Available at: https://www.sciencedirect.com/science/article/pii/S1041608017301735
   c. Zhang, X., Klassen, R.M. and Wang, Y. (2020) 'Academic self-efficacy and academic performance: A meta-analytic review', *BMC Medical Education*, 20(1), p. 95.
9. **Impact of purpose and values**
   a. **Purpose in Life and Associated Cognitive and Affective Mechanisms**
   Martela, F. and Steger, M.F. (2024) 'Purpose in life: A scoping review of associated cognitive and affective mechanisms', *Journal of Happiness Studies*. Available at: https://link.springer.com/article/10.1007/s10902-024-00771-6
   b. **The Relationship Between Meaning in Life and Subjective Well-Being**
   Disabato, D.J., Kashdan, T.B., Short, J.L. and Jarden, A. (2017) 'The relationship between meaning in life and subjective well-being: A meta-analysis', *Journal of Happiness Studies*, 18(3), pp. 905–919. Available at: https://link.springer.com/article/10.1007/s10902-014-9540-5
   c. **Purpose in Life as a Protective Factor Against Depression**
   Schippers, M.C. and Ziegler, N. (2023) 'Purpose in life as an asset for well-being and a protective factor against

depression: Evidence from longitudinal studies', *Frontiers in Psychology*, 14, p. 1250279. Available at: https://www.frontiersin.org/articles/10.3389/fpsyg.2023.1250279/full

10. **Values-driven behaviour and thriving**: Dela Cruz, A.J. (2021) 'The impact of values education on students' academic and personal growth: A qualitative study', *CMC Research Journal*, 5(2), pp. 45–60. Available at: https://research.cmc.edu.ph/index.php/journals/article/view/161

11. **Beyond-the-self goals and fulfillment**: Koltko-Rivera, M.E. (2006) 'Rediscovering the later version of Maslow's hierarchy of needs: Self-transcendence and opportunities for theory, research, and unification', *Review of General Psychology*, 10(4), pp. 302–317.

## Chapter 3: Stress Mastery—An Essential Skill for Betterment in a Fast-Paced World

1. **Collective beliefs about stress:** NPR, Robert Wood Johnson Foundation and Harvard School of Public Health (2014) Burden of stress in America survey. NPR/Robert Wood Johnson Foundation/Harvard School of Public Health. [Conducted 5 March – 8 April 2014, with 2,505 respondents].

2. **Beliefs more harmful:** Keller, A., Litzelman, K., Wisk, L.E., Maddox, T., Cheng, E.R., Creswell, P.D. & Witt, W.P. 2012, 'Does the perception that stress affects health matter? The association with health and mortality', *Health Psychology*, vol. 32, no. 5, pp. 677-684.

3. **Book:** McGonigal, K. 2015, *The Upside of Stress: Why Stress is Good for You, and How to Get Good at It*, Avery, New York.

4. **DHEA and Growth Index:**
    a. Boudarene, M., Legros, J.J. & Timsit-Berthier, M. 2001, 'Study of the stress response: Role of anxiety, cortisol, and DHEAs', *L'Encéphale*, vol. 28, no. 2, pp. 139–146.

b. Wemm, S., Koone, T., Blough, E.R., Mewaldt, S. & Bardi, M. 2010, 'The role of DHEA in relation to problem-solving and academic performance', *Biological Psychology*, vol. 85, no. 1, pp. 53–61.
5. **The Science of the challenge vs. threat response**
   a. Crum, A.J., Salovey, P. & Achor, S. 2013, 'Rethinking stress: The role of mindsets in determining the stress response', *Journal of Personality and Social Psychology*, vol. 104, no. 4, pp. 716-733.
   b. Crum, A.J., Akinola, M., Martin, A. & Fath, S. 2017, 'The role of stress mindset in shaping cognitive, emotional, and physiological responses to challenging social situations', *Anxiety, Stress & Coping*, vol. 30, no. 4, pp. 379-395.
6. **Fortune 500 company:** McGonigal, K. 2015, *The Upside of Stress: Why Stress is Good for You, and How to Get Good at It*, Avery, New York. Pp. 28-29.
7. **Heart Rate Variability (HVR) & stress resilience**: Shaffer, F. & Ginsberg, J.P. 2017, 'An overview of heart rate variability metrics and norms', *Frontiers in Neuroscience*, vol. 11, article 758.
8. **Smiling and stress reduction – even fake smiling**
   a. Kraft, T.L. & Pressman, S.D. 2012, 'Grin and bear it: The influence of manipulated facial expressions on the stress response', *Psychological Science*, vol. 23, no. 11, pp. 1372–1378.
   b. Wollmer, M.A., de Boer, C., Kalak, N., Beck, J., Götz, T., Schmidt, T., Hodzic, M. & Kruger, T.H.C. 2012, 'Facing depression with botulinum toxin: A randomized controlled trial', *Journal of Psychiatric Research*, vol. 46, no. 5, pp. 574–581.
9. **Deep breathing**
   a. **Respiratory Vagal Nerve Stimulation (rVNS) and relaxation**
      Zaccaro, A., Piarulli, A., Laurino, M., Garbella, E.,

Menicucci, D., Neri, B. and Gemignani, A. (2018) 'How breath-control can change your life: A systematic review on psychophysiological correlates of slow breathing', *Frontiers in Human Neuroscience*, 12, p. 397.

b. **Heart Rate Variability (HRV) and decision-making**
Bergland, C. (2019) 'Longer exhalations are an easy way to hack your vagus nerve', *Psychology Today*. Available at: https://www.psychologytoday.com/us/blog/the-athletes-way/201905/longer-exhalations-are-an-easy-way-to-hack-your-vagus-nerve

c. **Autonomic nervous system balance and slow breathing**
Ravindra, P. and Gupta, A. (2020) 'Physiology of long exhalation breathing techniques and their effects on autonomic nervous system balance', *PhilArchive*. Available at: https://philarchive.org/archive/RAVPOL

10. **Scientific research on power posing**
    a. Cuddy, A.J.C., Schultz, S.J. & Fosse, N.E. 2018, 'P-curving a more comprehensive body of research on postural feedback reveals clear evidential value for power-posing effects: Reply to Simmons and Simonsohn (2017)', *Psychological Science*, vol. 29, no. 4, pp. 656–666.
    b. Cuddy, A.J.C. 2012, *Your body language may shape who you are*, TED Talk, https://www.ted.com/talks/amy_cuddy_your_body_language_shapes_who_you_are.

11. **Scientific research on walking in green spaces**
    a. Bratman, G.N., Hamilton, J.P. & Gross, J.J. 2015, 'Nature experience reduces rumination and subgenual prefrontal cortex activation', *Proceedings of the National Academy of Sciences*, vol. 112, no. 28, pp. 8567–8572.
    b. Kjellgren, A. & Buhrkall, H. 2010, 'A comparison of the restorative effect of a natural environment with that of a

simulated natural environment', *Journal of Environmental Psychology*, vol. 30, no. 4, pp. 464–472.
   c. Martyn, P. & Brymer, E. 2016, 'The relationship between nature relatedness and anxiety', *Journal of Health Psychology*, vol. 21, no. 7, pp. 1436–1445.
12. **When-then plans**
   a. Gollwitzer, P.M. & Sheeran, P. 2006, 'Implementation intentions and goal achievement: A meta-analysis of effects and processes', *Advances in Experimental Social Psychology*, vol. 38, pp. 69–119.
   b. Milne, S., Orbell, S. & Sheeran, P. 2002, 'Combining motivational and volitional interventions to promote exercise participation: Protection motivation theory and implementation intentions', *British Journal of Health Psychology*, vol. 7, pp. 163–184.
13. **Lingering negative emotions:** Leger, K.A., Charles, S.T. & Almeida, D.M. 2018, 'Let it go: Lingering negative affect in response to daily stressors is associated with physical health ten years later', *Psychological Science*, vol. 29, no. 8, pp. 1288–1296.
14. **Expressive writing & emotional regulation**
   a. Pennebaker, J.W. 1997, 'Writing about emotional experiences as a therapeutic process', *Psychological Science*, vol. 8, no. 3, pp. 162-166.
   b. Pennebaker, J.W. & Smyth, J.M. 2016, *Opening Up by Writing It Down: How Expressive Writing Improves Health and Eases Emotional Pain*, 3rd edn, The Guilford Press, New York.
15. **Forgiveness and health outcomes**
   a. Worthington, E.L., Witvliet, C.V.O., Pietrini, P. and Miller, A.J. (2007) 'Forgiveness, health, and well-being: A review of the evidence for emotional versus decisional forgiveness', *Journal of Behavioral Medicine*, 30(4),

pp. 291–302. Available at: https://link.springer.com/article/10.1007/s10865-007-9105-8
   b. VanderWeele, T.J. and Chen, Y. (2020) 'Forgiveness and mental health: A cross-sectional study on mid-life adults', *BMC Psychology*, 8, p. 116. Available at: https://bmcpsychology.biomedcentral.com/articles/10.1186/s40359-020-00470-w
16. **The 'Tend-and-Befriend' stress response**
    a. Taylor, S.E., Klein, L.C., Lewis, B.P., Gruenewald, T.L., Gurung, R.A. & Updegraff, J.A. 2000, 'Biobehavioral responses to stress in females: Tend-and-befriend, not fight-or-flight', *Psychological Review*, vol. 107, no. 3, pp. 411-429.
    b. Taylor, S.E. 2006, 'Tend and befriend: Biobehavioral bases of affiliation under stress', *Current Directions in Psychological Science*, vol. 15, no. 6, pp. 273–277.
17. **The Power of Contribution & Oxytocin Release:** Zak, P.J. 2012, 'The Moral Molecule: How Trust Works', Dutton, New York.
18. **Bigger than self goals:** Abelson, J.L., Erickson, T.M., Mayer, S.E., Crocker, J., Briggs, H., Lopez-Duran, N.L. & Liberzon, I. 2014, 'Brief cognitive intervention can modulate neuroendocrine stress responses to the Trier Social Stress Test: Buffering effects of a compassionate goal orientation', *Psychoneuroendocrinology*, vol. 44, pp. 60–70.
19. **Meaningful Work as a Mediator Between Stress and Work Engagement**:
    a. Rahmi, T., Fitriana, E., Harding, D. & Agustiani, H., 2021. Stress and Work Engagement: Meaningful Work as Mediator. *In: Proceedings of the 2nd Progress in Social Science, Humanities and Education Research Symposium* (PSSHERS 2020).

b. Allan, B. A., Douglass, R. P., Duffy, R. D., & McCarty, R. J. (2016). Meaningful work as a moderator of the relation between work stress and meaning in life. *Journal of Career Assessment, 24*(3), 429–440.

## Chapter 4: The Four States of Mind—Your Choice in the Storm (or in the Face of Overwhelm)

1. **Losing control, controls us:** Seligman, M.E.P. 1972, *Learned Helplessness*, W.H. Freeman, San Francisco.
2. **Focus:** Rotter, J.B. 1966, 'Generalized expectancies for internal versus external control of reinforcement', *Psychological Monographs: General and Applied*, vol. 80, no. 1, pp. 1-28.
3. **Agency:** Bandura, A. 1997, *Self-efficacy: The exercise of control*, W.H. Freeman, New York.
4. **Disempowered and stuck.** Wood, R.E. & Bandura, A. 1989, 'Impact of conceptions of ability on self-regulatory mechanisms and complex decision making', *Journal of Personality and Social Psychology*, vol. 56, no. 3, pp. 407–415.
5. **Victim mode:** Abramson, L.Y., Seligman, M.E.P. & Teasdale, J.D. 1978, 'Learned helplessness in humans: Critique and reformulation', *Journal of Abnormal Psychology*, vol. 87, no. 1, pp. 49-74.
6. **The need for control:** Bwalya, A. (2024) 'Micromanagement: A comprehensive analysis', Global Scientific Journal, 12(7), pp. 29–39. Available at: https://www.researchgate.net/publication/382067762_MICROMANAGEMENT_A_COMPREHENSIVE_ANALYSIS
7. **Mental Flexibility:** Kashdan, T.B. & Rottenberg, J. 2010, 'Psychological flexibility as a fundamental aspect of health', *Clinical Psychology Review*, vol. 30, no. 7, pp. 865–878.
8. **Stepping into ownership:**
    a. Deci, E.L. & Ryan, R.M. 2000, 'The "what" and "why" of

goal pursuits: Human needs and the self-determination of behavior', *Psychological Inquiry*, vol. 11, no. 4, pp. 227–268.
   b. **Internally focused:** Duckworth, A.L., Peterson, C., Matthews, M.D. & Kelly, D.R. 2007, 'Grit: Perseverance and passion for long-term goals', *Journal of Personality and Social Psychology*, vol. 92, no. 6, pp. 1087–1101.
   c. **Steer our own experience:** Dweck, C.S. 2006, *Mindset: The new psychology of success*, Random House, New York.
9. **Nelson Mandela's mindset:** Stengel, R. 2009, *Mandela's Way: Lessons on Life, Love, and Courage*, Crown Publishing, New York.

## Chapter 5: The Anchor Within—Building Stability Through Empathy and Compassion

1. **Negative social exchange:** Rook, K.S., 2014. The health effects of negative social exchanges in later life. *Generations: Journal of the American Society on Aging*, 38(1), pp.15–23.
2. **Empathy and emotional regulation**: Eisenberg, N. 2000, 'Emotion, regulation, and moral development', *Annual Review of Psychology*, vol. 51, pp. 665-697.
3. **Benefits on wellbeing:** Neff, K.D. 2011, 'Self-compassion, self-esteem, and well-being', *Social and Personality Psychology Compass*, vol. 5, no. 1, pp. 1-12.
4. **Common Humanity & resilience**
   a. Neff, K.D. 2003, 'The development and validation of a scale to measure self-compassion', *Self and Identity*, vol. 2, no. 3, pp. 223-250.
   b. Neff, K.D. 2011, 'Self-compassion, self-esteem, and well-being', *Social and Personality Psychology Compass*, vol. 5, no. 1, pp. 1-12.
5. **The link between empathy and leadership effectiveness**:
   a. Goleman, D. 1998, *Working with Emotional Intelligence*, Bantam Books, New York.

 b. Boyatzis, R.E. 2011, 'Neuroscience and leadership: The promise of insights', *Ivey Business Journal*, vol. 75, no. 2, pp. 1-5.
6. **Microsoft's culture:** Nadella, S. 2017, *Hit Refresh: The Quest to Rediscover Microsoft's Soul and Imagine a Better Future for Everyone*, Harper Business, New York.
7. **Microsoft, empathy and business success:** Denning, S. (2021) 'How Microsoft's digital transformation created a trillion-dollar gain', *Forbes*, 20 June.
8. **Nadella CEO Rating:** Business Insider (2017) 'How Elon Musk, Jeff Bezos, Mark Zuckerberg, and 18 other top CEOs are rated by their employees', *Inc.*, 17 February. Available at: https://www.inc.com/business-insider/employees-rate-tech-ceo-elon-musk-jeff-bezos-satya-nadella-glassdoor.html
9. **Aging and negative social exchanges:** Newsom, J.T., McQueen, A., Rook, K.S., Krause, N. and Denning, E.C. (2022) 'A change for the worse: Negative social exchanges are associated with an accelerated decline in self-rated health over time', *Journal of Aging and Health*. Available at: https://doi.org/10.1177/08982643221083407
10. **Evidence for perspective switching:**
 a. **Perspective-Taking and Conflict Resolution**
Sklad, M., Irrmischer, M., Park, E., Versteegt, I. & Wignand, J., 2021. Perspective taking skills and conflict resolution. In: *Social and Civic Competencies Against Radicalization in Schools*. Cham: Springer, pp.75–96.
 b. **Perspective-Taking and Empathy Development**
Lamm, C., Batson, C.D. and Decety, J. (2007) 'The neural substrate of human empathy: Effects of perspective-taking and cognitive appraisal', *Journal of Cognitive Neuroscience*, 19(1), pp. 42–58. Available at: https://www.cbs.mpg.de/empathy-and-perspective-taking-how-social-skills-are-built

c. **Perspective-Taking and Stress Reduction**
   Batson, C.D., Early, S. and Salvarani, G. (1997) 'Perspective taking: Imagining how another feels versus imagining how you would feel', *Personality and Social Psychology Bulletin*, 23(7), pp. 751–758. Available at: https://doi.org/10.1177/0146167297237008

11. **Evidence for mentalisation**
    a. Luyten, P., Campbell, C., Allison, E. and Fonagy, P. (2020) 'The mentalizing approach to psychopathology: State of the art and future directions', *Annual Review of Clinical Psychology*, 16, pp. 297–325. Available at: https://doi.org/10.1146/annurev-clinpsy-071919-015355
    b. Asen, E. and Fonagy, P. (2017) 'Mentalization-based therapeutic interventions for families', *Journal of Family Therapy*, 39(2), pp. 207–222. Available at: https://www.researchgate.net/publication/263576573_Mentalization-based_Therapeutic_Interventions_for_Families

## Chapter 6: The Power Shift—How Ownership Redefines Control

1. **The CIA model:** Thompson, N. & Thompson, S. 2018, *The Social Work Companion*, Palgrave Macmillan, London.
2. **Accepting and letting go:** Kashdan, T.B. & Rottenberg, J. 2010, 'Psychological flexibility as a fundamental aspect of health', *Clinical Psychology Review*, vol. 30, no. 7, pp. 865-878.
3. **Emotional regulation**
   a. Troy, A.S. and Mauss, I.B. (2011) 'Resilience in the face of stress: Emotion regulation as a protective factor', *Resilience and Mental Health: Challenges Across the Lifespan*, pp. 30–44. Cambridge: Cambridge University Press.
   b. Razak, H.A., MacLeod, C., Rudaizky, D. & Notebaert, L., 2025. The role of emotion regulation in distinct measures of emotional resilience. *Cognitive Therapy and*

*Research*, [online] Available at: https://doi.org/10.1007/s10608-025-10581-6

4. **Taking ownership:** Deci, E.L. & Ryan, R.M. 2000, 'The "what" and "why" of goal pursuits: Human needs and the self-determination of behavior', *Psychological Inquiry*, vol. 11, no. 4, pp. 227-268.

5. **Lingering negative emotions:** Leger, K.A., Charles, S.T., Almeida, D.M., and Prather, A.A. (2018) 'Let it go: Lingering negative affect in response to daily stressors is associated with physical health years later', *Psychological Science*, 29(8), pp. 1283–1290.

6. **Broaden-and-build theory:** Fredrickson, B.L. 2004, 'The broaden-and-build theory of positive emotions', *Philosophical transactions of the Royal Society of London. Series B, Biological sciences*, vol. 359, no. 1449, pp. 1367-78.

7. **Negativity bias:** Rozin, P. & Royzman, E.B. 2001, 'Negativity bias, negativity dominance, and contagion', *Personality and Social Psychology Review*, vol. 5, no. 4, pp. 296-320.

8. **Gratitude:** Chowdhury, M.R., 2019. The neuroscience of gratitude and effects on the brain. *PositivePsychology.com*, 9 April. Available at: https://positivepsychology.com/neuroscience-of-gratitude/

9. **Laughter**
   a. Berk, L.S., Tan, S.A., Fry, W.F., Napier, B.J., Lee, J.W., Hubbard, R.W., Lewis, J.E. and Eby, W.C. (1989) 'Neuroendocrine and stress hormone changes during mirthful laughter', *The American Journal of the Medical Sciences*, 298(6), pp. 390–396.
   b. Manninen, S., Tuominen, L., Dunbar, R.I.M., Karjalainen, T., Hirvonen, J., Arponen, E., Hari, R., Jääskeläinen, I.P. and Nummenmaa, L. (2017) 'Social laughter triggers endogenous opioid release in humans', *The Journal of Neuroscience*, 37(25), pp. 6125–6131.

10. **Wonder:**
    a. Rudd, M., Vohs, K.D., and Aaker, J. (2012) 'Awe expands people's perception of time, alters decision making, and enhances well-being', *Psychological Science*, 23(10), pp. 1130–1136. Available at: https://doi.org/10.1177/0956797612438731
    b. Chirico, A., Glăveanu, V.P., Cipresso, P. & Riva, G., 2018. Awe enhances creative thinking: An experimental study. *Creativity Research Journal*, 30(2), pp.123–131.
    c. Piff, P.K., Dietze, P., Feinberg, M., Stancato, D.M., and Keltner, D. (2015) 'Awe, the small self, and prosocial behavior', *Journal of Personality and Social Psychology*, 108(6), pp. 883–899. Available at: https://doi.org/10.1037/pspi0000018

**Chapter 7: A Better Way—Moving Beyond Me Vs. You**

1. **Win-Win Matrix**: Covey, S.R. 1989, *The 7 Habits of Highly Effective People*, Free Press, New York.
2. **In 2011, BMW and Toyota joined forces**: BMW Group (2011) *BMW Group and Toyota agree to mid-to-long-term research collaboration in environment-friendly technologies.* Available at: https://www.press.bmwgroup.com/global/article/detail/T0123686EN
3. **BMW was a leader:** BMW Group (n.d.) *Company Profile.* Available at: https://www.bmwgroup.com/en/company.html
4. **Toyota was ahead of the curve:** Toyota Motor Corporation (2020) *Sustainability Data Book 2020.* Available at: https://global.toyota/en/sustainability/report/sdb/
5. **By 2013:** BMW Group (2013) *BMW Group and Toyota Motor Corporation deepen collaboration by signing binding agreements.* Available at: https://www.press.bmwgroup.com/global/article/detail/T0136503EN

6. **Set to launch in 2028:** BMW Group (2023) *Hydrogen pioneers: BMW Group and Toyota Motor Corporation take collaboration to the next level.* Available at: https://www.press.bmwgroup.com/global/article/detail/T0444790EN

## Chapter 8: Beneath the Surface—Why Trust, Safety, and Respect are Non-Negotiable

1. **The Impact of Trust on Workplace Performance:** Zak, P.J. 2017, 'The neuroscience of trust', *Harvard Business Review*, vol. 95, no. 1, pp. 84-90.
2. **New York Times Questions to fall in love:** Catron, M.W. (2015) 'To fall in love with anyone, do this', *The New York Times*, 9 January. Available at: https://www.nytimes.com/2015/01/11/fashion/modern-love-to-fall-in-love-with-anyone-do-this.html
3. **Diagnosing Trust Breakdowns: Character vs. Competence:** Covey, S.M.R. 2006, *The Speed of Trust: The One Thing That Changes Everything*, Free Press, New York. pp41-125.
4. **Psychological Safety & Performance in Organizations (McKinsey Study):** McKinsey & Company 2021, 'Psychological safety and the critical role of leadership', https://www.mckinsey.com/capabilities/people-and-organizational-performance/our-insights/psychological-safety-and-the-critical-role-of-leadership-development
5. **Psychological Safety & High-Performing Teams**
    a. Edmondson, A.C. 1999, 'Psychological safety and learning behavior in work teams', *Administrative Science Quarterly*, vol. 44, no. 2, pp. 350-383.
    b. Edmondson, A.C. 2019, *The Fearless Organization: Creating Psychological Safety in the Workplace for Learning, Innovation, and Growth*, Wiley, Hoboken.
    c. Google re:Work 2016, 'Project Aristotle: Understanding team effectiveness', https://rework.withgoogle.com/en/

guides/understanding-team-effectiveness#identify-dynamics-of-effective-teams

## Chapter 9: The Art of Alignment—Moving Beyond Stalemates to Shared Purpose

1. **The Concept of Moving from Positions to Purpose:** L Fisher, R., Ury, W. & Patton, B. 1981, *Getting to Yes: Negotiating Agreement Without Giving In*, Penguin Books, New York. pp.40-56.
2. **Clarity on roles:** Gratton, L. and Erickson, T.J. (2007) 'Eight ways to build collaborative teams', *Harvard Business Review*, November. Available at: https://hbr.org/2007/11/eight-ways-to-build-collaborative-teams
3. **Impact of clarity:** Gambill, T. (2024) 'How to "ACT" like a leader by creating alignment, clarity, and trust', *Forbes*, 10 April. Available at: https://www.forbes.com/sites/tonygambill/2024/04/10/how-to-act-like-a-leader-by-creating-alignment-clarity-and-trust
4. **The Positive No & Constructive Boundaries**: Ury, W. 2007, *The Power of a Positive No: How to Say No and Still Get to Yes*, Bantam Books, New York.
5. **Leading with yes**: Ury, W. 2007, *The Power of a Positive No: How to Say No and Still Get to Yes*, Bantam Books, New York. pp. 26-52.
6. **Hold and cold:** Harvard Business Review (2018) *Dealing with Difficult People*. Boston: Harvard Business Review Press. pp9-14.
7. **Building a Golden Bridge:** Ury, W. (2024) *Possible: How We Survive (and Thrive) in an Age of Conflict*. New York: Harper Business. Pp.119-203.

## Chapter 10: Unlocking Potential—Transforming How You See Challenges

1. **History.com Editors** (2010) 'Daredevil crosses Niagara Falls on tightrope', *HISTORY*. A&E Television Networks. Available at: https://www.history.com/this-day-in-history/daredevil-crosses-niagara-falls-on-tightrope
2. **References to support scarcity narrows attention and reduces creativity etc:**
   a. Goldsmith, K., Griskevicius, V. & Hamilton, R., 2020. Scarcity and consumer decision making: Is scarcity a mindset, a threat, a reference point, or a journey? *Journal of the Association for Consumer Research*, 5(4), pp.358–364.
   b. de Almeida, F., Scott, I.J., Soro, J.C., Fernandes, D., Amaral, A.R., Catarino, M.L., Arêde, A. & Ferreira, M.B., 2024. Financial scarcity and cognitive performance: A meta-analysis. *Journal of Economic Psychology*, 101, 102702. Available at: https://doi.org/10.1016/j.joep.2024.102702
3. **2019 Study:** Huijsmans, I., Ma, I., Micheli, L., Civai, C., Stallen, M. & Sanfey, A.G. 2019, 'A scarcity mindset alters neural processing underlying consumer decision making', *Proceedings of the National Academy of Sciences*, vol. 116, no. 24, pp. 11699-11704.
4. **Studies show abundance:**
   a. **Improved Relationships:** Putnam-Walkerly, K., 2020. The power of an abundance mindset for changemakers. *Leader to Leader*, 2020(98), pp.52–57. Available at: https://doi.org/10.1002/ltl.20547
   b. **Enhanced Creativity and Problem-Solving:** McNally, C., 2021. An abundance mindset might be the key to unlocking your creativity. *The Startup*, 15 December.
   c. **Increased Resilience and Adaptability:** Pavlov, A. & Lunov, V., 2023. Reframing prosperity: Abundance as the

universal master signifier in shaping human well-being and civilization's narrative (A multidisciplinary exploration). *SSRN*. Available at: https://doi.org/10.2139/ssrn.4555339

    d. **Higher Levels of Success:** Castrillon, C., 2025. How to develop an abundance mindset that fuels career growth. *Forbes*, 6 April. Available at: https://www.forbes.com/sites/carolinecastrillon/2025/04/06/how-to-develop-an-abundance-mindset-that-fuels-career-growth/

5. **Reframing emotions:** Troy, A.S., Shallcross, A.J., & Mauss, I.B. (2013). 'A person-by-situation approach to emotion regulation: Cognitive reappraisal can be beneficial or harmful, depending on the context.' *Psychological Science*, 24(12), 2505-2514.

6. **The Power of Yet & Growth Mindset:** Dweck, C.S. 2006, *Mindset: The New Psychology of Success*, Random House, New York. p.24.

## Chapter 11. Optimism—Opening New Doors to Opportunity and Momentum

1. **Martin Seligman's Research on Learned Optimism:** Seligman, M.E.P. 2006, *Learned Optimism: How to Change Your Mind and Your Life*, Vintage, New York.

2. **Optimism & Sales Performance (Insurance Study):** Seligman, M.E.P. & Schulman, P. 1986, 'Explanatory style as a predictor of productivity and quitting in life insurance sales agents', *Journal of Personality and Social Psychology*, vol. 50, no. 4, pp. 832-838.

3. **Optimism & Health Benefits:**

    a. Kubzansky, L.D., Sparrow, D., Vokonas, P. & Kawachi, I. 2001, 'Is the glass half empty or half full? A prospective study of optimism and coronary heart disease in the normative aging study', *Psychosomatic Medicine*, vol. 63, no. 6, pp. 910-916.

b. Segerstrom, S.C. & Sephton, S.E. 2010, 'Optimistic expectancies and cell-mediated immunity: The role of positive affect', *Psychological Science*, vol. 21, no. 3, pp. 448-455.

## Chapter 12: Inspired Action—Expanding Possibility Through Questions and Creative Problem-Solving

1. **Leadership and questions:** Hagel, J. (2021) 'Good leadership is about asking good questions', *Harvard Business Review*, 4 January. Available at: https://hbr.org/2021/01/good-leadership-is-about-asking-good-questions
2. **Question Thinking & Marilee Adams**:
    a. Adams, M. 2004, *Change Your Questions, Change Your Life: 12 Powerful Tools for Leadership, Coaching, and Life*, Berrett-Koehler Publishers, San Francisco.
    b. Adams, M. 2016, *Change Your Questions, Change Your Life: 12 Powerful Tools for Leadership, Coaching, and Life*, 4th en, Berrett-Koehler Publishers, San Francisco.
3. **Q-Storming:** Adams, M. 2016, *Change Your Questions, Change Your Life: 12 Powerful Tools for Leadership, Coaching, and Life*, 4th en, Berrett-Koehler Publishers, San Francisco. Pp127-139.
4. **SCAMPER Method & Bob Eberle**: Eberle, B. 1971, *SCAMPER: Games for Imagination Development*, Prufrock Press, Waco.
5. **Alex Osborn:** Osborn, A.F. 1953, *Applied Imagination: Principles and Procedures of Creative Thinking*, Charles Scribner's Sons, New York.
6. **The Power of Expansive Thinking (William Ury & The Circle of Possibility)**: Ury, W. 2022, *Possible: How We Survive (and Thrive) in an Age of Conflict*, HarperOne, New York.

## Chapter 13: Betterment Leadership—Building Cultures of Ownership and High Performance

1. **73% of enterprises:** Bendor-Samuel, P. 2019, 'Why Digital Transformations Fail: 3 Exhausting Reasons', *Everest Group Blog*.
2. **90% of acquisitions:** Christensen, C.M., Rising, C. & Waldeck, A. 2011, 'The Big Idea: The New M&A Playbook', *Harvard Business Review*.
3. **IT projects:** Flyvbjerg, B. & Budzier, A. 2011, 'Why Your IT Project May Be Riskier Than You Think', *Harvard Business Review*.
4. **According to McKinsey:** Bradley, C., Hirt, M. and Smit, S. (2018) 'Strategy to beat the odds', McKinsey Quarterly, 13 February. Available at: https://www.mckinsey.com/capabilities/strategy-and-corporate-finance/our-insights/strategy-to-beat-the-odds.
5. **Building a visionary company:** Collins, J.C. and Porras, J.I. (1996) 'Building your company's vision', *Harvard Business Review*, September-October.
6. **Research shows:** Sull, D., Homkes, R. and Sull, C. (2015) 'Why strategy execution unravels—and what to do about it', Harvard Business Review, 93(3), pp. 57–66.
7. **Only 29%** Leadership IQ (2020) 'The state of leadership development', *Leadership IQ*.
8. **Research from McKinsey:** Bucy, M., Schaninger, B., VanAkin, K. and Weddle, B. (2021) 'Losing from day one: Why even successful transformations fall short', *McKinsey & Company*. Available at: https://www.mckinsey.com/capabilities/people-and-organizational-performance/our-insights/successful-transformations

## Chapter 15: Betterment Beyond the Self—A Mission for a Better World

1. **Muhammad Yunus & Microfinance**: The story of Muhammad Yunus and how he pioneered the concept of microfinance, demonstrating how small, accessible loans could lift people out of poverty. His work with Grameen Bank revolutionised global financial inclusion and earned him the Nobel Peace Prize in 2006.
   a. Yunus, M. 1999, *Banker to the Poor: Micro-Lending and the Battle Against World Poverty*, PublicAffairs, New York.
   b. Yunus, M. 2007, *Creating a World Without Poverty: Social Business and the Future of Capitalism*, PublicAffairs, New York.
2. **Information about the Kindness Pandemic. The Kindness Pandemic (n.d.)** *The Kindness Pandemic*. Available at: https://www.thekindnesspandemic.org
3. **Patagonia's Business Model & Impact**: Patagonia redefined corporate responsibility by prioritising sustainability, ethical supply chains, and long-term environmental impact over short-term profits, setting a benchmark for conscious business practices.
   a. Chouinard, Y. 2005, *Let My People Go Surfing: The Education of a Reluctant Businessman*, Penguin, New York.
   b. Chouinard, Y. 2016, *Let My People Go Surfing: The Education of a Reluctant Businessman*, 2nd edn, Penguin, New York.

# Acknowledgements

There are far too many people to name who have shaped my journey and contributed, directly and indirectly, to the insights and experiences shared in this book. To each of you, thank you. Your influence is on part of every page.

To all the incredible clients I've had the privilege to partner with over the years—thank you. Your openness, trust, and commitment to growth have deeply informed this work. Through our shared challenges and triumphs, you've helped bring these practical insights to life. This book is better for the wisdom, courage, and collaboration you've brought to every conversation.

Deep thanks to the talented team who helped bring this book to life: Gail Tagarro The Book Writing Coach, for your thoughtful and steady hand as editor; Alicia Grady at Struck by Violet, for the stunning internal design that makes the content sing; and Ella Cantly, for your eagle eyes on fact-checking and referencing—I couldn't have done this without you.

To my family, your support is my anchor. Mum, your unwavering belief in me and the mindset you've role-modelled are gifts I carry with me every day. And most of all, to my beautiful husband Jonas—my partner in every sense. Your love, encouragement, and belief made the time, energy, and space for this book possible. This is as much yours as it is mine.

# About the Author

**Alison Earl** is a leading corporate adviser and behaviour change expert, helping organisations around the world accelerate success by unlocking leadership alignment and people transformation. She believes that alignment, ownership, and empowerment are not just beneficial but essential for turning strategies into reality.

Over her twenty-year career, Alison has shaped innovative strategies for global companies, built businesses from the ground up in Sydney, London, and New York, and been a repeat guest lecturer on behaviour change at the Harvard School of Public Health. She has facilitated transformational change in over fifty organisations worldwide, guiding them through uncertainty, growth, and reinvention.

Known for her ability to cut through complexity, Alison combines research, creative thinking, and real-world experience to help leaders build trust, collaboration, and shared commitment. Her approach blends mentoring, facilitation, and training to empower people to take ownership, make better decisions faster, and drive high performance.

At the heart of her work is a commitment to helping organisations thrive, not just by managing change, but by leveraging it as a catalyst for meaningful transformation.

www.ingramcontent.com/pod-product-compliance
Lightning Source LLC
Chambersburg PA
CBHW071950070526
44583CB00015B/1143